Third Edition · Volume II
A Practical Business Chinese Reader

基础实用商务汉语 下 册
（第三版）

关道雄（Daoxiong Guan）◎编著

北京大学出版社
PEKING UNIVERSITY PRESS

图书在版编目(CIP)数据

基础实用商务汉语. 下册 / 关道雄编著. —3 版. —北京: 北京大学出版社，2018.5

ISBN 978-7-301-29492-5

Ⅰ.①基… Ⅱ.①关… Ⅲ.①商务－汉语－对外汉语教学－教材 Ⅳ.①H195.4

中国版本图书馆CIP数据核字（2018）第 078339 号

书　　　名	**基础实用商务汉语（第三版）下册** **JICHU SHIYONG SHANGWU HANYU (DI-SAN BAN) XIA CE**
著作责任者	关道雄（Daoxiong Guan） 编著
责任编辑	孙　娴
标准书号	ISBN 978-7-301-29492-5
出版发行	北京大学出版社
地　　　址	北京市海淀区成府路 205 号　100871
网　　　址	http://www.pup.cn　新浪微博：@北京大学出版社
电子信箱	zpup@pup.cn
电　　　话	邮购部 62752015　发行部 62750672　编辑部 62753374
印 刷 者	北京大学印刷厂
经 销 者	新华书店
	787 毫米 × 1092 毫米　16 开本　17.25 印张　257 千字
	2000 年 9 月第 1 版　2003 年 9 月第 2 版
	2018 年 5 月第 3 版　2018 年 5 月第 1 次印刷
定　　　价	86.00 元

To our students whose love of Chinese encouraged us to complete this book.

第三版修订说明

《基础实用商务汉语》是一部以一般商务用途汉语（Chinese for General Business Purpose or CGBP）为学习内容的教材。它所服务的对象主要是已经学习了一年到一年半汉语课程、对基本的现代汉语语法结构已有所了解的汉语非母语的学习者。

本书第三版的修订工作主要涉及以下几个方面。

（一）将原有的十六课分为上下两册，可供两个学期使用。

体例上保持了"内容上既前后衔接又相对独立"和"前八课稍易，后八课较难"[1]的设计，但对原来全书各课的先后次序做了微调。教师也可以根据自己学生的具体情况，选择使用其中的一册。

（二）更新课文内容。

第三版每课的课文内容（即"对话"和"阅读短文"）均有程度不同的更新。其中《广告与促销》的课文完全重写；《招聘面试》和《工业园区》两课为新增，替换了原有的《文化异同》和《经济特区》两课。这样做的目的是为了使课文话题和内容能够更好地切合中国经济发展的现实情况以及实际商务活动中的典型场景，增加本教材的实用性。

（三）大幅更新全书每课的"练习与活动"。

第三版的"练习与活动"分为三大部分，即"词汇练习""句型练习"及"阅读、讨论和其他活动"。作者在设计、编写这些练习与活动时，融入了交际法、任务教学、合作学习等理念，同时也不排除使用一些比较传统的练习、活动方式。此次修订着重充实了"词汇练习"与"阅读、讨论和其他活动"两大部分的含量，增加（或改进）了多种不同类型的练习、任务和活动。另外，每课"练习与活动"的最后部分均新增了"快速复习"。"快速复习"以补充阅读的形式呈现。阅读内容实际是对本课对话或本课与前一课两课对话的整合、重写。阅读材料中尽可能不出现任何本课和本课以前各课没有出现过的生词。这样设计的目的是为了帮助学习者巩固已经学过的内容，同时提高教材中词汇的复现率。商务汉语教材词汇复现率一直是一个不容易解决的问题。《基础实用商务汉语》第三版在修订

1　见初版前言。

过程中对这一问题给予了更多的注意。作者一方面有意识地让一些商务词汇在前后课文中多次出现，另一方面通过新增加的"快速复习"以及其他各项练习与活动来提供多次操练这些商务汉语词汇的机会。这些做法在一定程度上确实提高了本教材词汇的复现率。

（四）增加听力材料。

除了原有的课文对话、阅读短文和生词录音以外，练习部分中的一些句型练习和每课的快速复习部分的短文也配了录音。所有录音材料均以 🎧 符号标出。

（五）新增了扫二维码查看课文英译和听录音的功能。

为了给使用者提供更多的方便，第三版新增了扫码听录音和查看课文英译的功能。每一课大标题旁均印有一个二维码，加注"听力材料"字样。扫描该码后可以看到这一课按编号排列的（即001、002）所有听力材料的完整录音目录。点击任意子目录，就可以在线收听录音材料。此外，每课对话和阅读短文前的二维码，加注"课文英译"字样。扫描该码后即可在线阅读相应的英译材料。使用者也可以从北京大学出版社网站的下载专区（http://www.pup.cn/dl/newsmore.cfm?sSnom=d203）下载相应的录音文件，从书后的"总附录"中查看所有课文英译。

（六）修订每课的附录。

本书第三版对所有的附录材料都做了更新、替换，尽可能使本教材的附录材料对教与学都有一些实际的用处。

《基础实用商务汉语》第三版总词汇表共列词汇 1113 个，句型总表共收句型 142 个。每课的课堂教学时间一般为 5—6 课时。建议教师根据实际的教学情况作出必要的调整。

《基础实用商务汉语》一书自 2000 年出版以来，收到海内外很多使用者的热心反馈。这些意见对于本书的修订无疑有莫大的助益。北京大学出版社一直对本书的编写、出版和修订给予充分的支持和帮助。第三版责编孙娴女士为修订提供了很多有益的建议。作者在此一并表示诚挚的感谢。

关道雄 dxguan@ucsb.edu
2017 年 5 月于美国加州大学
圣塔芭芭拉分校
东亚语言文化研究系

Preface to the Third Edition

A Practical Business Chinese Reader is a language textbook that teaches Chinese for General Business Purpose (CGBP). It aims to serve those non-Chinese speakers who have completed one to one and a half year of Chinese courses at the college level, as well as having an understanding of most of the basic modern Chinese grammatical structures.

The changes to the third edition of this textbook mainly cover the following:

1) Dividing 16 lessons into 2 volumes.

It preserves the design that "the contents of the lessons may be seen in the chronological order of events or as sixteen individual stories" and "the first eight lessons are more basic while the latter eight lessons are more advanced by comparison".[1] Nevertheless, the order of lessons in this edition has been adjusted slightly. Teachers may choose one of the two volumes for teaching based on the practical need from students.

2) Updated lesson content.

Of the lessons, "Advertising and Sales Promotion" has been completely rewritten; "Job Interview" and "Industrial Park" are newly added lessons, replacing "Cultural Similarities and Differences" and "Special Economic Zones". The purpose of doing so is for the topics and contents of the lessons to better represent the current state of Chinese economic development and typical scenarios in practical business activities, contributing to the practical usability of this textbook.

3) Large scale changes to the "Exercises and Activities" in each chapter.

In the third edition, the "Exercises and Activities" are split into three categories: "Vocabulary Exercises", "Sentence Pattern Exercises", and "Reading, Discussion, and Other Activities". In designing and composing these exercises and activities, the author blends the communicative approach, task-based teaching, cooperative learning, etc., while also keeping usage of some more traditional methods of exercises and activities. This edition heavily expands on the contents of "Vocabulary Exercises" and "Reading, Discussion, and Other Activities", adding (or enhancing) many different types of exercises, tasks, and activities. In addition, "Quick Review" was added to the last part of "Exercises and Activities" in each lesson. "Quick Review" is presented in the form of supplementary reading. The reading material is a simple combination and rewrite of the dialogues in the current lesson, or the current lesson plus the previous lesson. There are almost no vocabulary words new to the lesson or previous lessons appearing in this reading material. The goal of this design is to help students strengthen their grasp of material already learned, as well as raising the word recurrence frequency in the text. Word recurrence frequency has always been

---

1   See the preface, First Edition.

a difficult problem in Business Chinese teaching materials. *A Practical Business Chinese Reader* pays more care to this issue in the Third Edition. The author deliberately repeats some business Chinese vocabulary words throughout the text, while also providing opportunities for students to practice these words many times through the "Quick Review" and other exercises and activities. These approaches have indeed increased the word recurrence frequency in this text.

4) Adding more listening materials.

In addition to the original audio recordings of the dialogues, reading passages, and vocabulary words, new audio recordings have been provided for some Sentence Pattern Exercises and the Quick Review passages in each lesson. All audio materials have been marked with the 🎧 symbol.

5) Added functionality of scannable QR code to access English translations of the lessons and audio recordings.

To provide greater convenience for the user, the Third Edition has added scannable QR codes to access English translations of the lessons and audio recordings. The QR code next to the title of each chapter marked with "Audio Recordings" contains a complete list of all audio recordings for this chapter. After scanning the QR code, you can view the full list of contents for all audio materials (e.g., 001, 002) for each lesson. You can click the links to listen to the recordings. In addition, QR codes placed before Dialogues as well as Reading Passages of each lesson are marked with "English Translation". Scanning these codes will allow you to read the corresponding English translations online. Users can also download the audio recordings from the website of Peking University Press (http://www.pup.cn/dl/newsmore.cfm?sSnom=d203), and look up all English translations of the lessons from the General Appendix at the back of the book.

6) Editing the appendices to each lesson.

In the Third Edition, all appendices have been updated or replaced, enhancing the practical value of the appendix material to both teaching and learning.

In total, *A Practical Business Chinese Reader Third Edition* includes 1113 vocabulary words and 142 sentence patterns. Each lesson will need approximately 5 to 6 hours of instruction time. It is suggested that instructors make adjustments based on their own teaching circumstances.

Ever since *A Practical Business Chinese Reader* was published in 2000, I have received enthusiastic feedback from many users in China and abroad. These comments have been immensely beneficial to the editing and revision of this book. The Peking University Press has always been greatly supportive and helpful with the composition, publishing, and revision of this book. The editor for the Third Edition, Ms. Sun Xian, provided many beneficial suggestions. The author expresses sincere gratitude.

Daoxiong Guan (dxguan@ucsb.edu)
Department of East Asian Languages and Cultural Studies
University of California, Santa Barbara
May, 2017

第二版前言

《基础实用商务汉语》一书自 2000 年出版以来，先后为国内外一些学校选用作教材。其韩文版亦于 2002 年由韩国多乐园有限公司在首尔出版。此次修订再版，除了订正原稿中的错误并更换、补充了若干课文中的部分内容以外，主要对每课的练习作了大幅度的扩充和调整。修订后的词汇总表共收入生词 1040 个，句型总表共收入句型 154 个。

需要说明的是，本书的原作者之一遇笑容教授因为出任加州大学海外学习项目驻华中心主任，此次未能参与修订工作。但是本书得以成稿问世却是与她的长期关心、支持与参与分不开的。北京大学出版社的徐刚先生和郭力女士从本书的撰写到修订出力甚多，在此一并表示感谢。

关道雄

2003 年 3 月于美国加州大学

圣塔芭芭拉分校

东亚语言文化研究系

Preface to the Second Edition

Since it was first published in 2000, *A Practical Business Chinese Reader* has been adopted as a textbook by schools in China and overseas. The Korean edition (*Ok! Business Chinese*) was published by Darakwon Inc. at Seoul in 2002. This revised edition has corrected some mistakes and partially replaced or replenished content in several lessons. However, the majority of the revision was made to the exercises in each lesson. Almost all the exercises have been rewritten or redesigned. As a result, the number of the exercises in this book has increased by as many as 3-4 times. There are only slight changes in vocabulary and sentence patterns. A total of 1040 new words and 154 sentences patterns has been introduced in the revised edition.

It was very unfortunate that Professor Hsiao-Jung Yu, the co-author of the original edition of this book, could not work on the new version of the book this time. She was appointed as director of the UC EAP (University of California Education Abroad Program) Study Center at Beijing last year and has committed herself completely into this immense responsibility. There is no doubt that it would have been impossible for me to complete this book from the very beginning without her support, concern, and contribution. Many thanks also go to Mr. Xu Gang and Ms. Guo Li at Peking University Press. Their continuous support and help have made the revision successful.

Daoxiong Guan
Department of East Asian Languages and Cultural Studies
University of California, Santa Barbara
March, 2003

初版前言

近年来，商务汉语在海外汉语教学中逐渐引起了相当的注意。在美国，目前已经有不少大学相继开设了商务汉语课程。一些大学甚至正在计划、酝酿开设层次不同、训练重点不同的系列商务汉语课。显然，商务汉语正开始成为对外汉语教学中的新热点。

商务汉语课的出现无疑与中国经济的迅速发展有着密切的关系。可以肯定地说，只要中国经济继续保持良好的发展趋势，商务汉语课的发展将是非常有潜力的。但是，作为一门新课程或者说新领域，商务汉语面临着众多急需解决的问题。其中，编写出版适合对外汉语教学所使用的商务汉语课教材的任务尤为迫切。这就是我们编写《基础实用商务汉语》的起因。

《基础实用商务汉语》一书的主要适用对象定位为至少已经学习了一年到一年半汉语、对主要的现代汉语语法结构已有所了解的学生。其已经掌握的词汇量应当在一千字左右，即大致相当于《汉语水平词汇与汉字等级大纲》中甲级词的水准。在编写体例与架构上，《基础实用商务汉语》一书共分为十六课，以一个美国商务代表团访问中国为线索，依次介绍了商务谈判的各项主要环节和其他相关的商务、社交活动。内容上既前后衔接又相对独立，以便任课教师根据需要调整自己的课程教学安排。就难易程度而言，前八课稍易，后八课较难。每课包括：

1. 主题对话；

2. 阅读短文；

3. 词汇和句型；

4. 练习和活动；

5. 附录。

全书最后编有总附录，包括全部课文的英译、词汇总表、句型总表、重要网址、中国地图和主要参考书目。全书共计列出生词 1010 个，句型 152 个。通过这本课本的学习，学生可望达到中级或中级以上的汉语水平。

把本书设计在上述的汉语水平层次上是基于这样的考虑。我们认为，商务汉语的学习应该在已经初步具有了一定的汉语语言能力的基础上进行。商务汉语课不需要也不应该在"商务"的名目之下再教授发音、识字或是最基本、最常用的汉语词汇和语法。如果要那样做的话，势必会模糊一般对外汉语课和商务汉语课的界限。商务汉语课应该是一门具有特定目标、特定内容的对外汉语语言课程。它所提供的是现代汉语中常用的商务词汇的知识以及与此相关的社会、文化知识，培养学生在汉语语言环境中进行商务活动所需要的语言交际技能。作为对外汉语课程中的一种，商务汉语与普通汉语课存在着密切的联系。但是商务汉语课的教学目的显然有别与普通汉语课。其教材与教法也应当具有自己的特色。换句话说，商务汉语课必须在其教学内容上提供普通汉语课无法提供的语言、文化知识，才能真正成为一门独立的、无法替代的课程。

基于上述的想法，我们在《基础实用商务汉语》一书的总体设计和具体编写中做了以下的尝试：

（一）注重培养学生在实际汉语语言环境中进行商务活动的语言能力。

能力语言教学法是近二三十年来在美国外语教学界一再讨论及推行的外语教学理论。能力语言教学法强调培养外语学习者实际的语言交流能力，把从书本上学到的语言知识及时地（即时地）运用在真实的生活情境之中。为了在商务汉语课中达到这一目的，《基础实用商务汉语》的课文选题力求概括最具代表性、最有普遍意义的实际商务活动。课文对话的编写力求真实而生动、实用且不乏风趣，尽可能避免单调的或教科书式的语言。每一课的练习与活动的设计均旨在鼓励学生的主动参与。在帮助学生理解课文内容的同时，尽量利用多种形式，为学生提供在真实（或模拟真实）的语境中操练、使用该课词汇与句型的机会。每课的附录则结合课文的需要，提供相关的中文商业信函、文件、表格等实例，以期帮助学生熟悉实际商务活动中可能接触到的这类材料，取得学以致用的效果。

（二）重视相关文化背景知识的介绍。

将文化背景、风俗民情、社交礼仪乃至思维方式的介绍融入外语教学之中的文化、语言融合教学法也是近年来欧美语言教学界讨论的重点之一。这种教学理论的一个明显的好处就是使学习外语的人可以通过语言的学习来了解文化、通过了解文化来提高其外语水平。我们觉得商务汉语教学有必要与文化知识的介绍相结合。了解中国人的思想、行为模式以及在待人接物上的种种习惯，将有助于在实际商务活动中有效的沟通与交流，避免某些不必要的误会。基于这样的认识，《基础实用商务汉语》一书在每课的主题对话之外，又安排了一篇阅读短文。其内容是与该课主题对话相关的社会背景、文化背景信息。换言之，本书每一课的主题对话是以具体的商务活动设立单元，而每课的阅读短文则是以介绍文化背景设立单元。在文体上，前者是口语，后者是书面语。这样不但可以同时训练学生的会话和阅读能力，同时也增加了学生的学习兴趣。

（三）从商务汉语的角度出发，合理挑选课文词汇和句型。

在从事对外汉语教学的实践中，我们深深感到课本词汇的合理甄选和使用是非常值得重视的一个问题。编写一本汉语教材，应该仔细审慎地考虑它所准备使用的字、词和词组。在决定哪些字词应该介绍给学生、哪些应该列为必需掌握的生词的时候，编写者应该尽量避免主观性和随意性。对外汉语课本中词汇的取舍标准无疑应该建立在科学统计的基础上。商务汉语课本更不能例外。根据《汉语水平词汇与汉字等级大纲》的统计，对外汉语教学基础阶段的词汇量应当以3000词为界标。根据我们的分析，在这3000个词中，有可能被收入任何一本商务汉语词典的词大约在百分之一左右。因此，一本理想的商务汉语教材所提供的基本词汇，应当能够最直接地反映出其不同与一般汉语课本的特征。在《基础实用商务汉语》一书的编写中，我们决定以《汉语水平词汇与汉字等级大纲》的甲级词表为界线。甲级词表共收词1033个，都是现代汉语中使用频率最高的基本常用词，也是初学者在基础阶段应该首先掌握的词汇。这样一个词汇量正好符合我们为本书使用者设定的汉语水平起点。因此，凡是被收入甲级词表的词汇，在这本教材中均被编者视为学生已经掌握的词汇，不再列入生词部分。必须说明的是，由于我们还缺乏商务汉语词汇使用频率方面的统计资料，因此在选择这方面的词汇的时候，本书可能有不少考虑不周的地方。我们真诚地盼望读者提出批评和建议。

　　《基础实用商务汉语》一书的内容和体例由关道雄与遇笑容拟定。关道雄负责主题对话、阅读短文、生词表、句型表的编写以及全书的统稿，遇笑容负责每课练习与活动的设计和编写。课文的英文翻译由史香侬（Shannon Lee Du）承担。中国江西财经大学经济文化传播系的熊焰、陈秀平教授审读了本书的初稿，并且为本书的附录搜集、提供了一些有用的信息和原始材料。陈毓贤女士（Susan Chan Egan, 原美国Scudder, Stevens & Clark, Inc. 资深证券分析师）为书中涉及的专业词汇的英汉对译解决了不少难题。在此一表示衷心的感谢。我们还应该特别感谢审读本书的北京大学出版社的郭力女士和徐刚先生。因为他们的关心和帮助，本书才能够得以顺利出版。

　　本书的初稿曾在加州大学圣塔芭芭拉分校试用。这使我们有机会在实践中对这本教材做出修改。在此我们也想对我们的学生表示由衷的谢意。正是他们对汉语学习的强烈兴趣和热爱给了我们编写本书的动力。

关道雄、遇笑容
2000 年 5 月于加州大学
圣塔芭芭拉分校
东亚语言文化研究系

Preface to the First Edition

In recent years, Business Chinese has drawn increasing attention in the field of overseas Chinese teaching. In the United States, some universities are already offering Business Chinese courses. Others are even considering or planning to offer series of Business Chinese courses at different levels, each placing the emphasis on various aspects. Obviously, Business Chinese is becoming a popular new course in the field of teaching Chinese as a foreign language.

The popularity of Business Chinese is a by-product of China's economy, which has grown rapidly in the last decade. There is no doubt that Business Chinese has a tremendous potential as long as China's economy maintains this positive trend and continues growing. On the other hand, Business Chinese as a newborn course is facing a number of questions that have to be solved without delay. What is most urgent and crucial now is to compile textbooks that properly fit the needs of Business Chinese in the field of teaching Chinese as a foreign language. That was our intention in writing this textbook, A Practical Business Chinese Reader.

A Practical Business Chinese Reader is designed for those who have completed at least one year to one and a half years of Chinese study at the college level and have gained a good knowledge of basic grammar in modern Chinese as well as around a 1,000-word vocabulary in Chinese, equivalent to the beginning level in Guidelines of Chinese Proficiency and the Degree of Difficulty of Chinese Characters. We believe that Business Chinese should be taught beyond the beginning level. There is no need to teach pronunciation, character writing or beginning level vocabulary and grammar in a Business Chinese course. Although there are similarities and connections between Business Chinese and other Chinese language courses, the goal of Business Chinese certainly is different than other Chinese language courses, and so is its content. Business Chinese courses train students to develop their communication skills both in oral and written forms in order to conduct business in a Chinese language environment. The emphasis is placed on the usage of business terms in modern Chinese and on language proficiency in a business context as well as on business related social-cultural awareness.

By following the progress of an American business delegation in China, A Practical Business Chinese Reader has developed sixteen lessons in all to introduce some typical business activities and business related social events in the Chinese business world. The contents of the lessons may be seen in the chronological order of events or as sixteen individual stories so that instructors may adjust their teaching plans according to their own needs. In terms of difficulty, the first eight lessons are more basic while the latter eight lessons are more advanced by comparison. However, these sixteen lessons, should they all be used, are sufficient for one semester or two quarters. Each of the sixteen lessons in the book contains the following sections:

1. Dialogues: The dialogues in each lesson are set at various authentic sites in China. The scenarios are intended to be typical of those encountered by foreigners conducting business in P. R. China. Authentic language of modern Chinese, which occurs in realistic business contexts, is employed to the greatest extent in order to provide the most efficient examples for students to imitate and eventually enhance their Chinese language proficiency.

2. Reading Passages: The reading passage in each lesson is a short essay, in which the topic of the lesson is further explored. The reading passages are intended to sketch some general pictures of cultural background in Chinese society and its business world. In the terms of language style, the reading passages in the book are in written form while the dialogues present a more lifelike spoken style.

3. Vocabulary and Patterns: The book presumes prior competence or mastery of about a 1000-word vocabulary. The Glossary of Beginning Level in Guidelines of Chinese Proficiency and the Degree of Difficulty of Chinese Characters, which has a 1033-word vocabulary of the most frequently used words, has been adopted as the measure to establish the vocabulary glosses for each lesson. The words that are not covered in this 1033-word vocabulary glossary are considered as new words for the book. Due to the fact that there is no supporting data of lexicostatistics in business Chinese, it was very difficult to decide what vocabulary items should be included. In order to better equip students with useful business terms in Chinese, a great effort has been made to select proper vocabulary words from a practical standpoint of conducting business. We therefore would welcome the input of teachers and students alike, so that we can continue to best meet the needs of the changing context of Business Chinese in the classroom. The patterns are another component of this section. Normally eight to ten patterns are presented in each lesson. There are certain important patterns that students may have been exposed to in their prior study but that they might not have mastered. Each pattern heading is followed by two examples. The first one is drawn from either the Dialogues or the Reading passage while the second one serves as an additional example.

4. Exercises and Activities: Exercises and activities are designed to reinforce newly introduced vocabulary and patterns as well as to help students in understanding the content of the dialogues and the reading passage in each lesson. Some questions posed in this section require students to do research in business related topics by using various media sources, including the internet, while some questions are intended to lead students into discussions of cultural differences. Instructors

may choose to use these exercises in whole or in part, as written homework or as in-class oral exercises.

5. Appendix: Appendixes in each lesson provide examples of business documents in Chinese as well as other useful information such as a Customs Declaration Form, a Product Catalogue, an Order Sheet, a Letter of Credit, a Letter of Intent, a Contract, and Common Chinese Signs etc. Some of them are duplicates of the originals.

The book has also complied a General Appendix, which contains a complete English translation of all dialogues and reading passages, vocabulary, patterns, useful web sites, a map of China, and a bibliography. There are 1010 new words and 152 sentence patterns introduced in the book. All the texts, vocabulary and patterns are printed in both traditional and simplified characters. Through study of this textbook, students may attain an intermediate level of Chinese or higher.

This book was designed by Daoxiong Guan and Hsiao-jung Yu. Daoxiong Guan wrote the dialogues and the reading passages. He also made vocabulary and pattern glossaries and took the responsibility for finalizing the whole book. Hsiao-jung Yu created the exercises and activities. Shannon Lee Du translated all of the dialogues and the reading passages into English. We want to thank Professor Xiong Yan and Chen Xiuping (Jiangxi Finance and Economy University), who not only provided some valuable materials and examples of business documents but also proofread the first draft of the book. Our gratitude also goes to Mrs. Susan Chan Egan (Chartered Financial Analyst, former Vice President at Scudder, Stevens & Clark, Inc.). Her special knowledge in business solved many problems that we encountered during translating business terms into English. We owe a special thanks to Ms. Guo Li and Mr. Xu Gang (Peking University Press), who proofread the whole book. It would have been impossible to publish this book without their continuous support. Finally, we want to express our gratitude to our students at University of California, Santa Barbara. It was their love of Chinese that encouraged us to complete this book.

Daoxiong Guan
Hsiao—jung Yu
Department of East Asian Languages and Cultural Studies
University of California, Santa Barbara
May, 2000

主要人物
Main Characters

 美 方

|史强生|
美国国际贸易公司亚洲地区总裁
Johnson Smith, CEO of Asia Region,
American International Trading Company

白琳|
美国国际贸易公司亚洲地区总裁助理
Lynn Petty, Assistant to CEO of Asia Region,
American International Trading Company

 中 方

|王国安|
中国东方进出口公司总经理
Wang Guo'an, President,
China Eastern Import & Export Corporation

李信文|
中国东方进出口公司副总经理
Li Xinwen, Vice President,
China Eastern Import & Export Corporation

|张 红|
中国东方进出口公司公共关系部主任
Zhang Hong, Director of Public Relations,
China Eastern Import & Export Corporation

目　录
Table of Contents

3

9 交货和付款
Delivery and Payment

　　通过前两天的洽谈，中美双方已经初步商定了新订单。现在，交货时间和付款方式是他们最关心的问题。今天上午双方要就这些问题举行进一步的会谈。

（一）对 话 Dialogue

课文英译

1. 交货时间 Delivery Schedule

史强生：我想今天我们应该讨论这批订单的交货时间问题。

李信文：好。不知道您对交货时间有什么具体要求？

史强生：您知道服装的季节性很强。这次我们向贵公司订购的毛衣和牛仔裤，都要在今年秋季投放市场。李先生，您能在八月上旬交货吗？

李信文：八月上旬？史先生，您不是开玩笑吧？去年我们是九月才交货的。我们目前的生产计划已经安排满了。

史强生：（认真地）不是开玩笑。九月、十月是毛衣的销售旺季。去年我们的商品比别人晚进入市场两个星期，结果吃了亏。今年我可不想再错过机会了。

李信文：可是要我们马上调整生产计划、增加产量确实有困难。

白　琳：李先生，我知道这个交货时间的确是紧了一些，可是我们也有我们的难处啊。李先生，咱们是老朋友了，请您帮帮忙、想想办法吧。

李信文：白小姐，我是想帮您的忙，也想帮自己的忙，可是要提前一个多月交货实在不太容易。

白　琳：我有一个想法。我们能不能把这些服装分成两次交货？八月上旬交一半，九月上旬交另外一半。Johnson，你觉得行吗？

史强生：嗯，这是一个解决的办法。李先生，您说呢？

李信文：让我考虑考虑……我得给王总打个电话。我们先休息一下儿吧？

史强生、白　琳：好！

课文英译

2. 付款方式 Method of Payment

李信文：对不起，让你们久等了。刚才我跟王总联系了一下儿。我们可以接受分两次交货的安排……

史强生：那太好了！谢谢！

李信文：不过，我必须说明我们对付款方式的要求。

史强生：当然，我也很关心这个问题。请问，贵公司打算采用哪种方式？

李信文：我们一般采用信用证付款方式。但是这次贵方要求提前交货，这对
　　　　我们的资金周转有一定影响，所以我们要求贵公司预付百分之三十
　　　　的货款，其余的货款采用即期信用证。

史强生：百分之三十的预付货款，我可以通过美国花旗银行电汇给您。其余
　　　　的货款，我们是不是可以采用承兑交单或者其他的分期付款方式？

李信文：很抱歉，我们目前不接受这些付款方式。为了不影响交货时间，请
　　　　您务必在装运前三十天开出信用证。

白　琳：李先生，您可真厉害！说到钱，您一点儿情面也不讲！

李信文：（笑）您没听过这样一句中国话吗？"亲兄弟，明算账"嘛！

白　琳：（笑）不对！您这是"一手交钱，一手交货"！

词汇（一）　Vocabulary (1)

1.	付款	fù kuǎn	to make payment; payment
2.	通过	tōngguò	by means of; through
3.	商定	shāngdìng	to settle through discussion
4.	方式	fāngshì	manner; mode; way; method
5.	进一步	jìnyíbù	go a step further
6.	季节性	jìjiéxìng	seasonal
	季节	jìjié	season
7.	强	qiáng	strong
8.	上旬	shàngxún	the first ten days of the month
	旬	xún	a period of ten days
9.	开玩笑	kāi wánxiào	to joke; to make fun of

10.	旺季	wàngjì	peak sales period; busy season
11.	错过	cuòguò	to miss; to let slip by
12.	难处	nánchù	difficulty; problem
13.	提前	tíqián	in advance; beforehand
14.	实在	shízài	really; indeed; truly
15.	想法	xiǎngfǎ	idea; opinion; view
16.	分成	fēnchéng	divide into; split up into
17.	采用	cǎiyòng	to select for use; to employ; to adopt
18.	信用证	xìnyòngzhèng	letter of credit (L/C) (A letter from one bank to another bank, by which a third party, usually a customer, is able to obtain money.)
	信用	xìnyòng	credit
19.	资金周转	zījīn zhōuzhuǎn	capital turnover; flow of funds; circulation of funds
20.	预付	yùfù	to pay in advance
21.	货款	huòkuǎn	payment for goods
22.	其余	qíyú	the rest; the remainder
23.	即期信用证	jíqī xìnyòngzhèng	letter of credit at sight (An L/C at Sight is a letter of credit that is payable immediately – more or less – after the seller meets the requirements of the letter of credit. This type of L/C is the quickest form of payment for sellers.)
24.	电汇	diànhuì	to wire money; telegraphic transfer (T/T)
25.	承兑交单	chéngduì jiāodān	documents against acceptance bill (D/A) (A bill of exchange sent by an exporter with other shipping documents to an agent who will not release the documents until the bill of exchange has been signed/accepted by the person receiving the goods. This is used when the bill of exchange is a period bill and must be paid by a specified date.)

26.	分期付款	fēn qī fù kuǎn	to pay in installments; payment in installments
27.	抱歉	bàoqiàn	be apologetic; to feel sorry about
28.	务必	wùbì	must; should
29.	装运	zhuāngyùn	to load and transport; to ship
30.	开出	kāichū	to write out; to make out (a check, etc.)
31.	厉害	lìhai	tough; sharp; formidable
32.	说到	shuōdào	to speak of; to mention; when it comes to...
33.	不讲情面	bùjiǎng qíngmiàn	to have no consideration for sb.'s feelings
	情面	qíngmiàn	feelings; sensibilities; "face"
34.	亲兄弟，明算账	qīn xiōngdì, míng suàn zhàng	Even blood brothers keep careful accounts.
35.	一手交钱，一手交货	yì shǒu jiāo qián, yì shǒu jiāo huò	Literally, "One hand hands over the money; one hand hands over the goods"; to deliver (only) when the cash is in hand.

专有名词 / 特殊名词 Proper Nouns / Special Nouns

花旗银行	Huāqí Yínháng	Citibank

句型（一） Sentence Patterns (1)

1. 通过……　　by means of; through

例：❶ 通过前两天的洽谈，中美双方已经初步商定了新订单。

❷ 通过这次访问，史先生交了很多新朋友。

2.（你）对……有什么要求？
What demands/requirements do (you) have concerning...?

例：❶ 您对交货时间有什么具体要求？

❷ 请问，贵公司对我们的产品质量还有什么要求？

3.（你）不是……吧？
(A rhetorical question. For example, you are joking, aren't you?)

例：❶ 您不是开玩笑吧？

❷ 那家公司不是把我们的订单忘了吧？

4. A 比 B 早 / 晚 V. + amount of time
A V. + amount of time earlier/later than B

例：❶ 去年我们的商品比别人晚进入市场两个星期。

❷ 对不起，日本公司的报盘比您的报盘早到了几天，我们已经签订了合同。

5. 把 Obj. 分成……　　to divide obj. into...

例：❶ 我们能不能把这些服装分成两次交货？

❷ 我们可以采用分期付款的方式，把这批货款分成六个月付。

6. 说到……　　speak about; when it comes to...; when... is mentioned

例：❶ 说到钱，您一点儿情面也不讲！

❷ 说到那些皮夹克的质量，这位客户变得很生气。

（二）阅读短文 Reading Passage

中国的银行和人民币
Chinese Banks and Renminbi

课文英译

　　中国的国家中央银行是中国人民银行。全国性的商业银行主要分成两大类型：一类是国有商业银行，它们是中国工商银行、中国建设银行、中国农业银行和中国银行，又称"四大行"；另一类是股份制商业银行，重要的有招商银行、交通银行、浦发银行等等。外国人到中国做生意，往往都会跟这些银行中的某一家打交道。

　　中国的法定货币是人民币。它的单位分为元、角、分三种。一元等于十角，一角等于十分。人民币的面值一共有十三种：分为一百元、五十元、二十元、十元、五元、二元、一元、五角、二角、一角、五分、二分和一分。不过有些面值的人民币已经很少使用了。目前，人民币仅限于中国国内流通使用。在对外贸易中，中外双方一般使用美元、日元、欧元、英镑等国际通行的硬通货进行结算；使用汇付、托收、信用证等国际通行的方式支付货款。2001年，中国正式加入世界贸易组织。随着经济的迅速发展和金融改革，中国开始尝试在国际贸易中用人民币结算。不少中国商业银行都已进入了海外金融市场。2015年国际货币基金组织宣布人民币成为它的国际储备货币。人民币国际化的步伐正在逐渐加快。

词汇（二） Vocabulary (2) 005

1.	全国性	quánguóxìng	national; nationwide
2.	类	lèi	type; kind
3.	称	chēng	to call; to name
4.	股份制	gǔfènzhì	shareholding system; joint-stock system
5.	打交道	dǎ jiāodào	have dealings with; come into contact with
6.	法定	fǎdìng	legal; stipulated by law
7.	货币	huòbì	currency; money
8.	单位	dānwèi	unit in measurement; organization (*see L.4b)
9.	等于	děngyú	be equal to; the same as
10.	面值	miànzhí	face value; denomination
11.	仅	jǐn	only
12.	限于	xiànyú	be limited/confined to
13.	国内	guónèi	interior (of a country); domestic
14.	流通	liútōng	to circulate
15.	对外	duìwài	foreign; external
16.	日元	rìyuán	Japanese yen
17.	欧元	ōuyuán	euro
18.	英镑	yīngbàng	pound
19.	通行	tōngxíng	prevalent; of general use; current
20.	硬通货	yìngtōnghuò	hard currency
21.	结算	jiésuàn	to settle/close an account
22.	汇付	huìfù	remittance (e.g. 电汇 T/T, 信汇 M/T, 票汇 D/D)
23.	托收	tuōshōu	collection; to collect (e.g. 承兑交单 D/A, 付款交单 D/P)
24.	支付	zhīfù	to pay (money); defray
25.	加入	jiārù	to join; accede to

26.	随着	suízhe	along with; in pace with
27.	金融	jīnróng	banking; finance
28.	尝试	chángshì	to attempt; to try
29.	海外	hǎiwài	overseas
30.	宣布	xuānbù	to announce; to declare
31.	储备	chǔbèi	reserve; to reserve
	储备货币	chǔbèi huòbì	reserve currency (The reserve currency is commonly used in international transactions and often considered a hard currency or safe-haven currency.)
32.	国际化	guójìhuà	internationalization
33.	步伐	bùfá	pace
34.	加快	jiākuài	to speed up; to accelerate

专有名词 / 特殊名词 Proper Nouns / Special Nouns

1.	中国人民银行	Zhōngguó Rénmín Yínháng	People's Bank of China
2.	中国工商银行	Zhōngguó Gōngshāng Yínháng	Industrial and Commercial Bank of China
3.	中国建设银行	Zhōngguó Jiànshè Yínháng	China Construction Bank
4.	中国农业银行	Zhōngguó Nóngyè Yínháng	Agricultural Bank of China
5.	中国银行	Zhōngguó Yínháng	Bank of China
6.	招商银行	Zhāoshāng Yínháng	China Merchants Bank
7.	交通银行	Jiāotōng Yínháng	Bank of Communications
8.	浦发银行	Pǔfā Yínháng	SPD Bank, a short form for Shanghai Pudong Development Bank（上海浦东发展银行）
9.	世界贸易组织	Shìjiè Màoyì Zǔzhī	World Trade Organization; WTO（世贸组织）
10.	国际货币基金组织	Guójì Huòbì Jījīn Zǔzhī	International Monetary Fund; IMF

句型（二） **Sentence Patterns (2)**

1. 跟……打交道   come into contact with...; have dealings with...

例：① 外国人到中国做生意，往往都会跟这些银行中的某一家打交道。

     ② 跟这家公司打交道常常让我头疼。

2. 仅限于   be limited to...

例：① 目前人民币仅限于中国国内流通使用。

     ② 信用证付款方式仅限于我们的老客户。

3. 在……中   in...; within...

例：① 在对外贸易中，双方一般使用美元、日元、欧元、英镑等国际通行的硬通货进行结算。

     ② 在昨天的会谈中，我们讨论了很多问题。

4. 随着   along with; in pace with; as...

例：① 近年来随着经济的发展和金融改革，中国开始尝试在国际贸易中用人民币结算。

     ② 随着出口的增加，我们公司的生意越来越好。

（三）练习与活动 Exercises & Activities

I. 词汇练习 Vocabulary Exercises

1. 组词。你可以参考总附录中的词表。

Build upon the following words. You may refer to the Vocabulary List in the General Appendix.

例：（ 具 ）体　　　　（ 身 ）体

（1）交（　　　）　　交（　　　）　　交（　　　）　　交（　　　）

（2）订（　　　）　　订（　　　）　　订（　　　）

（3）出（　　　）　　出（　　　）　　出（　　　）

（4）预（　　　）　　预（　　　）　　预（　　　）

（5）（　　　）款　　（　　　）款　　（　　　）款

（6）（　　　）定　　（　　　）定　　（　　　）定

（7）（　　　）费　　（　　　）费　　（　　　）费

（8）（　　　）心　　（　　　）心　　（　　　）心

（9）（　　　）货　　（　　　）货　　货（　　　）　　货（　　　）

2. 为列在左边的词找出它们的反义词，把每个反义词的号码和英文意思写在括号的空格里。

Match the words on the left with their antonym on the right. Write down the number of the antonym and its English equivalent in the spaces provided.

例：旺季（# 2 ；　off season　）

（1）对外（#　　；　　　　　　　）

（2）提前（#　　；　　　　　　　）

（3）上旬（#　　；　　　　　　　）

（4）旺季（#　　；　　　　　　　）

（5）失败（#　　；　　　　　　　）

1. 下旬

2. 淡季（dànjì）

3. 放慢

4. 国内

5. 推后

（6）加快（#　　；_____）

（7）付款（#　　；_____）

（8）海外（#　　；_____）

6. 对内

7. 成功

8. 收款

3. 阅读下面的句子，根据拼音提示写出汉字。

Please read the following sentences and write down the missing characters according to the *pinyin*.

（1）按照 _____ 规定的时间，分几次付 _____，这种付款 _____
　　　　　 hétóng　　　　　　　　　　　　　　huòkuǎn　　　　　　　　 fāngshì

叫做 _____ 付款。
　　　 fēn qī

（2）买方（进口商）向银行 _____ 开出信用证，保证通过 _____ 向卖
　　　　　　　　　　　　 shēnqǐng　　　　　　　　　　　　　　　 yínháng

方（出口商）_____。这就是 _____ 贸易常采用的 _____
　　　　　　　 fù kuǎn　　　　　　 guójì　　　　　　　　　　 xìnyòngzhèng

付款方式。

（3）承兑交单是国际 _____ 采用的另一种 _____。_____ 地
　　　　　　　　　　 màoyì　　　　　　　　 fùkuǎn fāngshì　 dàzhì

说，进口商（买方）_____ 银行开出汇票（Bill of Exchange; Bank's
　　　　　　　　　　 tōngguò

Acceptance Bill）交给出口商（卖方），_____ 在 _____ 的时间
　　　　　　　　　　　　　　　　　　　　　 bǎozhèng　　　 guīdìng

_____，这就是 _____；_____ 在收到这样的汇票以后把
　 fù kuǎn　　　　　　 chéngduì　　 chūkǒushāng

提货单（delivery order, D/O）交给 _____，这就是 _____。
　　　　　　　　　　　　　　　　　 jìnkǒushāng　　　　　　 jiāo dān

4. 🎧 *007* **用中文回答下面的问题。**

Answer the following questions in Chinese.

（1）你知道哪些商品有季节性？什么时候是它们的销售旺季？

_____

（2）在中文里，一个月的前十天叫什么？（第二个十天呢？最后十天呢？）

_____

（3）"亲兄弟，明算账"和"一手交钱，一手交货"是什么意思？什么时候可以用这两句话？你可以举出例子吗？

_____

（4）根据本课的阅读短文，在对外贸易中，中外双方通常使用哪些货币？为什么使用这些货币？

_____

（5）写出本课提到的付款方式。（你还知道别的付款方式吗？）

_____

_____

II. 句型练习（一）　Sentence Pattern Exercises (1)

1. 🎧 *008* **东方电脑公司的李总打算找一位新经理。下面的问题是李总打算在面试的时候问申请人的问题。如果你能用"通过……"很好地回答下面的问题，你当经理一定没问题。**

Eastern Computer Company's President Li is looking for a new manager. The questions below are what President Li will ask the job applicants during the job interview. If you can answer these questions well by using the pattern of"通过……", you are certainly qualified for this job.

（1）你打算怎样了解市场行情？

_____

（2）你打算怎样提高产品质量？

_____

（3）你打算怎样推销产品？

_____

（4）你打算怎样吸引更多的顾客？

_____

2. **你在跟一位买主洽谈明年的毛衣订单。请用"对……有什么要求"向你的客户询问下面的问题。你的客户会用"说到……"回答你的问题。**

A buyer and you are discussing next year's purchase of sweaters. Ask your client the following questions by using the pattern of "对……有什么要求". Your client will answer you by using the pattern of "说到……".

（1）问题一：毛衣的设计或式样

你：_____

客户：_____

（2）问题二：产品的质量

你：_____

客户：_____

（3）问题三：交货时间

你：_____

客户：_____

（4）问题四：付款方式

你：_____

客户：_____

3. 完成下面的对话并用"不是……吧"提出你的猜测（cāicè / conjecture, guess）或者疑问（yíwèn / doubt, question）。

Please complete the following dialogues by using the pattern "不是……吧" to express your guesses or doubts.

（1）甲：上个星期陈厂长胖了十磅！

乙：_____

（2）甲：听说小张当了花旗银行的总裁！

乙：_____

（3）甲：卖方说，如果我们付现金，一条牛仔裤只要三块钱！

　　　乙：_____

（4）甲：真奇怪，已经到了会谈的时间了，为什么对方代表还没有来？

　　　乙：_____

4. 🎧 _010_ 用"A 比 B 早 / 晚 + V. + amount of time"回答下面的问题。
   Answer the following questions by using the pattern of "A 比 B 早 / 晚 + V. + amount of time".

   （1）白小姐昨天已经到达北京了。史先生明天才能到达北京。他们谁先到达北京？
   　　　早几天？

   　　_____

   （2）合同要求七月一日交货，可是那家公司到七月十五日才交货。交货时间晚了
   　　　多少天？

   　　_____

   （3）我们公司订购的秋季毛衣这个月上旬可以进入市场。他们公司订购的毛衣这个
   　　　月下旬才能进入市场。哪家公司的毛衣能先进入市场？早多长时间？

   　　_____

   （4）采用信用证的付款方式，卖方一般七天就可以收到货款；采用承兑交单，可能
   　　　要等一个月才能收到货款。承兑交单收到货款的时间大概要晚多久？

   　　_____

5. 根据下面的问题，用"把……分成"造句。*复习：比较"把……分成"（本课）、
   "把 sth. V. 成……"（第4课）和"A 分为……"（第7课），看看它们是不是一样。
   **Use the pattern of "把……分成" to accomplish the following tasks. *Review: please
   compare the pattern of "把……分成" in this lesson with the pattern of "把 sth. V.
   成……" in Lesson 4 and the pattern of "A 分为……" in Lesson 7.**

   （1）怎样用中文告诉中方卖主，你希望"make an installment payment of 1 million
   　　　dollars over 10 months"？

   　　_____

（2）怎样用中文通知中方买主，你计划 "deliver 20,000 dozens of sweaters in several shipments" ？

_____

（3）怎样用中文说明，你计划 "divide your company into two smaller companies" ？

_____

（4）怎样让中方谈判代表知道，你希望 "discuss this issue in two steps" ？

_____

III. 句型练习（二） **Sentence Pattern Exercises (2)**

1. 🎧 *1011* 请用 "跟……打交道" 回答下面的问题。
   Answer the following questions by use the pattern of "跟……打交道".

（1）一般来说，你喜欢跟什么样的人打交道？

_____

（2）做生意的时候，你喜欢跟什么样的公司（/客户）打交道？

_____

（3）你不喜欢跟什么样的公司打交道？

_____

（4）到中国做生意的外国人常会跟什么单位（/部门）打交道？

_____

2. 🎧 *1012* 用 "仅限于" 改写下面的句子。
   Rewrite the following sentences by using the pattern of "仅限于".

（1）今天晚上的招待会只邀请本公司最重要的客户参加。

_____

（2）参加明天会议的人都是局长以上的官员。

_____

（3）这次会谈只讨论交货时间问题。

_____

（4）很抱歉，我们目前接受的支付方式是汇付和信用证。

_____

3. 用 "在……中" 回答下面的问题。

Answer the following questions by using the pattern of "在……中".

（1）在你考察过的城市中，你对投资哪个城市感兴趣？

_____

（2）在跟你的公司打交道的客户中，哪一位最重要？

_____

（3）在昨天的会谈中，双方讨论了哪些问题？

_____

（4）在双方讨论的问题中，哪个问题最重要？

_____

4. 用 "随着" 完成下面的句子。

Complete the following sentences by using the pattern of "随着".

（1）随着 _____，这家高新科技公司产品的
知名度越来越高。

（2）随着 _____，这家民营企业收到的订单
越来越多。

（3）随着 _____，这家外资企业在中国的业
务越来越好。

（4）随着 _____，这个地区吸引了越来越多
的外国公司和厂家。

IV. 阅读、讨论和其他活动 Reading, Discussion and Other Activities

1. 🎧 014 根据课文对话回答问题。
Answer the following questions according to the dialogues in this lesson.

（1）今天中美双方要讨论什么问题？

_____

（2）美方希望中方什么时候交货？为什么？

_____

（3）中方有什么困难？

_____

（4）白琳提出来什么样的解决办法？

_____

（5）李经理为什么要给王总打电话？

_____

（6）中方接受了分两次交货的建议吗？

_____

（7）中方要求美方怎样付款？

_____

（8）中方接受承兑交单的付款方式吗？

_____

（9）为什么白琳说李先生"可真厉害"？

_____

2. 🎧 015 根据阅读短文回答问题。
Answer the following questions according to the Reading Passage in this lesson.

（1）中国的国家中央银行叫什么？

_____

（2）中国主要的商业银行有哪些？

_____

（3）人民币的单位分为哪几种？

_____

（4）人民币最大的面值是多少？最小的面值是多少？

_____

（5）目前在国际贸易中，人民币是硬通货吗？

_____

（6）根据本课的阅读短文，在对外贸易中，中外双方通常使用哪些货币？
为什么使用这些货币？

_____

（7）为什么阅读短文里说"人民币国际化的步伐正在逐渐加快"？

_____

3. 角色扮演。Role-playing.

你刚跟一家服装厂洽谈订购了一大批夏季服装。现在你们开始讨论交货时间的问题。为了跟别人竞争，你的公司希望能早一点儿把这批服装投放市场。可是服装厂觉得提前交货有困难。请根据这些内容写一个对话并表演。请先复习本课的对话，注意谈判双方在表达询问、试探（shìtàn / to sound out）、质疑（zhìyí / to question）、解释（jiěshì / to make explanations）、建议、折中（zhézhōng / to compromise）、让步（ràng bù / to yield, to give in）、拒绝（jùjué / to decline）或遗憾时的方式，体会双方说话的语气和态度。这对你写对话会有帮助。

You are a buyer purchasing summer clothing from another clothing factory. You have just placed a big order. Now, you are discussing the delivery schedule. Your company wants to have these clothes on the market earlier due to competition. However, the clothing factory feels that it is difficult for them to deliver the goods beyond their regular schedule. Write a short dialogue describing such a situation and act it out with your classmates. Please review the dialogues in this lesson, paying attention to how these negotiators make inquiries, sound out and question, make explanations and suggestions, compromise or yield, and decline or show regret. Try to get a feeling about the manner of speaking （i.e. "tone" and "attitude"） from both sides of the negotiators. This will help you to create a "professional negotiation".

4. 🎧 016 快速复习。**Quick review.**

Ⓐ 阅读下面的短文，复习学过的词汇和句型。

Read the following text and review vocabularies and sentence patterns that you have learned.

> 　　在这两天的谈判中，中美双方就秋季的订单讨论了很多具体问题。其中包括产品的品种、数量、价格等。除了在一两种产品的价格上有不同意见以外，双方对洽谈结果都非常满意。今天他们还进一步讨论了订单的付款方式和交货时间问题。因为美方考虑到他们订购的服装产品季节性很强，为了能赶在销售旺季前投放市场，所以提出了提前交货的要求。中方在认真考虑以后，同意了美方的要求。双方决定把这次的秋季订单分成两次交货，八月上旬交一半的货，九月上旬交另一半的货。中方的李经理又联系了服装厂的陈厂长，请他马上调整生产计划。不过，中方为了不让自己的资金周转受到影响，要求美方预付百分之三十的货款，其余的货款采用即期信用证的方式支付。美方接受了中方的要求。谈判结束后，白小姐对李先生说："你可真厉害！说到钱的时候，一点儿情面都不讲！"李先生笑了，他知道白小姐是跟他开玩笑。他告诉白小姐，这就是中国人常说的，"亲兄弟，明算账"。

Ⓑ 问答 Q & A：

（1）在这两天的谈判中，双方具体讨论了哪些问题？

_____

（2）他们洽谈的问题都取得了满意的结果吗？（有什么问题没有谈成功？）

_____

（3）为什么美方要求服装订单提前交货？

_____

（4）双方最后决定什么时候交货？

_____

（5）李经理联系陈厂长要他做什么？

_____

（6）中方要求怎样付款？为什么？美方同意不同意？

_____

（7）白琳小姐生李先生的气了吗？

_____

（四）附录　　Appendix

1. 信用证样本 Letter of Credit

中国工商银行
INDUSTRIAL AND COMMERCIAL BANK OF CHINA

信　用　证（副本）

开证日期　　　年　月　日

开证申请人	全　　称		受益人	全　　称	
	地址、邮编			地址、邮编	
	账　　号			账　　号	
	开 户 行			开 户 行	

开证金额	人民币（大写）	亿 千 百 十 万 千 百 十 元 角 分

有效日期及有效地点 _____

通知行名称及行号 _____

运输方式：_____

分批装运：允许□　不允许□　　付款方式：□　延期付款□　议付□

转　　运：允许□　不允许□

货物运输起止地：自 _____ 至 _____　议付行名称及行号：_____

最迟装运日期：____ 年 ___ 月 ___ 日　付款期限：即期□　运输单据日后 ____ 天

货物描述：_____

受益人应提交的单据：_____

其他条款：_____

　　本信用证依据中国人民银行《国内信用证结算办法》和申请人的开证申请书开立。本信用证为不可撤销，不可转让信用证。我行保证在收到单证相符的单据后，履行付款的责任。如信用证系议付信用证，受益人开户行应将每次提交单据情况背书记录在正本信用证背面。

开证行地址：_____　　　　邮箱：_____

电传：_____

电话：_____

传真：_____　　编押：_____　　开证行签章：_____

2. 信用证流程示意图 Flowchart of Letter of Credit

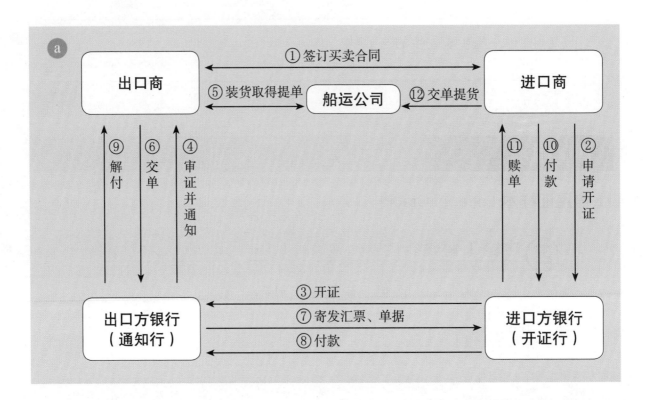

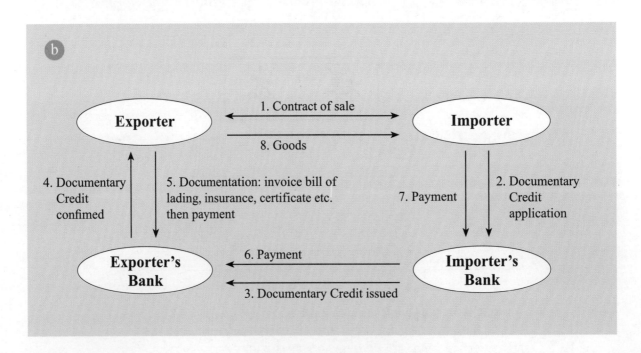

3. 订货单实例 Order Sheet

中国长江家电公司：

　　贵公司的报盘及货样分别于五月十日和五月二十日收到。十分感谢贵方对我方询盘迅速回复。我方愿接受贵方报盘。现随函寄去 17029 号订单，请按此订单细则发货是盼。

1. 商品详情：

订单编号：17029

序号	产品名称	规格型号	数量	单价（元）	单位	金额（元）
01	超薄高清智能电视	CJ17A/32 英寸	2000	1,100	台	2,200,000
02	超薄高清智能电视	CJ17L/60 英寸	3000	5,600	台	16,800,000
总计金额（人民币大写）：壹仟玖佰万元整						19,000,000

2. 包装：

　　外包装用标准出口木板箱，内衬防水材料，金属片加固箱角。内包装用防震塑料泡沫打包。

3. 装运：

　　2017 年 7 月 1 日前装船。起运港：中国上海；目的港：新加坡。由卖方代保水渍险。

4. 付款：

　　信用证付款。2017 年 7 月 10 日前由买方通过新加坡银行开具以中国长江家电公司为收益人的不可撤销信用证。

　　　　　　　　　　　　　　　　　　新加坡新亚国际电子器材公司
　　　　　　　　　　　　　　　　　　2017 年 5 月 22 日

4. 微信支付与支付宝 WeChat Pay & Alipay

10 销售代理
Sales Agents

中美双方刚刚就交货时间和付款方式达成了协议。史强生和白琳对此都非常满意。现在双方要就东方公司作为美方在中国的销售代理问题继续进行洽谈。

（一）对话 Dialogue

1. 独家代理 Sole Agency

王国安： 史先生、白小姐，李经理告诉我，今天上午你们就今年秋季的新订单达成了协议。我非常高兴。请问，贵公司对此满意吗？

史强生： 我们对协议非常满意，尤其是我们双方能够顺利地解决了交货时间的问题，这对我们非常重要。王总经理，谢谢您的关照！

王国安：您别客气！贵公司是我们的老客户，我们应该尽力满足您的要求。

白　琳：（笑）王总经理，这次我们公司可是购买了您四百多万美元的东西。您打算跟我们买点儿什么呢？

李信文：（笑）白小姐，我看您才是真厉害。告诉您，今天下午王总就是来谈在中国经销贵公司产品这件事的。

王国安：是这样的。今年我们东方公司第一次代理销售贵公司的节能空调、环保洗衣机等家用电器产品，市场销路很好。我们希望进一步扩大在这方面的合作。

史强生：好啊，这也是我们这次来中国的目的之一。王先生，您有什么具体的打算？

王国安：我们希望成为贵公司在中国的独家代理。

史强生：您知道我们目前跟广东的一家公司也有代理销售空调的协议。把独家代理权给你们恐怕会影响我们跟那家公司的其他生意。

李信文：史先生，我们公司在国内各地都有很好的销售网点。如果我们有独家代理权，一定会做得更好！

史强生：这样吧，我们可以把洗衣机的独家代理权给你们。另外，我们还有一种节能家用洗碗机，打算在中国市场试销。如果你们愿意的话，也想请贵公司独家代理。王先生、李先生，你们看怎么样？

王国安、李信文：行！一言为定！

课文英译

2. 资信调查和佣金 Credit Check and Commission

史强生：王先生，既然贵公司将成为我们的独家代理，我们就还需要再了解一下儿贵公司的资信情况。

王国安：有关我方的资信情况，您可以向中国银行北京分行查询。

史强生：您也一定知道，作为独家代理，东方公司必须同意在我们的协议有效期之内不代理其他公司的同类产品。

王国安：对，这一点我们很清楚。

史强生：贵方想要提取多少佣金？

王国安：代理经销外国产品，我们一般提取百分之十的佣金。

史强生：百分之十太多了！我认为百分之八更合理。

王国安：如果贵公司愿意分担一半的广告费用，我们可以把佣金降低到百分之八。

史强生：贵公司能保证我们每年有多少出口额？

王国安：去年洗衣机的销售总额是两百五十万。如果独家代理，我们每年至少可以进口贵公司五百万美元的洗衣机。不过，洗碗机是第一次在中国试销。销路怎么样还不清楚。我们需要先做一个市场调查，然后才能决定。

史强生：这样吧，我们可以先签订一个一年的独家代理协议，看看我们的产品是不是受欢迎。

白　琳：我想中国的女士们一定会喜欢用洗碗机。

李信文：（笑）你错了，白小姐！在中国现在洗碗的都是男人！

词汇（一）　Vocabulary (1) D002

1.	达成	dáchéng	to reach (an agreement, etc.)
2.	协议	xiéyì	agreement
3.	作为	zuòwéi	as; to act/serve as
4.	独家代理	dújiā dàilǐ	sole/exclusive (sales) agent/agency
5.	关照	guānzhào	to look after; concern and care
6.	尽力	jìnlì	to do all one can; to do one's best
7.	满足	mǎnzú	to satisfy; to meet (a demand/request, etc.)
8.	百万	bǎiwàn	million
9.	经销	jīngxiāo	to sell/distribute on commission
10.	节能	jiénéng	energy-saving
11.	空调	kōngtiáo	air conditioner
12.	环保	huánbǎo	environment (al) protection (the short form for "环境保护huánjìng bǎohù"); environment-friendly
13.	洗衣机	xǐyījī	washing machine
14.	家用电器	jiāyòng diànqì	household appliances
	电器	diànqì	electrical equipment/appliance
15.	扩大	kuòdà	to expand; to enlarge; to extend
16.	独家代理权	dújiā dàilǐquán	right of the sole agency
17.	各地	gèdì	various places/localities
18.	销售网点	xiāoshòu wǎngdiǎn	commercial networks
19.	洗碗机	xǐwǎnjī	dishwasher
	洗碗	xǐ wǎn	to wash dishes
20.	资信	zīxìn	credit; (capital) credibility

21.	佣金	yòngjīn	commission
22.	将（要）	jiāng (yào)	be about to; will
23.	查询	cháxún	to inquire about
24.	有效期	yǒuxiàoqī	duration/term of validity
25.	之内	zhīnèi	within
26.	提取	tíqǔ	to draw; to collect
27.	分担	fēndān	to share responsibility for (a task/duty/etc.)
28.	费用	fèiyòng	cost; expenses
29.	出口额	chūkǒu'é	value of exports; export quota
	额	é	a specified quantity
30.	销售总额	xiāoshòu zǒng'é	gross sales
31.	至少	zhìshǎo	at (the) least
32.	市场调查	shìchǎng diàochá	market survey
33.	受欢迎	shòu huānyíng	be well-received; popular
34.	女士	nǚshì	woman; lady; Ms.; Miss

专有名词 / 特殊名词 Proper Nouns / Special Nouns

| 广东 | Guǎngdōng | a province in southeast China |

句型（一）　Sentence Patterns (1)

1. 就……达成（了）协议　reach an agreement on...

例：① 中美双方刚刚就交货时间和付款方式达成了协议。

② 我们已经就明年的订单达成了协议。

2. 作为……　as...; act / serve as...

例：① 今天双方要就东方公司作为美方在中国的销售代理问题进行洽谈。

② 作为中方谈判代表，我还有一个问题。

3. 可是 + V. (or Adj.)　(to emphasize the tone of the speaker)

例：① 王总经理，这次我们公司可是购买了您两百多万美元的东西。

② 无论您怎么说，这个报盘可是太高了！

4. 有关……的情况　with regard to the situation of...

例：① 有关我方的资信情况，建议您向中国银行北京分行查询。

② 我想向各位介绍一下儿有关这种产品销售代理的基本情况。

5. 在……之内　within...

例：① 东方公司必须同意在我们的协议有效期之内不代理其他公司的同类产品。

② 我们将在三天之内通知您我们的决定。

（二）阅读短文 Reading Passage

外国货在中国
Foreign Goods in China

课文英译

　　随着中外贸易的迅速发展，越来越多的外国产品进入了中国。从衣食住行到高科技产品，中国人对外国货的兴趣越来越浓。毫无疑问，人口众多的中国是一个非常有潜力的巨大市场。外国厂商正面临着一次难得的商业机会。可是，人地生疏的外国公司在中国做生意并不是一件容易的事。进入中国市场的外国产品也有不同的命运：有的赚钱，有的赔本，有的还因为盗版产品和山寨产品而遭受经济损失。为了在中国市场的竞争中取得成功，许多外国厂商委托资信可靠的中国公司作为代理，销售它们的产品。一般说，代理可分为三种，即总代理、独家代理和普通代理。总代理可以全权代表外国厂商在代理协议商定的地区进行各种商业活动和拥有指定分代理的权利。独家代理拥有在商定地区经销指定产品的专卖权，同时不能经销其他厂家的同类产品。普通代理有生产商许可，销售指定的产品，提取佣金，但没有专卖权。因此厂商也可以签约若干个代理商同时代理销售同一产品。总之，销售代理不但可以为外国厂商提供便利的销售网点、降低产品销售成本，而且有利于迅速打开市场、建立品牌知名度。这是一种对双方都有利的商业经营方式。

词汇（二）　Vocabulary (2)

1.	衣食住行	yī shí zhù xíng	clothing, food, shelter and transportation; basic necessities for life
2.	浓	nóng	strong; dense
3.	毫无疑问	háowú yíwèn	without a doubt; undoubtedly
4.	人口众多	rénkǒu zhòngduō	to have a very large population
	人口	rénkǒu	population
	众多	zhòngduō	numerous
5.	潜力	qiánlì	potential
6.	巨大	jùdà	huge; tremendous
7.	厂商	chǎngshāng	manufacturer; firm; commercial corporation
8.	面临	miànlín	to face; be faced with; be up against
9.	难得	nándé	rare; hard to come by; seldom
10.	人地生疏	rén dì shēngshū	be unfamiliar with the place and the people; be a complete stranger
11.	并不	bìng bù	not at all, by no means
12.	命运	mìngyùn	fate; destiny
13.	赚钱	zhuàn qián	to make money; to make a profit
14.	盗版产品	dàobǎn chǎnpǐn	illegal copy; pirated products
	盗版	dàobǎn	piracy; pirated edition
15.	山寨产品	shānzhài chǎnpǐn	imitating reproduction
	山寨	shānzhài	knockoff; to make a knockoff product; (literally, mountain stockade/stronghold)
16.	遭受	zāoshòu	to incur (losses, etc.); to sustain; to suffer
17.	损失	sǔnshī	loss; to lose

18.	委托	wěituō	to entrust
19.	可靠	kěkào	reliable; dependable; trustworthy
20.	即	jí	namely; to be (with emphasis)
21.	总代理	zǒngdàilǐ	general agent/agency
22.	普通代理	pǔtōng dàilǐ	commission agent/agency
23.	全权	quánquán	with full authority; full/plenary powers
24.	拥有	yōngyǒu	to possess; to have; to own
25.	指定	zhǐdìng	to appoint; to assign
26.	分代理	fēndàilǐ	sub-agent
27.	专卖权	zhuānmàiquán	exclusive right to sell sth.; a monopoly right
28.	许可	xǔkě	permission; to permit; to allow
29.	签约	qiān yuē	to sign a contract
30.	若干	ruògān	a certain number/amount
31.	同一	tóngyī	same; identical
32.	便利	biànlì	convenient
33.	有利	yǒulì	beneficial; advantageous

句型（二）　Sentence Patterns (2)

1. 从……到……　　from...to...

例：❶ 从衣食住行到高科技产品，中国人对外国货的兴趣越来越浓。

　　❷ 从南到北，代表团参观了很多地方。

2. 面临……　　to face/be faced with...; be up against

例：❶ 外国厂商正面临着一次难得的商业机会。

　　❷ 我们的产品正面临着新的竞争。

3. 并不　　not at all; by no means (*for emphasizing negation)

例：❶ 在中国做生意并不是一件容易的事。

　　❷ 很抱歉，本公司并不打算签订这个合同。

4. （……）即……　　namely; to be (with emphasis)

例：❶ 代理可分为三种，即总代理、独家代理和普通代理。

　　❷ 中国的国家中央银行即中国人民银行。

5. A 有利于 B　　A is beneficial/helpful to B

例：❶ 签约销售代理有利于迅速打开市场。

　　❷ 改革开放政策有利于中国经济的发展。

（三）练习与活动 Exercises & Activities

I. 词汇练习 Vocabulary Exercises

1. 连词比赛。Matching games.

按照拼音找出相应的英文并将标示该英文的字母填进"？"栏，再写出汉字。

Match each *pinyin* with its English equivalent by filling in the corresponding letter into the "?" box, and then writing Chinese characters into the "汉字" box.

* 第一场 Game one:

	PINYIN	汉字	?
1	dújiā dàilǐ		
2	jiāyòng diànqì		
3	jiénéng		
4	fēndān		
5	chūkǒu'é		
6	jīngxiāo		
7	tíqǔ		
8	cháxún		
9	shìchǎng diàochá		
10	xiéyì		

	English equivalent
A	energy-saving
B	to sell on commission
C	exclusive (sales) agent
D	to draw; to collect
E	household appliances
F	market survey
G	agreement
H	to inquire about
I	value of exports
J	to share responsibility for

* 第二场 Game two:

	PINYIN	汉字	?
1	qiān yuē		
2	wěituō		
3	qiánlì		
4	sǔnshī		
5	dàobǎn		
6	fēndàilǐ		
7	chǎngshāng		
8	zhuānmàiquán		
9	fǎngzhìpǐn		
10	pǐnpái		

	English equivalent
A	potential
B	a monopoly right
C	to sign a contract
D	brand name
E	imitation; replica
F	manufacturer
G	sub-agent
H	pirated edition
I	to entrust
J	loss; to lose

2. 组词。Build upon the following words.

例：提前　→　　提前付款　　　　　　提前交货

（1）达成　→ _____　　_____

（2）满足　→ _____　　_____

（3）扩大　→ _____　　_____

（4）提取　→ _____　　_____

（5）分担　→ _____　　_____

（6）面临　→ _____　　_____

（7）遭受　→ _____　　_____

（8）拥有　→ _____　　_____

3. 用中文解释以下生词的意思，然后造句。

Explain the following in Chinese, then make a sentence for each of them.

例：省力：不用花很多力气，很方便

这件事很省力，一点儿也不麻烦。

（1）关照： _____

_____

（2）尽力： _____

_____

（3）资信： _____

_____

（4）佣金： _____

_____

（5）查询： _____

_____

（6）销售总额： _____

_____

（7）市场调查：_____

_____

（8）将（要）：_____

_____

（9）委托：_____

_____

（10）全权：_____

_____

（11）许可：_____

_____

（12）人地生疏：_____

（13）人口众多：_____

_____

（14）毫无疑问：_____

_____

4. 阅读下面的句子，根据拼音提示写出汉字。
Please read the following sentences and write down the missing characters according to the _pinyin_.

（1）作为 _____ 的代理商，我们会尽力 _____ 顾客的要求，保证 _____
　　　　 shòu huānyíng　　　　　　　　　　　　 mǎnzú　　　　　　　　 tígōng

最好的服务。

（2）贵公司必须同意在协议的 _____ 之内不 _____ 销售其他公司的
　　　　　　　　　　　　　　 yǒuxiàoqī　　　　　　　 dàilǐ

_____ 产品。
　 tónglèi

（3）按照 _____ 的结果，_____ 空调和 _____ 洗衣机等家用
　　　　　shìchǎng diàochá　　　　　jiénéng　　　　　　huánbǎo

　　_____ 产品的市场 _____ 很好。今年的销售 _____ 至少可以有
　　diànqì　　　　　　　　xiāolù　　　　　　　　　　zǒng'é

五 _____！
　　bǎiwàn

（4）谢谢您的 _____。我们已经向银行 _____ 了那家公司的 _____
　　　　　　guānzhào　　　　　　　　　　cháxún　　　　　　　　　zīxìn

情况。

（5）"如果贵公司能够 _____ 在 _____ 的销售 _____，_____
　　　　　　　　　　　kuòdà　　　gèdì　　　　　　wǎngdiǎn　　　jìnlì

提高 _____。我们可以同意 _____ 百分之十的要求，并 _____
　　xiāoshòu'é　　　　　　　　yòngjīn　　　　　　　　　　　　fēndān

百分之二十五的广告 _____。""这听起来更 _____。我们 _____
　　　　　　　　　　　fèiyòng　　　　　　　　　　hélǐ　　　　jiēshòu

你们的条件。_____！"
　　　　　　yìyán-wéidìng

（6）那家公司已经得到我方的 _____。他们是我们最重要的 _____。我
　　　　　　　　　　　　　　xǔkě　　　　　　　　　　　　kèhù

们必须 _____ 他们 _____ 的 _____。
　　　　shǐ　　　bǎi fēn zhī bǎi　　　mǎnyì

II. 句型练习（一）　Sentence Pattern Exercises (1)

1. 🎧 *007* 请用"就……达成了协议"回答下面的问题。
Answer the following questions by using the pattern of "就……达成了协议".

（1）在昨天的谈判中，双方就什么问题达成了协议？

_____

（2）长城服装厂的陈厂长跟他的竞争对手就什么达成了协议？

_____

（3）听说东方公司希望作为贵公司在中国的独家代理。你们双方已经洽谈过了吗？

是啊，_____

（4）最近中国跟哪个国家进行过贸易洽谈？谈了一些什么问题？谈得圆满吗？

_____

2. 🎧 008 请用"作为……"回答下面的问题。

Answer the following questions by using the pattern of "作为……".

（1）如果请你做我们玩具产品的销售代理，你希望提取多少佣金？

_____

（2）如果你是一家公司的总经理，你打算怎样管理公司的业务？

_____

（3）为什么生产厂家常常要做市场调查？

_____

（4）外国人（/外国公司）在中国做生意最大的问题是什么？

_____

3. 🎧 009 把"可是"放进下面的句子中可以加强说话人的语气。想一想把"可是"放在哪儿才合适？（最多可以放入九个"可是"）如果有时间，请复习第 2 课的"可 + Adj. + 了"。

Where should you insert the word "可是" into the following sentences to emphasize the tone of the speaker?（ *up to 9 "可是" in total）In the meantime, you may want to review "可 + Adj. + 了" in Lesson 2.

（1）贵厂生产的洗碗机太方便了！

（2）那种新型空调真不便宜！

（3）交易会上的新产品太多了，一个小时真看不过来！

（4）甲：百分之十的佣金太高了！

乙：可是我觉得很合理。别忘了，我方分担了一半的广告费用呢！

（5）甲：听说那家公司的销售网点有一些问题。你们别上当啊！

乙：不对吧？我们做了资信调查以后，才决定委托他们做我们的独家代理。

4. 🎧 *010* 在新闻发布会上，史强生总裁宣布了跟中国东方进出口公司的新合同，还用英文回答了提问。请你用"有关……的情况"，写出他的回答。

After he announced a new contract with China Eastern Import & Export Corporation at a news conference, Mr. Smith took some questions from the audience. The following are his answers in English. Please rewrite（not translate）his answers in Chinese by using the pattern of "有关……的情况".

（1）记者：您能告诉我们贵公司新型洗碗机的价格吗？

Mr. Smith: You might look in our product catalogue for the information on wholesale price and retail price.

_____

（2）记者：请问，除了家用电器以外，贵公司还有哪些产品？

Mr. Smith: You can go to our company's website（i.e. go online）to find the information about our other products.

_____

（3）记者：请问，贵公司去年的销售总额是多少？

Mr. Smith: I am sorry. I can't tell you the information about the last year's gross sales of our company at this moment.

_____

（4）记者：您认为东方公司目前的销售网点能满足贵公司的要求吗？

Mr. Smith: It would be better to have Mr. Li, the manager of Eastern Corporation, answer this question.

_____

5. 完成下面带"在……之内"的句子。

Complete the following sentences with the pattern of "在……之内".

（1）本厂计划在三年之内 _____。

（2）双方代表将在本星期之内 _____。

（3）在合同有效期之内，_____。

（4）在产品的质量保证期之内，_____。

III. 句型练习（二） **Sentence Pattern Exercises (2)**

1. 用"从……到……"改写下面的句子。

Rewrite the following sentences by using the pattern of "从……到……".

（1）李经理这个星期每天都有会谈和宴会。

_____

（2）进口和出口的生意，那家公司都做。

_____

（3）这家商店不但代理销售服装、玩具，而且代理销售电脑和汽车。

_____

（4）昨天的会谈时间非常长。双方代表讨论了交货、付款、总代理权和明年的访问等等问题。

_____

2. "面临"和"面对"（第5课）的意思一样，但是"面临"常常用在比较抽象的意思中。请完成下面有"面临……"的句子，熟悉它的用法。

"面临" and "面对" (Lesson 5) are similar to each other. However, "面临" is often used in an abstract sense. Complete the following sentences with the pattern of "面临……".

（1）因为面临其他厂家的竞争 _____。

（2）虽然那家大型国有企业的改革面临很多困难 _____。

（3）当一家企业的发展面临挑战的时候 _____。

（4）即使面临着这样难得的商业机会 _____。

3. 🎧 D12 用"并不"对下面的问题给出否定的回答。

Make negative answers to the following questions by using the pattern of "并不".

（1）在中国家庭里，总是女士洗碗，对吗？

_____

（2）普通代理可以全权代表厂家和享有产品专卖权，对不对？

_____

（3）听说贵公司打算明年开始代理销售家电产品。这是真的吗？

_____

（4）听说那家企业的知名度很高，产品也很受欢迎。我们要跟他们签约合作吗？

_____

4. 🎧 D13 "即"的意思跟"就是"一样。请用"……即……"回答下面的问题。

The word "即" and the word "就是" have same meaning. Please answer the following questions by using the pattern of "……即……".

（1）底价的意思是什么？

_____

（2）什么是报盘和还盘？

_____

（3）人民币的单位分为几种？是什么？（You may refer to Lesson 9's Reading Passage）

_____

（4）什么是"世贸组织"？它的英文是什么？（You may refer to Lesson 9）

_____

5. 🎧 用 "A 有利于 B" 回答下面的问题。
D14

Answer the following questions by using the pattern of "A 有利于 B".

（1）为什么很多外国厂商委托中国公司作为产品销售代理？

_____。

（2）取得独家代理权对代理商有什么好处？

_____。

（3）引进最新的高科技对一个老企业有什么好处？

_____。

（4）到中国做生意为什么应该了解中国人的文化传统？

_____。

IV. 阅读、讨论和其他活动　Reading, Discussion and Other Activities

1. 🎧 根据课文对话回答问题。
D15

Answer the following questions according to the dialogues in this lesson.

（1）美方对什么非常满意？

_____

（2）为什么今天下午王总经理也来参加会谈？

_____

（3）王总经理希望怎样扩大跟美方的合作？

_____

（4）为什么美方不想把销售空调的独家代理权给东方公司？

_____

（5）美方可以向谁查询东方公司的资信情况？

_____

（6）东方公司希望提取多少佣金？佣金可以降低一些吗？

_____

（7）如果作为独家代理，东方公司每年能进口多少美元的洗衣机？

_____

（8）东方公司计划为哪种产品做一个市场调查？为什么？

_____

（9）今天的洽谈，双方达成了哪些协议？

_____

（10）* 附加题（*extra question）

请跟你的同学讨论一下儿：你们觉得这种节能洗碗机在中国会有很好的销路吗？为什么？

_____

_____

2. 小任务。Tasks.

Ⓐ 本课的阅读短文介绍了三种不同的代理。现在请你想一想它们有什么不同，然后上网找出一家通过销售代理在中国做生意的外国公司并写一份小报告。你的报告应该包括：

（1）这家外国公司的名字和它的简单介绍；
（2）中国代理商的名字和它的简单介绍；
（3）它们在中国销售什么产品；
（4）采用了哪种代理方式；
（5）外国公司使用中国代理商是不是一个好办法？

The Reading Passage in this lesson introduces 3 types of agent/agency. Now think about the differences among these 3 types of agent/agency, then use the internet to find a foreign company that sells products in China through an agent. Please write a short report about your findings. Your report should include the following:

(1) The name of the foreign company and a brief introduction about this company;
(2) The name of the Chinese company (as an agent) and a brief introduction about this company;
(3) What products do they sell in China?
(4) What type of the agent/agency has been adopted?
(5) Is it a good idea for a foreign company to have a sales agent in China?

B 你知道最近在市场上有什么山寨产品或者盗版产品吗？请找出 1-2 个例子，然后写一个小报告。在你的报告里，请你说一说：

（1）介绍你找到的例子。

（2）你觉得山寨（盗版）产品好不好？为什么？

（3）你会买它们吗？为什么？

（4）如果你的产品被"山寨"了，你会怎么办？

Have you heard any imitation reproductions or pirated products on the market recently? Please provide 1-2 examples and present it/them in class. Your report should include the following:

(1) Tell about your findings (i.e. the knockoff product or pirated product).

(2) Do you like this kind of products and why?

(3) Would you be willing to purchase a knockoff product or pirated product for any reason? Why?

(4) What will you do if your (/your company's) product has been illegally copied?

3. 🎧 快速复习。**Quick review.**

A 阅读下面的短文，复习学过的词汇和句型。

Read the following text and review vocabularies and sentence patterns that you have learned.

　　在过去的几天中，中美双方代表进行了多次洽谈，讨论了从产品价格、付款方式到交货时间等问题。虽然在洽谈过程中，双方有一些不同的意见，但是这些问题最后都得到了圆满解决。今天东方公司又向美方提出了独家代理销售美方家电产品的要求。可是美方告诉东方公司，节能空调的代理权已经给了广东的一家公司，在代理协议有效期内，美方不能把独家代理权交给东方公司。通过一个上午的洽谈，双方最后达成了协议。协议包括：

　　第一，美方同意从明年开始由东方公司在中国独家代理销售环保洗衣机和节能家用洗碗机。

　　第二，考虑到洗碗机产品是第一次在中国市场试销，中美双方同意先签订一年的洗碗机独家代理协议。洗衣机独家代理的有效期为三年。

第三，中方同意明年至少进口和销售五百万美元的洗衣机产品。

第四，双方同意以上两种产品的代理佣金是百分之八。

第五，如果中方能够满足以上第三条的要求，美方同意分担百分之五十的广告费用。

双方代表对谈判结果都非常满意。史强生和白琳发现，要想在这样的国际商务活动中取得成功，耐心的交流和沟通是少不了的。

B 选择正确的答案　Choose the correct answer based on the paragraphs above.

（1）在过去几天的洽谈中，双方讨论了哪些问题？

　　a 产品价格和付款方式
　　b 产品价格和代理销售
　　c 产品价格、付款方式和代理销售
　　d 产品价格、付款方式和交货时间

（2）过去几天的洽谈进行得顺利吗？

　　a 比较顺利，结果圆满
　　b 比较顺利，可是有一些问题
　　c 虽然有一些问题，可是都圆满解决了

（3）通过洽谈，美方同意把什么产品的独家代理权给东方公司？

　　a 环保洗衣机和节能家用洗碗机
　　b 环保洗衣机、节能空调和家用洗碗机
　　c 家电产品和环保洗衣机、节能家用洗碗机

（4）这些产品的代理权有效期是多久？

　　a 洗碗机和洗衣机都是一年
　　b 洗衣机和洗碗机都是三年
　　c 洗衣机是三年，洗碗机是一年
　　d 洗衣机和空调是三年，洗碗机是一年

（5）中方同意明年进口、销售多少美元的洗衣机？

    a 五百万美元以上

    b 差不多五百美元

    c 最多五百万美元

    d 五百万美元或者更多

（6）美方同意分担一半的广告费用的条件是什么？

    a 中方提取百分之八的佣金

    b 中方能够满足协议第三条的要求

    c 中方提取百分之八的佣金，同时中方能够满足协议第三条的销售额

（四）附录　　Appendix

1. 独家代理证书 Sole Agent Certificate

2. 代理商授权证书 Certificate of Authorization

3. 经销商洽谈日 The Dealer Day

4. 资信证明书 Certificate of Credit

中国工商银行
INDUSTRIAL AND COMMERCIAL BANK OF CHINA

资 信 证 明 书（正本）
Certificate of Creditworthiness（original）

号码： 陕A 00009893

日 期：Date:二○○九年四月十五日

陕西省动物卫生监督所/陕西建华招投标代理咨询有限责任公司：

截止 2009 年 4 月 12 日（即该日我行营业终了结帐时）止，西安德图仪器有限公司在中国工商银行西安市南关支行（所属）雁塔路支行开立账户，账号为（3700023009024511008）的资金往来中未发生开具空头支票、印鉴（支付密码）不符、变造支票、变造汇票、无理拒付等违反我行结算纪律情况。

仅此证明，下无正文。

银行签章
Bank's Seal

有权签字人
Authorized Signature

提示：阅读本证明书时请同时阅知证明书背面"声明"。
Note: Please read this certificate in conjunction with "Statement" on the back of the certificate.

11 广告与促销
Advertising and Sales Promotion

在昨天的谈判中，中美双方达成了协议，决定一起分担在中国的广告费用。因为今天中午史先生和白小姐就要坐高铁离开北京去上海了，所以今天的洽谈开始得很早。双方代表就广告策划和销售策略等问题进行了讨论。

（一）对 话 Dialogue

1. 广告策划 Advertisement Planning

（在长城酒店小会议室）

白 琳：李先生，您到得真早！用过早餐了吗？

李信文：谢谢，我吃过早饭了。中午你们还要坐高铁去上海，所以我想早点儿过来。我们可以有多一点儿时间，就怎样做好产品的广告宣传和销售交换一下儿意见，制定一个初步方案。史先生，不知道您有什么看法。

史强生：这次的广告是为我们的家电产品正式进入中国市场宣传造势，我认为首先应该突出我们的品牌形象。

李信文：我完全同意。节能、环保是这个品牌产品的优势和卖点。我们的广告一定要有效地传达出这些信息。

白　琳：李先生，您对中国市场的情况比我们熟悉，广告策划又是您的强项，您有什么具体建议呢？

李信文：我在想我们可以邀请一位著名影星担任品牌形象代言人。

史强生：嗯，利用名人效应应该是一个不错的方法，不过费用可能会比较高吧？

李信文：这样吧，费用的问题让我先找一家有经验的广告公司咨询一下儿，然后再做进一步讨论和决定。除非费用在合理范围之内，否则我们将采用其他的办法。

课文英译

2. 销售策略 Sales Strategy

史强生：我想了解一下儿，除了刚才谈到的产品广告宣传以外，贵公司还有什么更多的具体打算吗？有什么需要我们配合的？

李信文：为了迅速打开市场，我方计划搞一次大型促销活动，扩大宣传造势的效果，建立品牌知名度。

史强生：您觉得这个促销活动的规模应该有多大？

李信文：我主张把这个促销活动分为两个阶段进行。首先在全国各大城市进行产品促销活动。如果市场销路好，我们再把促销活动范围扩大到中小城市。如果销路不够好的话，我们可以对销售策略进行及时调整。

白　琳：对不起，我想问一句：贵公司的官网也会同时推出相应的促销活动
　　　　吧？

李信文：是的。我们会在网上推出更多的优惠活动。比如，免费送货上
　　　　门、延长产品保修期和"买一送一"等等。

白　琳：（笑）听起来很有吸引力。我就最喜欢"买一送一"了！

词汇（一）　Vocabulary (1) 🎧 D02

1.	促销	cùxiāo	to promote sales; sales promotion
2.	高铁	gāotiě	high-speed rail
3.	策划	cèhuà	planning; to plan
4.	策略	cèlüè	strategy; tactics
5.	宣传	xuānchuán	propaganda; to promote; to give publicity to
6.	制定	zhìdìng	to draw up; to formulate; to establish
7.	方案	fāng'àn	scheme; plan; project
8.	造势	zào shì	to put spin on sth.; to build up publicity
9.	突出	tūchū	to give prominence to; to protrude
10.	形象	xíngxiàng	image
11.	卖点	màidiǎn	selling point
12.	有效	yǒuxiào	effective; effectively
13.	传达	chuándá	to pass on; to convey; to deliver
14.	熟悉	shúxi	be familiar with
15.	强项	qiángxiàng	key strength; specialty
16.	影星	yǐngxīng	movie star

17.	担任	dānrèn	to serve as; to take charge of
18.	代言人	dàiyánrén	spokesperson
19.	名人效应	míngrén xiàoyìng	celebrity effect
	名人	míngrén	famous person; celebrity
	效应	xiàoyìng	effect
20.	除非	chúfēi	unless
21.	范围	fànwéi	scope; range; area
22.	否则	fǒuzé	otherwise
23.	配合	pèihé	to coordinate with; to cooperate and support
24.	大型	dàxíng	large-scale
25.	效果	xiàoguǒ	effect; result
26.	规模	guīmó	scale; scope
27.	阶段	jiēduàn	phase; stage; period
28.	及时	jíshí	in time; promptly
29.	官网	guānwǎng	official website
30.	相应	xiàngyìng	relevant; corresponding
31.	优惠活动	yōuhuì huódòng	promotions; favorable offers
	优惠	yōuhuì	preferential; favorable
32.	比如	bǐrú	for instance; for example
33.	送货上门	sòng huò shàng mén	home delivery
34.	延长	yáncháng	to extend
35.	保修期	bǎoxiūqī	warranty period
36.	买一送一	mǎi yī sòng yī	buy one and get one free

句型（一）　Sentence Patterns (1) *003*

1. 离开 A 去 / 回 B　　to leave A for/to return to B

例：❶ 今天中午史先生和白小姐就要坐高铁离开北京去上海了。

❷ 他已经离开这家公司回大学读工商管理硕士（MBA）了。

2. 就……进行讨论 / 交换意见
to have discussions on/to exchange opinions on

例：❶ 双方代表就广告策划和销售策略等问题进行了讨论。

❷ 在今天的晨会上，大家就怎样做好产品的广告宣传和市场销售交换了意见。

3. 对……熟悉　　to be familiar with...

例：❶ 您对中国市场的情况比我们熟悉。

❷ 对不起，我们对这种产品的行情不太熟悉。

4. 除非……，否则……　　unless...., otherwise...

例：❶ 除非费用在合理范围之内，否则我们将采用其他的办法。

❷ 除非对方的资信可靠，否则我们不会跟他们做这笔生意。

（二）阅读短文 Reading Passage

广告和中国人的心理
Advertisements and the Chinese Mentality

课文英译

　　做生意离不开广告。好广告不但能帮助厂商打开市场销路，而且有利于建立产品的知名度。一般说，年轻人喜欢新潮和时尚，中老年人注重物美价廉，这大概是通常的规律。不过，在中国做广告还一定要了解中国人的文化传统和价值观。长城、黄河、中国龙、孔子、天安门等是中国国家和文化的象征。中国的消费者往往不能接受用这些形象开玩笑或者搞怪。相反，一些以中国人喜闻乐见的形式来传达产品信息的外国商业广告通常都能取得很好的宣传效果。例如，可口可乐和百事可乐的名字让喜欢讨吉利的中国人一听就喜欢。"车到山前必有路，有路必有丰田车"是丰田汽车在中国的广告。它以借用中国俗语的方式来巧妙地宣传自己的产品，使中国消费者一见就过目不忘。另外值得注意的是，中国人在传统上总觉得产品本身才是最好的广告。"酒香不怕巷子深"。如果你的东西真得非常好，就不用担心没有人买。在中国消费者看来，过分夸张、过分漂亮的广告有时是不可信的。"王婆卖瓜，自卖自夸"，谁不喜欢说自己的产品是最好的呢？

词汇（二） Vocabulary (2)

1.	心理	xīnlǐ	mentality
2.	离不开	líbukāi	cannot do without; unable to separate from
3.	新潮	xīncháo	new trend; trendy
4.	时尚	shíshàng	fashion; fashionable; stylish
5.	中老年	zhōnglǎonián	middle and old age
	中年	zhōngnián	middle age
	老年	lǎonián	old age
6.	注重	zhùzhòng	to attach great importance to; to pay attention to
7.	物美价廉 / 价廉物美	wùměi-jiàlián/ jiàlián-wùměi	(said of merchandise) excellent quality and reasonable price
8.	规律	guīlù	law; regular pattern
9.	价值观	jiàzhíguān	value system
10.	龙	lóng	dragon
11.	象征	xiàngzhēng	symbol; to symbolize
12.	消费者	xiāofèizhě	consumer
	消费	xiāofèi	to consume
13.	往往	wǎngwǎng	often; frequently; to more often than not
14.	搞怪	gǎo guài	to do weird things; to make funny jokes
15.	相反	xiāngfǎn	opposite; contrary; on the contrary
16.	喜闻乐见	xǐwèn-lèjiàn	love to see and hear
17.	形式	xíngshì	form; shape
18.	讨吉利	tǎo jílì	to seek good fortune (through auspicious sayings, etc.)
	讨	tǎo	to demand; to ask for; to seek
	吉利	jílì	good luck/fortune; auspicious; lucky

19.	车到山前 必有路	chē dào shān qián bì yǒu lù	When the carriage reaches the mountain, there will surely be a road.... Things will take care of themselves when the time comes.
20.	借用	jièyòng	to borrow; to use sth. for another purpose
21.	俗语	súyǔ	common saying; slang
22.	巧妙	qiǎomiào	ingenious; skillful; clever
23.	过目不忘	guò mù bú wàng	to have sth. imprinted in one's memory; to have a photographic memory; very impressive
24.	值得	zhídé	to deserve; to be worth
25.	本身	běnshēn	itself; oneself
26.	酒香不怕 巷子深	jiǔ xiāng bú pà xiàngzi shēn	If your wine really tastes good, you don't need to worry that your wine shop is located at the end of a narrow lane; Good wine needs no bush... No matter where you are, people will find you if your product is good.
	香	xiāng	fragrant; aroma
	巷子	xiàngzi	lane; narrow road
27.	过分	guòfèn	excessive(ly); over(ly)
28.	不可信	bù kě xìn	cannot be trusted; untrustworthy
29.	王婆卖瓜， 自卖自夸	Wángpó mài guā, zì mài zì kuā	When old lady Wang sold melons, she was always overstating her goods...A salesman always says that his products are the best.

专有名词 / 特殊名词 Proper Nouns / Special Nouns

1.	黄河	Huáng Hé	Yellow River
2.	天安门	Tiān'ānmén	Tian'anmen (i.e. Gate of Heavenly Peace)
3.	可口可乐	Kěkǒu-Kělè	Coca-Cola
4.	百事可乐	Bǎishì Kělè	Pepsi
5.	丰田	Fēngtián	Toyota

句型（二）　Sentence Patterns (2)

1. A 离不开 B　　A cannot do anything well without B; A is inseparable from B

例：❶ 做生意离不开广告。

　　❷ 放心！那家公司离不开我们的产品。

2. 以……的形式（/ 方式）来 + V. + sth.
do sth. in the form of; do sth. by way of

例：❶ 这家公司的广告往往以中国人喜闻乐见的形式来传达产品信息。

　　❷ 它以借用中国俗语的方式来巧妙地宣传自己的产品。

3. 一……就……　　as soon as; once...then...

例：❶ 可口可乐的名字让喜欢讨吉利的中国人一听就喜欢。

　　❷ 丰田车的广告借用了中国俗语，使中国消费者一见就过目不忘。

4. 值得注意的是……　　What is worth noting is...

例：❶ 值得注意的是，中国人在传统上总觉得产品本身才是最好的广告。

　　❷ 值得注意的是，我们的产品正面临着新的竞争。

5. 在……看来　　in the view of...

例：❶ 在中国消费者看来，过分夸张的广告常常是不可信的。

　　❷ 在很多外国厂商看来，到大城市投资更有吸引力。

6. 谁不 V. …… 呢？
Who doesn't + V. ...? (*to form a rhetorical question. It means "everyone does" "no exception")

例：❶ 谁不喜欢说自己的产品是最好的呢？

　　❷ 谁不想买到又便宜又好的东西呢？

（三）练习与活动　Exercises & Activities

I. 词汇练习　Vocabulary Exercises

1. 组词。你可以参考总附录中的词表。

Build upon the following words. You may refer to the Vocabulary List in the General Appendix.

例：（具）体（身）体

（1）策（　　）　　策（　　）

（2）形（　　）　　形（　　）

（3）保（　　）　　保（　　）　　保（　　）

（4）代（　　）　　代（　　）　　代（　　）

（5）效（　　）　　效（　　）　　效（　　）　　效（　　）

（6）有（　　）　　有（　　）　　有（　　）　　有（　　）

（7）方（　　）　　方（　　）　　方（　　）　　方（　　）

（8）（　　）定　　（　　）定　　（　　）定

（9）（　　）星　　（　　）星　　（　　）星

（10）（　　）时　　（　　）时　　（　　）时

2. 用下列词汇填空。

Fill in the blanks by using the words given below. Each word can be used only once.

Ⓐ　配合　有效　形象　造势　卖点　传达　突出　宣传　担任

（1）这次的产品广告一定要 ＿＿＿＿＿＿ 我们的品牌 ＿＿＿＿＿＿。

（2）环保和节能是新产品的 ＿＿＿＿＿＿。我们的广告 ＿＿＿＿＿＿ 一定要
＿＿＿＿＿＿ 地 ＿＿＿＿＿＿ 出这些信息。

（3）公司邀请了一位著名影星 ＿＿＿＿＿＿ 产品代言人，＿＿＿＿＿＿ 今年的新产
品宣传 ＿＿＿＿＿＿ 活动。

Ⓑ　满意　官网　保修期　策略　送货上门　调整　规模　相应　优惠

（4）这次促销活动的 _____ 很大。公司的 _____ 也会推出 _____ 的 _____ 活动。

（5）公司对目前的促销活动不太 _____，我们必须及时 _____ 我们的销售 _____。

（6）在网上购买的产品，不但可以免费 _____，而且可以免费延长 _____。

Ⓒ　注重　价值观　喜闻乐见　形象　象征　值得

（7）广场舞是中国很多中老年人 _____ 的一种活动。

（8）龙的 _____ 是中国和中国人的 _____。

（9）我们的 _____ 可能不同，但是我们都觉得 _____ 和宣传传统文化是一件 _____ 做的事。

Ⓓ　不可信　消费者　离不开　新潮　效应　形式　促销　信息　过份

（10）这次大 _____ 活动将以"买一送一"的 _____ 吸引更多的 _____。

（11）在服装设计方面，_____ 跟搞怪并不一样。

（12）做好市场销售工作 _____ 消费者 _____。

（13）你的这些信息 _____ 夸张了名人 _____，我觉得 _____。

3. 小测试：下面的这些词，哪些你能"过目不忘"？请写出它们的英文意思和拼音。
Pop Quiz. Can you memorize（"过目不忘"）the following words? Please write down the English equivalents and pronunciations（*pinyin*）for these words.

（1）a. 高铁　b. 产品　c. 品牌　d. 名牌　e. 名人　f. 著名

English equivalent	Pronunciation (*pinyin*)
a. _____	_____

b._____   _____

c._____   _____

d._____   _____

e._____   _____

f._____   _____

（2） g.有效　　h.效果　　i.效应　　j.价值　　k.价格　　l.物美价廉

| English equivalent | Pronunciation (*pinyin*) |

g._____   _____

h._____   _____

i._____   _____

j._____   _____

k._____   _____

l._____   _____

（3） m.策划　　n.策略　　o.消费　　p.消费者　　q.免费　　r.喜闻乐见

| English equivalent | Pronunciation (*pinyin*) |

m._____   _____

n._____   _____

o._____   _____

p._____   _____

q._____   _____

r._____   _____

（4）s.制定　t.方案　u.时尚　v.新潮　w.搞怪　x.官网

English equivalent	Pronunciation (*pinyin*)
s.＿＿＿＿＿＿	＿＿＿＿＿＿
t.＿＿＿＿＿＿	＿＿＿＿＿＿
u.＿＿＿＿＿＿	＿＿＿＿＿＿
v.＿＿＿＿＿＿	＿＿＿＿＿＿
w.＿＿＿＿＿＿	＿＿＿＿＿＿
x.＿＿＿＿＿＿	＿＿＿＿＿＿

4. **本课的阅读短文中用了以下成语和俗语。请你想一想它们的意思，试着用中文回答下面的问题。**

The following Chinese idioms and old sayings are used in the Reading Passage of this lesson. Please think over their meanings again and try to answer the questions in Chinese below.

（1）你认为哪些产品"**物美价廉**"？请举出两个例子，并且告诉你的朋友在哪里可以买到它们。

＿＿＿＿＿＿＿＿＿＿＿＿＿＿＿＿＿＿＿＿

＿＿＿＿＿＿＿＿＿＿＿＿＿＿＿＿＿＿＿＿

（2）阅读短文中说，"许多以中国人**喜闻乐见**的形式来传达产品信息的外国商业广告往往都能取得很好的宣传效果"。你能举出一个这样的例子吗？

＿＿＿＿＿＿＿＿＿＿＿＿＿＿＿＿＿＿＿＿

＿＿＿＿＿＿＿＿＿＿＿＿＿＿＿＿＿＿＿＿

（3）"**过目不忘**"一般有两个意思。第一个是"非常好的记忆力"。第二个是"印象深刻"。你能用这两个不同的意思造句吗？

＿＿＿＿＿＿＿＿＿＿＿＿＿＿＿＿＿＿＿＿

＿＿＿＿＿＿＿＿＿＿＿＿＿＿＿＿＿＿＿＿

（4）日本的汽车厂商用"**车到山前必有路**，有路必有丰田车"给他们的丰田汽车做广告。你知道它原来是哪两句话吗？原来的意思是什么？丰田广告的意思是什么？请上网或者用你的词典查查看。

_____

_____

（5）你觉得什么时候（／什么情况下）可以用"**酒香不怕巷子深**"这句话？你能举出一个这样的例子吗？

_____

_____

（6）"**王婆卖瓜，自卖自夸**"这句话有什么意思？在你看来，做广告应该自夸吗？为什么？

_____

_____

II. 句型练习（一）　Sentence Pattern Exercises (1)

1. 助理白小姐将跟她的老板史强生总裁去中国。白小姐准备了一份日程表。现在她要把日程表发给中方。请用"**离开 A 去／回 B**"写出白小姐安排的旅行计划。

Miss Lynn Petty is going to accompany her boss, Johnson Smith, on a business trip to China, and she has already arranged a preliminary schedule (below). Now she will send the itinerary to Chinese counterparts. Please use the pattern "离开 A 去／回 B" to write down her travel plan.

China Trip Preliminary Schedule

Date	Departure City	Arrival City	Transportation	
June 30 (Fri)	Los Angeles (LAX)	Beijing (PEK)	UA7617 (nonstop)	✈
July 5 (Wed)	Beijing	Shanghai	CRH/G3	🚆
July 8 (Sat)	Shanghai (PVG)	Shenzhen(SZX)	MU5333 (nonstop)	✈
July 10 (Mon)	Shenzhen (SZX)	Los Angeles (LAX)	CA1894/UA199 (1 stop)	✈

（1）_____

（2）_____

（3）_____

（4）_____

2. 句型"就……进行讨论""就……交换意见"跟第 8 课的句型"就……进行谈判"和第 10 课的句型"就……达成协议"非常相似。请复习第 8 课和第 10 课的有关练习，再用本课的句型和学过的词汇回答下面的问题。例如：促销、广告、策划、策略、方案、宣传造势、代言人、品牌形象、范围、效果、优惠活动、费用、佣金、价格、交货时间、付款方式、进一步、仔细、继续、打交道，等等。

The sentence patterns of "就……进行讨论" and "就……交换意见" are very similar to the pattern "就 …… 进行谈判" in Lesson 8, and the pattern "就……达成协议" in Lesson 10. Please review the patterns and relevant exercises in Lesson 8 and Lesson 10, then answer the following questions by using the patterns of "就……进行讨论" or "就……交换意见" as well as words learned from this lesson and previous lessons. For instance, 促销、广告、策划、策略、方案、宣传造势、代言人、品牌形象、范围、效果、优惠活动、费用、佣金、价格、交货时间、付款方式、进一步、仔细、继续、打交道，etc.

（1）Mr. Bean: 你觉得中方希望跟总裁见面的目的是什么？

　　　Miss Smart: 我认为 _____。

（2）小　方：听说下个星期一我们市场部又要跟咨询公司开会了。

　　　老　陈：是啊。老板希望 _____。

（3）白　琳：王总，您觉得这份订单还有什么问题吗？

　　　王国安：不好意思，我觉得我们应该 _____。

（4）小　方：经理，我刚收到代理商的邮件，他们对这次的促销方案有不同的看法。

　　　李经理：这样吧，我们马上安排一个视频会议，_____
　　　_____。

（5）牛先生😎：谢小姐，我听说老板派你去跟那位著名影星见面。这太好了！你能帮我要一个签名（qiānmíng / autograph）吗？

　　　谢小姐☹：_____。

3. 完成下面带"对……熟悉"的句子。

Please complete the following sentences with the pattern "对……熟悉".

（1）因为白琳对 ＿＿＿＿＿＿＿＿＿＿＿＿＿＿＿＿ 很熟悉，所以公司派她去中国洽谈生意。

（2）公司决定由李先生担任销售部经理是一个合理的决定。大家都知道他对 ＿＿＿＿＿＿＿＿＿＿＿＿＿＿ 非常熟悉。＿＿＿＿＿＿＿＿＿＿＿ 是他的强项。

（3）因为对 ＿＿＿＿＿＿＿＿＿＿＿＿＿ 既不够熟悉又不够了解，这家外国企业在中国的发展 ＿＿＿＿＿＿＿＿＿＿＿＿＿＿＿。

（4）我对 ＿＿＿＿＿＿＿＿＿＿＿＿＿ 比较熟悉，可是（我）对 ＿＿＿＿＿＿＿＿＿＿ 并不熟悉。我 ＿＿＿＿＿＿＿＿＿＿＿＿＿＿＿＿ 。

4. 用"除非……，否则……"完成下面的句子。

Please complete the following sentences with the pattern "除非……，否则……".

（1）除非贵公司的报价在 ＿＿＿＿＿＿＿ 范围之内，＿＿＿＿＿＿＿＿＿＿＿＿＿＿＿＿ 。

（2）除非第一个阶段的销售不好，＿＿＿＿＿＿＿＿＿＿＿＿＿＿＿＿＿＿＿＿＿ 。

（3）＿＿＿＿＿＿＿＿＿＿＿＿＿＿＿＿＿＿＿＿＿＿＿＿＿ ，否则我方将不会增加投资。

（4）＿＿＿＿＿＿＿＿＿＿＿＿＿＿＿＿＿＿＿＿＿＿＿＿ ，否则我们的产品将面临更多的竞争。

III. 句型练习（二）　Sentence Pattern Exercises (2)

1. 用"A 离不开 B"回答下面的问题。

Answer the following questions with the pattern "A 离不开 B".

（1）如果想在一场商业谈判中取得成功，你认为离不开什么？

＿＿＿＿＿＿＿＿＿＿＿＿＿＿＿＿＿＿＿＿＿＿＿＿＿＿＿＿＿＿＿＿

（2）如果说做生意离不开广告，那么你认为做广告离不开什么？

＿＿＿＿＿＿＿＿＿＿＿＿＿＿＿＿＿＿＿＿＿＿＿＿＿＿＿＿＿＿＿＿

（3）如果想随时了解市场信息，你认为一定离不开什么？

_____

（4）你觉得外国企业想在中国顺利发展一定离不开什么？

_____

（5）如果你想在一家中国企业工作，你觉得一定离不开什么本领？

_____

2. 请用"以……的形式（来）+ verb + sth." 或者 "以……的方式（来）+ verb + sth." 把下面的句子翻译成中文。

Please translate the following sentences into Chinese by using the pattern "以……的形式（来）+ V. + sth." or "以……的方式（来）+ V. + sth."

（1）We have decided to promote sales of this year's new products in the form of "buy one and get one free."

_____

（2）He can deal with different clients by the most effective methods. He is the best sales manager in our company.

_____

（3）We still don't know how (in what way) the other party plans to cooperate with us.

_____

（4）That television commercial has effectively delivered the information about the product in the form that Chinese consumers love (to hear and see).

_____

3. 白琳只在上海待了一天。她的日程安排得非常紧。她到了上海以后，立刻跟上海进出口贸易公司的张经理见面会谈，接着跟服装厂洽谈明年的订货合同。吃了中饭以后，她去考察家用电器厂。晚上跟张经理、陈厂长吃饭，然后游览外滩（Wàitān / the Bund），最后给男朋友打电话。请用"一……就"写出她在上海的活动。

Miss Lynn Petty spent only one day in Shanghai. She had a very tight schedule. Once she arrived in Shanghai, she immediately held a meeting with Manager Zhang from Shanghai Import & Export Trading Company, and then had a negotiation with the clothing factory regarding next year's purchase contract. After lunch, she visited a house appliances plant. In the evening, she had dinner with Manager Zhang and Factory Director Chen, then went sightseeing at Shanghai Bund. Finally, she made a phone call to her boyfriend. Please write down her activities in Shanghai by using the pattern of "一……就".

（1）白小姐一到上海就 _____ ;

（2）_____ ;

（3）_____ ;

（4）_____ ;

（5）_____ ;

（6）_____ 。

4. 🎧 009 根据下面的要求，用"值得注意的是"造句。

Accomplish the following tasks by using the pattern of "值得注意的是".

（1）你觉得那家代理商的销售网点不但不够多而且也不够合理。请用"值得注意的是"的句型说出你的意见。

_____

（2）你从市场调查发现，越来越多的消费者喜欢外国产品和名牌产品。用"值得注意的是"的句型说出你的发现。

_____

（3）请用"值得注意的是"的句型提醒中方谈判代表，因为新的经济政策，你的公司不得不调整投资计划。

_____

（4）你觉得跟中国人做生意的时候（最）值得注意的是什么？

_____

5. 🎧 009 用"在……看来"回答下面的问题。

Answer the following questions by using the pattern of "在……看来".

（1）在一般消费者看来，什么样的商品最值得花钱买？

_____

（2）在很多厂家看来，什么样的产品值得生产？

_____

（3）在外国投资人看来，应该选择什么样的地区投资？

_____

（4）在中国政府看来，怎样才能迅速、有效地发展经济？

_____

（5）在你看来，中国目前的经济情况怎么样？

_____

6. 🎧 010 "谁不 V. ……呢？"被用来构成反诘句，强调"每个人都"和"没有例外"的意思。请用这一句型改写下面的句子。

The sentence pattern "谁不 V. ……呢" is used to form a rhetorical question and it emphasizes "everyone does" and "there is no exception", etc. Please rewrite the following sentences by using this pattern.

（1）人人都喜欢听吉利的话。

_____

（2）物美价廉的商品，男女老少都会愿意买。

_____

（3）做广告的时候，每个厂商都喜欢说自己的产品好。

_____

（4）我们都知道：做生意的时候大家都希望赚钱。

_____

IV. 阅读、讨论和其他活动　Reading, Discussion and Other Activities

1. 🎧 011 根据课文对话回答问题。

Answer the following questions according to the dialogues in this lesson.

（1）美方代表今天计划要去哪儿？他们离开以前还有什么事要做吗？

（2）李信文先生为什么很早就来找史先生和白琳？

_____

（3）史强生认为这次广告宣传的目的应该是什么？

_____

（4）这个品牌产品的优势和卖点是什么？

_____

（5）李信文对这次广告宣传活动有什么建议？

_____

（6）史强生总裁对李先生的建议有什么看法？

_____

（7）除了产品广告宣传以外，中方还有别的计划吗？

_____

（8）为什么中方主张把促销活动分为两个阶段？

_____

（9）在中方公司的官网上会有哪些相应的促销活动？

_____

2. 根据本课的阅读短文选出最合适的答案。

Choose the most appropriate answers for the following questions according to the Reading Passage in this lesson.

（1）什么可以帮助建立产品的知名度？

    a 做生意
    b 打开市场销路
    c 厂商
    d 好广告
    e 文化传统

（2）一般来说，中老年人买东西的时候＿＿＿＿＿＿＿＿＿＿＿＿＿＿＿。

    a 喜欢又美又便宜的东西

    b 喜欢又便宜又好的东西

    c 不喜欢时尚和新潮的东西

    d 不喜欢外国产品

（3）为什么中国人喜欢可口可乐和百事可乐的名字？

    a 因为它们的名字又好听又有名

    b 因为中国人喜欢喝它们

    c 因为它们的名字是非常好的广告

    d 因为它们的名字很吉利

（4）为什么丰田汽车的广告可以使中国消费者过目不忘？

    a 因为丰田车物美价廉

    b 因为消费者都知道丰田车

    c 因为它的广告很有名，中国人都喜欢

    d 因为它的广告巧妙地借用了一个有名的中国俗语

（5）一般来说，能取得很好的宣传效果的外国广告＿＿＿＿＿＿＿＿＿＿＿＿。

    a 都有长城、黄河、中国龙、孔子或者天安门

    b 都注重中国人的文化传统和价值观

    c 都是中国人喜闻乐见的有名俗语

    d 都不开玩笑或者搞怪

（6）"王婆卖瓜，自卖自夸"的意思是＿＿＿＿＿＿＿＿＿＿＿＿。

    a 王婆很喜欢自己卖的瓜

    b 王婆卖的瓜是最好的瓜

    c 王婆卖的瓜不是最好的瓜

    d 无论瓜好不好，王婆都不应该说自己的瓜是最好的瓜

    e 无论瓜好不好，王婆总是说自己的瓜是最好的瓜

3. 思考与讨论。Points for Discussion.

（1）找一个广告，说说它的长处和短处。你也可以使用本课附录中的"广告实例"。

Find one advertisement as an example to discuss its strong points and shortcomings. You may use those examples in this lesson's Appendix for your discussion too.

（2）本课的阅读短文谈到了中国人对广告的心理。在你自己的文化里，人们对商品广告的态度是什么？什么样的广告能够吸引消费者？请写一篇短文，比较不同文化中人们对商品广告的态度。

In the Reading Passage of this lesson, you learned what points are important to take into consideration in order to make advertisements appealing to Chinese customers. Do you find these points to be valid in your culture as well? Please write a short essay comparing the differences you have noticed in this regard.

4. 小任务。Tasks.

用中文为一个具体的产品或者服务设计一个广告。你可以使用多媒体的形式完成你的任务。

Use Chinese to design an advertisement for a specific product or service. You may use multimedia to complete your work.

5. 快速复习。Quick review.

Ⓐ 阅读下面的短文，复习学过的词汇和句型。

Read the following text and review vocabularies and sentence patterns that you have learned.

在昨天的谈判中，中美双方代表讨论了东方公司在中国代理销售美方家电产品的问题。通过差不多一天的谈判，双方达成了协议。从明年开始，东方公司将在中国独家代理销售美方的环保洗衣机和节能洗碗机。中方保证将尽力扩大国内市场，进口、销售更多的美方产品。美方同意中方提取百分之八佣金的要求，也同意分担一半的广告宣传费用。今天上午双方代表进一步讨论了明年的销售策略，就怎样更好地宣传产品和突出品牌形象交换了意见。双方代表认为，既然节能和环保是产品的两大卖点，那么广告宣传就一定要有效地传达出这些信息。中方代表还建议邀请一位著名影星担任产品的形象代言人，利用名人效应，为产品进入中国市场宣传造势。不过，考虑到这样做的费用可能会比较高，所以东方公司市场部将先找一家有经验的广告公司咨询一下儿费用问题，然后再做决定。今天的洽谈到快十一点半才结束。双方最后就明年的产品宣传和销售制定了一个初步方案。午饭以后，美方代表坐高铁离开了北京去上海。

Ⓑ 问答 Q & A：

（1）中美双方昨天讨论了什么问题？今天讨论了什么问题？

_____

（2）昨天的洽谈花了多长时间？今天的呢？

_____

（3）在昨天达成的协议中，中国做了什么保证？

_____

（4）在昨天达成的协议中，美方同意了什么？

_____

（5）在今天的洽谈中，双方认为明年的产品广告应该怎样宣传造势？

_____

（6）为什么东方公司市场部要找一家广告公司咨询费用问题？

_____

（7）今天的洽谈有结果吗？

_____

（四）附录　　　**Appendix**

广告实例 Samples of Advertisements

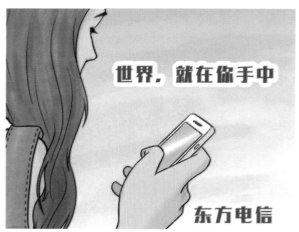

12 在交易会
At a Trade Fair

在东方公司公共关系部主任张红的陪同下，史强生和白琳昨天从北京坐高铁到了上海。今天上午，他们去参观了上海商品交易会。

（一）对 话 Dialogue

课文英译

1. 在家电展区 At the Exhibition Zone of Household Appliances

白 琳：啊，这儿真大！张主任，听说有一千多家厂商参加了这届交易会，是吗？

张 红：是啊，这是今年国内规模最大的交易会之一。不但全国各地都有厂商参加，而且还有不少外国公司参展。史先生、白小姐，这本小册子上有参加交易会的厂商介绍。

史强生：（看小册子）嗯，纺织、服装、家电、手机、自行车、玩具……参展的企业和产品可真不少！不过，我最感兴趣的是家电产品和纺织服装。哈，家电展区就在那边。我们过去看看吧！（走到展位前）

厂商甲：先生您好！这边是我们今年新推出的多功能空调。我给您介绍、展示一下儿吧？

史强生：现在市场上的空调产品很多。您这款产品有什么特点？

厂商甲：您看，我们这个产品的外形设计简洁、时尚，有五种颜色可供消费者选择。产品体积小，制冷效果好。除了制冷以外，还可以除湿、制暖和净化空气，而且非常节能。

史强生：这么多功能，价格是多少呢？

厂商甲：我们一共有三个型号，零售价都在市场上同类产品的价格以下。批发价更优惠。您请稍等，我给您拿一份产品资料，供您参考。

史强生：谢谢！（对白琳）看起来在中国做生意竞争很激烈啊！

课文英译

2. 在纺织、服装展区 At the Exhibition Zone of Textile and Clothing

厂商乙：张主任，您好、您好！好久不见了，您也是来参加交易会的吗？

张　红：不是。我是陪这两位客人来的。这位是美国国际贸易公司亚洲地区总裁史先生，这位是白小姐。他们对您的产品很感兴趣。

厂商乙：史先生、白小姐，幸会、幸会！欢迎光临，欢迎光临！

白　琳：我们刚才看了好几家公司的丝绸产品，可是就数您这儿的品种最多、设计最漂亮。

厂商乙：谢谢您的夸奖！实话对您说，我们的丝绸产品获得过多次国家优质产品金奖。要是您对中国丝绸（产品）感兴趣的话，您算是找对地方了！市场上那些廉价的山寨货可是没法儿跟我们的比！（拿出两本小册子）这是我们公司的产品目录。您看，既有传统式样，又有时尚新潮的设计。请二位过目！

史强生：（看目录）不错，这些产品的确很有吸引力，式样新、价格也很有竞争力。请问，您的这些产品都有现货供应吗？

厂商乙：保证都有。史先生，如果您打算现在就订货的话，我还可以给您打九五折。

史强生：今天恐怕不行。我还得再考虑考虑。也许明天我们会再来跟您洽谈。

厂商乙：没关系、没关系。生意不成情义在，这次不行下次行！这是我的名片，欢迎您随时跟我们联系！

张　红：（开玩笑）喂，您不是想把我的客户挖走吧？

厂商乙：（笑）哪儿的话！大家在这儿都是做生意嘛！

词汇（一）　Vocabulary (1)

1. 陪同	péitóng	to accompany
2. 展区	zhǎnqū	exhibition section/zone
3. 届	jiè	a measure word for periodic terms or events; session (of a conference, etc.)
4. 参展	cān zhǎn	a short form for 参加展览 (i.e., take part in an exhibition)
5. 小册子	xiǎocèzi	booklet
6. 纺织	fǎngzhī	textiles
7. 展位	zhǎnwèi	booth (at an exhibition)
8. 多功能	duōgōngnéng	multifunction
功能	gōngnéng	function
9. 特点	tèdiǎn	characteristic; peculiarity
10. 外形	wàixíng	appearance; external form; outside type
11. 简洁	jiǎnjié	succinct; simple and neat; to-the-point
12. 供	gōng	to supply; provide; to be for (the use/convenience of)
13. 体积	tǐjī	bulk; size; volume
14. 制冷	zhìlěng	to refrigerate; to cool; cooling
15. 除湿	chúshī	to dehumidify
16. 制暖	zhìnuǎn	to make warm; to heat; heating
17. 净化	jìnghuà	to purify
18. 型号	xínghào	model; type; "model number"
型	xíng	model; type
19. 以下	yǐxià	below; under
20. 稍等	shāoděng	to wait a moment

21.	参考	cānkǎo	to consult; to refer to
22.	看起来	kàn qilai	it seems; it looks as if
23.	丝绸	sīchóu	silk; silk cloth
24.	数	shǔ	to count; to be reckoned as exceptionally (good/bad/etc.)
25.	夸奖	kuājiǎng	praise; to praise; to commend
26.	实话	shíhuà	(the) truth
27.	获得	huòdé	to gain; to win; to achieve
28.	优质	yōuzhì	high quality; top quality
29.	金奖	jīnjiǎng	gold medal
30.	算是	suànshì	considered to be
31.	廉价	liánjià	low-priced; cheap
32.	没法（儿）	méifǎ (r)	no way; can do nothing about it
33.	现货	xiànhuò	merchandise on hand; goods in stock
34.	供应	gōngyìng	to supply (goods/merchandise/materials); supply
35.	订货	dìng huò	to order goods
36.	九五折	jiǔwǔ zhé	5 % discount
	打折	dǎ zhé	to make a discount
37.	生意不成情义在	shēngyi bù chéng qíngyì zài	Friendly relations should exist between buyer and seller even if they fail to clinch a deal.
38.	挖走	wāzǒu	to dig out and take away
	挖	wā	to dig; to scoop

句型（一）　Sentence Patterns (1)　

---

1. 在 sb.（的）陪同下
in the company of...; accompanied by sb. (*formal expression)

例：❶ 在张红的陪同下，史强生和白琳从北京坐飞机到了上海。

　　❷ 在马局长的陪同下，美国代表团昨天参观了高新科技产品交易会。

---

2. ……供 + sb. + 选择（/ 参考 etc.）
to be provided to sb. for choosing (/consulting, etc.)

例：❶ 这种空调（机）有五种颜色供消费者选择。

　　❷ 这份产品资料供您参考。

---

3. 看来 / 看起来　　it looks like...; to appear; to seem

例：❶ 看起来，参加交易会是进入中国市场的一个好办法。

　　❷ 这次的谈判看来很成功。

---

4. 就数……　　be reckoned as (the best/worst/etc.)

例：❶ 我们刚才看了好几家公司的丝绸产品，可是就数您这儿的最多、最漂亮。

　　❷ 在这届交易会上，就数这家公司的产品最受欢迎。

---

5. 算是……　　considered to be...

例：❶ 要是您对中国丝绸感兴趣的话，您算是找对地方了！

　　❷ 那家民营企业可以算是一家很大的公司。

（二）阅读短文 **Reading Passage**

课文英译

中国的交易会
Chinese Trade Fairs

交易会，又叫博览会，是厂商展销产品、交流信息、开展对外贸易和吸引外资的重要方式之一。为了推动经济的发展，每年中国都会定期举行若干国际交易会或者博览会。这些交易会的规模有的大有的小，类型也不完全一样。其中，历史最长、规模最大的是中国进出口商品交易会。它一年两次，分别在春季和秋季在广州举行，所以又简称广交会。很多中国厂商都以能够在广交会上展出自己的产品为荣。可以说，广交会是了解中国经济发展的一个窗口。每年九月在厦门举办的中国国际投资贸易洽谈会（简称投洽会），则是中国最重要的国际投资博览会。厦门投洽会以投资洽谈为主题，全面介绍当年的各类招商项目，是投资中国的桥梁。除此之外，重量级的交易会还有中国（北京）国际服务贸易交易会（简称京交会）和中国国际高新技术成果交易会（深圳，简称高交会）。

对于想到中国做生意、投资的外国厂商来说，参加中国的交易会无疑是熟悉中国市场、获得最新商业信息的有效途径。如果你想从中国进口商品，交易会应该是你能买到物美价廉产品的好地方。由于参展的厂商多，难免竞争激烈。许多厂商往往以降低价格、提供各种优惠条件的办法来吸引买主。你可别错过这样的好机会啊！

词汇（二）　Vocabulary (2)

1.	博览会	bólǎnhuì	exhibition; fair
2.	展销	zhǎnxiāo	to exhibit and sell
3.	开展	kāizhǎn	to develop; to launch; to expand
4.	定期	dìngqī	at regular intervals; periodically; regular; periodic
5.	春季	chūnjì	spring (season)
6.	简称	jiǎnchēng	be called sth. for short; abbreviation
7.	以……为荣	yǐ……wéi róng	consider/regard...as an honor
8.	展出	zhǎnchū	to exhibit; to display
9.	窗口	chuāngkǒu	window
10.	举办	jǔbàn	to conduct; to hold; to run
11.	则是	zé shì	then; and so (*to indicate consequence or result, used in formal writing)
12.	主题	zhǔtí	subject; theme
13.	全面	quánmiàn	overall; comprehensive
14.	当年	dāngnián	the same year; that very year
15.	各类	gèlèi	various kinds; various categories
16.	招商	zhāoshāng	inviting investments; investments
17.	项目	xiàngmù	item; project; program
18.	桥梁	qiáoliáng	bridge
19.	除此之外	chú cǐ zhī wài	other than this; in addition to this
20.	重量级	zhòngliàngjí	heavyweight; important; influential
21.	成果	chéngguǒ	achievement; positive result
22.	无疑	wúyí	beyond a doubt; undoubtedly
23.	途径	tújìng	way; channel
24.	由于	yóuyú	due to; as a result of; because of
25.	难免	nánmiǎn	hard to avoid

专有名词 / 特殊名词 Proper Nouns / Special Nouns

1.	中国进出口商品交易会	Zhōngguó Jìn-chūkǒu Shāngpǐn Jiāoyìhuì	China Import and Export Fair
2.	广州	Guǎngzhōu	*a city name*
3.	厦门	Xiàmén	*a city name*
4.	中国国际投资贸易洽谈会	Zhōngguó Guójì Tóuzī Màoyì Qiàtánhuì	China International Fair for Investment and Trade
5.	中国（北京）国际服务贸易交易会	Zhōngguó (Běijīng) Guójì Fúwù Màoyì Jiāoyìhuì	China Beijing International Fair for Trade in Services
6.	中国国际高新技术成果交易会	Zhōngguó Guójì Gāoxīn Jìshù Chéngguǒ Jiāoyìhuì	China Hi-Tech Fair

句型（二） Sentence Patterns (2)

1. 以……为荣／主题   consider/regard ... as an honor/a subject

例：❶ 很多中国厂商都以能够在广交会上展出自己的产品为荣。

　　❷ 每年九月的厦门投洽会以投资洽谈为主题。

2. 除此之外，（……）还／也……   in addition to this, (...) also...

例：❶ 除此之外，重量级的交易会还有中国（北京）国际服务贸易交易会。

　　❷ 这星期我要参加交易会。除此之外，我也打算去考察几家工厂。

3. 难免   hard to avoid

例：❶ 由于参加广交会的厂商多，难免竞争激烈。

　　❷ 如果你不了解市场行情，做生意的时候难免吃亏上当。

4. 以……的办法   use the method of ...

例：❶ 厂商往往以提供各种优惠条件的办法来吸引买主。

　　❷ 这家公司打算以分期付款的办法，引进新的组装线。

（三）练习与活动 Exercises & Activities

I. 词汇练习 Vocabulary Exercises

1. 字谜。 Crossword puzzle.

请根据下面的提示，猜一猜是哪个生词，把它的拼音填进下面的空格里，在旁边写出汉字，最后找出谜底。

Read each clue first, and then fill in the boxes with *pinyin* of the word you guessed. You may write the characters next to each clue. Once you fill out all the boxes, find out what "the wonder word" is.

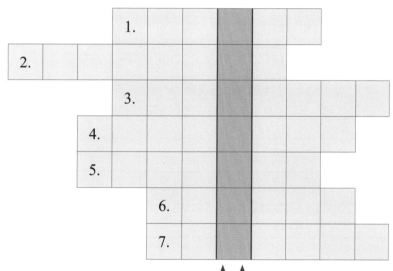

The wonder word

＊提示 (Clues)：　　　　　　　　　　　　　　　　　　　**汉字**

（1）跟"以上"相反的意思　　　⟶

（2）价格非常低，一点儿也不贵　　　⟶

（3）跟别的厂商一起，展出自己的产品　　　⟶

（4）使空气或者水变干净　　　⟶

（5）真话，不夸张的话　　　⟶

（6）降低价格销售　　　⟶

（7）非常好的质量　　　⟶

2. 写出本课中跟"交易会""博览会"有关的词汇。

Write down any words and expressions in this lesson's vocabulary list associated with "交易会" or "博览会".

_____

_____

_____

3. 用中文解释以下词汇的意思，然后造句。

Use Chinese to explain the meaning of the following words, then make a sentence.

例：频繁："很多很多次"的意思。

李经理频繁地给对方打电话，总算把事情安排好了。

（1）参展：_____

_____

（2）简称：_____

_____

（3）夸奖：_____

_____

（4）特点：_____

_____

（5）廉价：_____

_____

（6）展位：_____

_____

（7）净化：_____

_____

（8）无疑：_____

_____

（9）实话：_____

_____

（10）没法（儿）：_____

_____

（11）途径：_____

_____

（12）无疑：_____

_____

（13）展销：_____

_____

（14）重量级：_____

_____

II. 句型练习（一） Sentence Pattern Exercises (1)

1. 🎧 007 "在⋯⋯（的）陪同下"一般用在比较正式的场合。请复习、比较"陪"在第 5 和 7 课的用法，再用这个句型改写下面的句子。

The pattern of "在⋯⋯（的）陪同下" usually is only used in a formal situation. Please review the word "陪" in Lesson 5 & 7, and then use this pattern to rewrite the following sentences.

（1）昨天下午，李经理跟美国贸易代表团一起坐飞机到达了上海。

_____

（2）晚上，上海外贸局马局长邀请美国客人一起出席了文艺晚会。

_____

（3）今天上午，李经理带美国贸易代表团参观了上海国际纺织品交易会。

_____

（4）午饭后，马局长和李经理陪代表团访问了上海丝绸厂。

_____

2. 请用"……供＋sb.＋选择（/参考 etc.）"把下面的句子翻译成中文。

Please translate the following sentences into Chinese by using the pattern of "……供＋sb.＋选择 (/参考 etc.)".

（1）This air conditioner has 3 models for customers to choose from.

_____

（2）I would like to give you this booklet of our products for your reference.

_____

（3）Manger Lee suggests that we should draw up at least 2 plans to provide our client for comparing and choosing.

_____

（4）Before I can make up my mind, where can I find more specific information for my reference?

_____

3. 🎧 D08 根据下面的要求，用"看来"或者"看起来"完成下面的任务。

Use the pattern of "看来" or "看起来" to accomplish the following tasks.

（1）说一说你对目前经济的意见。

_____

（2）你觉得最新型号的苹果手机怎么样？

_____，不过 _____

_____

（3）你参观了一个古董车（gǔdǒngchē / vintage car）展览。你觉得它们的外形设计怎么样？

_____

（4）你的公司决定参加一个中国交易会，计划申请（shēnqǐng / to apply）一个标准展位（size 3m × 3m）。现在经理把展位图拿给你看，然后问你的意见。你的回答是：

_____，不过 _____

_____

4. 🎧 *D09* **根据下面的要求，用"就数"完成下面的任务。**
Use the pattern of "就数" to accomplish the following tasks.

（1）用"就数"的句型说出今年最受欢迎的汽车。

_____

（2）用"就数"的句型说出一家最有名的高科技公司。

_____

（3）用"就数"的句型说出一家最大的银行。

_____

（4）用"就数"的句型说出一个中国最大的交易会。

_____

5. **根据下面的要求，用"算是"回答问题。**
Use the pattern of "算是" to accomplish the following tasks.

（1）史先生打算去中国投资。因为他不太了解中国的情况，所以想听听你的意见。请你用"算是"的句型告诉他在什么地方投资比较好、投资什么比较合适。（为什么？）

_____

_____

（2）到了中国以后，史先生想给他的太太买一些纪念品（jìniànpǐn / souvenir），所以他又跟你请教（qǐngjiào / ask for advice）应该买什么和应该去哪儿买。请你用"算是"的句型告诉他什么东西是值得买的纪念品，哪儿的东西物美价廉。

_____

_____

（3）听了你的回答以后，史先生非常高兴。他说："I have finally found the right person who knows everything（about China）."请你把他的这句话翻译成中文。

_____

_____

III. 句型练习（二）   **Sentence Pattern Exercises (2)**

1. 根据下面的要求，用"以……为荣"或者"以……为主题"造句。
Use the pattern of "以……为荣" or the pattern of "以……为主题" to accomplish the following tasks.

（1）用"以……为荣"的句型说出某个公司最有名的一种产品。

_____

（2）用"以……为荣"的句型说出你最骄傲（jiāo'ào / to be proud）的一件事。

_____

（3）用"以……为主题"的句型说出明天的会谈将要讨论的内容。

_____

（4）用"以……为主题"的句型说出某个国际交易会的主题或者重点（zhòngdiǎn / focal point）。

_____

2. 🎧 句型"除此之外，（……）还/也……"跟第4课的句型"除了……以外，还……"非常相似。请先复习这两个句型，再用其中的一个句型改写下面的句子。

The pattern "除此之外,（……）还/也……" is very similar to the pattern "除了……以外，还……" in Lesson 4. Please review these 2 patterns first, then rewrite the following sentences by using one of these 2 patterns.

（1）这次交易会我们没有参展。一方面是因为太忙，另一方面是因为没有新产品。

_____

（2）明天美方代表的活动很多。既要考察一家工厂，又要参观新产品博览会，还要出席宴会。

_____

（3）这三天的洽谈非常成功。我们签订了两份合同，还获得了空调机的独家代理权。

（4）在宴会上，不但史先生喝了茅台酒，白琳小姐也喝了一小杯。大家都很开心。

_____

3. 用"难免"完成下面的句子。

Complete the following sentences by using the pattern of "难免".

（1）到中国去做生意和投资难免 _____

（2）给产品做广告难免 _____

（3）不了解市场行情的厂商难免 _____

（4）推销山寨产品难免 _____

4. ∩ 011 用"以……的办法"回答下面的问题。

Answer the following questions by using the pattern of "以……的办法".

（1）如果你要在交易会上订货，你打算怎样付款？

_____

（2）如果你的公司刚生产了一种新产品，你打算怎样打开销路？

_____

（3）如果你是一家私营企业的总裁，你打算怎样提高你的企业效益？

_____

（4）如果你的公司有资金周转的问题，你打算怎样解决这个麻烦？

_____

IV. 阅读、讨论和其他活动　Reading, Discussion and Other Activities

1. ∩ 012 根据课文对话回答问题。

Answer the following questions according to the dialogues in this lesson.

（1）为什么说这个交易会是"今年国内规模最大的交易会之一"？

_____

（2）史先生最想看哪些展品？

_____

（3）史先生看到的新型空调机有哪些功能？

_____

（4）史先生为什么觉得在中国做生意竞争很激烈？

_____

（5）那位丝绸厂商为什么告诉史先生和白小姐"您算是找对地方了"？

_____

（6）史强生和白琳觉得这位厂商的丝绸产品怎么样？（为什么？）

_____

（7）在课文对话中有两家中国厂商的代表。你觉得哪位厂商更善于做生意？为什么？

_____

（8）你觉得史先生回到美国以后，会不会跟这两位厂商联系？为什么？

_____

2. 🎧 **根据本课的阅读短文回答问题。**
Answer the following questions based on the Reading Passage.

（1）中国规模最大的商品交易会是什么？每年的什么时候举行？

_____

（2）为什么说厦门投洽会是"投资中国的桥梁"？

_____

（3）目前在中国举行的"重量级"交易会还有哪些？

_____

（4）为什么对跟中国有贸易关系的厂商来说，参加中国的国际商品交易会是一个好办法？

_____

3. 思考与讨论。Points for Discussion.

　　在本课的"对话"中，我们看到了两位中国厂商代表。在读了他们跟史强生等人的对话以后，你是否（shìfǒu / whether or not）发现这两位厂商代表的说话风格（fēnggé / style）和表达（biǎodá / expression）方式有一些不同？请思考以下的问题并跟你的同学交流、讨论：

　　There are 2 representatives from different Chinese companies. After you read the dialogues in the lesson, have you realized that there are some differences between these 2 representatives in speaking style and their way of expression? Please think about the questions below and share your thoughts with your classmates.

（1）比较两位厂商代表在介绍自己产品的时候的语气、用词和表达方式，找出两个人的不同。

（2）如果你做生意的话，你喜欢跟哪位厂商代表打交道？为什么？

4. 小任务。Tasks.

从下面的任务中选择一个，然后和你的同学一起完成它。

Please choose one of the 2 tasks below and accomplish it with your classmates.

Ⓐ 利用图书馆或者上网，找出一个在中国（或者在你们国家）举办的国际交易会的信息。然后写一篇短文，介绍一下儿这个交易会的情况。请你尽量多用在本课学到的词汇和句型。

Using the library and/or the Internet, find out some information about an international trade fair in China (or your country). Write a short essay giving a general introduction to this fair. Use as many new words and patterns from this lesson as possible.

Ⓑ 你在一家美国公司工作。目前总公司正在考虑进入中国市场。你的老板刚收到了一份从中国发来的邮件。他大致能猜出来是什么，不过他想知道更具体的内容。他把这个任务交给了你。请按照下面的要求做：

You work for an American company. Recently, the company is considering to enter the Chinese market. Your boss just received an email from China. He only has a vague idea about what it is, but wants to know more about it. So he assigns you to this task. Please follow the instructions below:

（1）仔细阅读下面的材料。你可以使用词典。

（2）找出以下的信息，并把它们用英文写出来：

- 洽谈会的名称
- 洽谈会的日期
- 洽谈会的地点
- 洽谈会的规模

- 报名日期
- 洽谈会的实际组织单位
- 联系方式
- 怎样获得更多的信息

（3）查一查："得中原者得天下"这句话有什么特别的意思？

想一想：为什么用这句话作为这个洽谈会的广告词？请写出你的答案。

（4）把你的看法告诉老板：你觉得公司应该参加这个洽谈会吗？为什么？

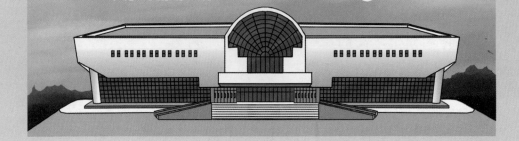

第十届中国河南国际投资贸易洽谈会
THE 10th CHINA HENAN INTERNATIONAL INVESTNENT & TRADE FAIR

2017 年4月8 – 15日郑州中原国际博览中心
河南省人民政府、中国国际贸易促进委员会主办
河南省商务厅、河南省贸促会承办
香港中华总商会、香港厂商联合会、香港总商会协办
四大主题展区，2100个国际标准展位
综合展区、投资洽谈区、进出口贸易区、外商投资企业成果展区
报名参展敬请于2017年1月31日前与河南国际投洽会办公室联系
地址：河南省郑州市文化路115号
邮编：450003
电话：0371–35763278
传真：0371–35763288
电子邮件：touqiaban@hotmail.com

得中原者得天下

河南人民欢迎国内外各界人士来河南参会、旅游、投资、合作
更多详情请查看：www.henan-trade.gov.cn

5. 🎧 *D14* **快速复习**。**Quick review.**

Ⓐ 阅读下面的短文，复习学过的词汇和句型。

Read the following text and review vocabularies and sentence patterns that you have learned.

上午在北京，下午到上海。白琳觉得时间过得非常快。

昨天一早，东方公司的李信文先生就赶到白琳和史强生住的酒店，跟他们讨论有关明年的广告策划和销售策略等问题。李信文对中国市场的情况很熟悉，而且广告策划是他的强项，所以他提了不少很好的建议供美方参考。这些建议包括突出新产品的卖点和优势，邀请著名影星担任品牌形象代言人，分两个阶段在全国推出大型促销活动和网上促销活动等等。白琳认为这些建议都很合理。她觉得李信文是一个工作效率很高的人。每次跟他打交道都让白琳觉得很愉快。

今天，陪同史先生和白小姐到上海的张红主任又陪他们参观了今年的上海商品交易会。张红告诉他们，这届交易会以科技创新（chuàngxīn / innovation）为主题，有一千多家国内外厂商参加，参展的产品都是今年投放市场的新产品和新设计，有些产品已经获得了优质金奖。史先生和白小姐对家电和服装产品特别感兴趣，他们看了差不多几十个展位，拿了不少产品资料，获得了很多有用的信息。白琳觉得参加中国的交易会真是一种很有意思的经验。她听说广交会是中国规模最大的商品交易会。她希望下次能有机会去那儿亲眼看一看。

Ⓑ 问答 Q & A:

（1）昨天白琳、史强生是在哪儿跟李信文见面的？为什么见面？

_____

（2）李信文提了哪些建议？

_____

（3）李信文为什么能够提供这些很好的建议？

_____

（4）白琳喜欢跟李信文打交道、谈生意上的事吗？为什么？

_____

（5）谁陪史先生和白小姐到上海看交易会？

_____

（6）这个交易会的主题是什么？展出的是什么？

_____

（7）对于史先生和白小姐来说，参观这个交易会有什么收获（shōuhuò / gains,
results）？

_____

（8）为什么白琳想去广交会？

_____

（9）为什么白琳觉得时间过得真快？

_____

（四）附录 **Appendix**

1. 展位申请表 Exhibition Application Form

<table>
<tr><td colspan="6" align="center">展位申请表（代合约）
Exhibition Application Form (Equal to contract)</td></tr>
<tr><td colspan="6">展会名称：中国·北京外国留学生专场招聘会
Recruitment Exhibition for Foreign Students in Beijing, P. R. China</td></tr>
<tr><td>展会地点
Location of Exhibition</td><td></td><td></td><td>展会日期
Date of Exhibition</td><td colspan="2"></td></tr>
<tr><td>公司名称
Company Name</td><td colspan="5"></td></tr>
<tr><td>公司地址
Company Address</td><td colspan="5"></td></tr>
<tr><td>联系人
Contact Person</td><td colspan="2"></td><td>联系电话
Contact Number</td><td colspan="2"></td></tr>
<tr><td>手机 Mobile</td><td colspan="2"></td><td>传真 Fax</td><td colspan="2"></td></tr>
<tr><td>电子邮件
E-mail</td><td colspan="2"></td><td>邮编 Post Code</td><td colspan="2"></td></tr>
<tr><td>所属行业 Industry</td><td colspan="5"></td></tr>
<tr><td>公司性质
Company Type</td><td>国有
State-owned</td><td>私营
Private</td><td>独资
Solely
Foreign-owned</td><td>合资
Joint Ventures</td><td>其他
Others</td></tr>
<tr><td>公司现有员工数量
Number of Employee</td><td colspan="2"></td><td>参展人数
Number of Conferee</td><td colspan="2"></td></tr>
<tr><td>计划招聘职位
Recruitment Position</td><td colspan="5"></td></tr>
<tr><td>计划招聘人数
Recruitment Planning</td><td colspan="5"></td></tr>
<tr><td rowspan="2">展位租赁明细
Details</td><td>展位号
Table NO.</td><td>面积
Size</td><td>展位费
Service Fee</td><td>特殊要求
Special Request</td><td>备注
Remarks</td></tr>
<tr><td></td><td></td><td></td><td></td><td></td></tr>
<tr><td>费用总额（人民币）
Total Cost (RMB)</td><td colspan="5"></td></tr>
</table>

2. 展位信息 Exhibition Booth Information

【展位规格及收费标准】

类别	标准展位（9 m²）	标改展位（9 m²）	室内光地收费（36 m² 起租）
国内企业	RMB 9,800 元	RMB 12,800 元	RMB 1,000 元 /m²
国外企业	$ 3,000 元	$ 4,000 元	$ 300 元 /m²
标准展位配置	标准展位配置包括三面围板、地毯、一张洽谈桌（信息台）、两把椅子、两只射灯、一只电源插座（220 V / 5 A）、中英文公司名称楣板。		
室内光地	室内光地含展期内使用面积和使用空间，不包括标准展位配置。		

3. 广交会快照 A Snapshot of China Import and Export Fair

13 招聘面试
Job Interview

为了进一步扩大在中国的业务，美国国际贸易公司决定招聘一位派驻中国的业务代表。通过初步电话面试，公司人力资源部筛选出三位优秀的申请人。他们中间的一位马杰目前正在上海。史强生和白琳到达上海以后，立刻安排了对他的正式面试。

（一）对 话 Dialogue

1. 介绍个人背景 Introducing Personal Background

（在旅馆套房的客厅。门铃响，白琳开门）

马　杰：您好！ I am Jack Martin.

白　琳：Hello, Jack! 请进、请进！

马　杰：谢谢！

白　琳：（让）我来介绍一下儿。这位是我们公司亚洲（地）区总裁，

97

Johnson Smith 先生。Johnson, 这位是 Jack Martin。

马　杰：I am much honored to meet you, sir.

史强生：（握手）你好。请坐。谢谢你从浦东赶过来面试。路上堵车吗？

马　杰：我是坐地铁过来的，很方便。我觉得非常荣幸有这样的面试机会。

史强生：那么，我们就开始吧。首先，请你介绍一下儿你自己的背景和经历。

马　杰：我应该用中文说吗？

史强生：对。这是一个派驻在中国的工作，要求申请人有中英文双语能力，尤其是应该有用中文跟中国客户交流和沟通的能力。

马　杰：好的。我叫 Jack Martin, 我的中文名字是马杰。我是美国人。两年前（我）从西雅图的华盛顿大学毕业，我的专业是市场营销。我目前在上海现代商贸公司工作。

史强生：这是一家什么样的企业？你的具体工作是什么？

马　杰：这是一家跨境电商公司，就在上海自贸区。我在公司的物流部工作，负责跟海外供应商的联系和沟通。

白　琳：你的中文很流利。请问你学了几年中文了？

马　杰：大概六七年了吧。我从高中的时候开始学中文。在大学期间我也一直上中文课。因为我相信学好中文一定会对我将来的工作有帮助。

史强生：（微笑）看来你在语言学习上做了一个很好的决定。好，接下来请你详细说一说你还有哪些经验吧。

2. 经验和技能 Experiences and Skills

课文英译

马　杰：从大二开始到毕业，我一直利用假期在亚马逊打工。开始的时候在客服部，后来在市场部。大学三年级的时候我参加了学校的海外学习项目，到北京大学学习了一个学期。学习期间，我还在北京的一家电商企业实习了三个月。

史强生：嗯，作为一个外国实习生，你具体做什么？

马　杰：我被分配在市场部，参加了一个新产品促销项目。我们有一个项目团队，具体工作包括市场调查、制定促销方案和联系客户等等。这个实习工作让我学到了很多有用的东西。大学毕业的时候，我决定再到中国工作一段时间。很幸运，我申请到了现在这份工作。（直）到这个月为止，我在上海已经工作了快两年了。

史强生：那么，你为什么申请我们这个职位呢？

马　杰：我在网上仔细看了对这个职位的要求和说明，我的理解是这个工作的职责涉及营销、物流、客服多个方面。这对于我来说不但是一个很好的挑战，而且也是一个增加专业知识、提高业务能力的好机会。我觉得这份工作可以让我更好地发挥我的专业特长，也对我个人今后的职业发展更有利。

史强生：做这份工作，你觉得你的强项是什么？

马　杰：我对电商的运营模式比较熟悉，在物流和客服方面也积累了一些经验。除此之外，因为已经在中国工作了两年，我对中国市场和中国消费者也比较了解。

史强生：嗯，很好。最后一个问题：你会愿意长期在中国工作吗？

马　杰：嗯……这个问题不太容易回答。这样说吧，我非常喜欢在中国工作。我希望能在这里至少工作、生活三到五年。

史强生：好，今天的面试就到这里。我们会在两个星期之内通知你最后的决定。谢谢你！

马　杰：谢谢，再见！

词汇（一） Vocabulary (1) 002

1.	招聘	zhāopìn	to invite applications for a job; recruitment
2.	面试	miànshì	interview; to interview
3.	派驻	pàizhù	to dispatch; to accredit
4.	筛选	shāixuǎn	to filter; to screen out; to select
5.	申请人	shēnqǐngrén	applicant
	申请	shēnqǐn	to apply; application
6.	背景	bèijǐng	background
7.	门铃	ménlíng	doorbell
8.	堵车	dǔ chē	traffic jam
9.	地铁	dìtiě	subway; metro
10.	荣幸	róngxìng	honored (to have the privilege of...)
11.	经历	jīnglì	to go through; to experience; experience
12.	双语	shuāngyǔ	bilingual
13.	能力	nénglì	ability; capability
14.	市场营销	shìchǎng yíngxiāo	marketing
15.	跨境电商	kuàjìng diànshāng	cross-border e-commerce
	跨境	kuàjìng	cross-border
	电商	diànshāng	e-business; e-commerce (a short form for 电子商务)
16.	物流	wùliú	logistics
17.	海外	hǎiwài	overseas
18.	供应商	gōngyìngshāng	supplier
19.	接下来	jiē xialai	then; next
20.	详细	xiángxì	detailed; thorough(ly)
21.	经验	jīngyàn	experience

22.	技能	jìnéng	skill; technical ability
23.	假期	jiàqī	vacation
24.	客服	kèfú	customer service (a short form for 顾客服务)
25.	实习	shíxí	to intern; to practice; internship
	实习生	shíxíshēng	trainee; intern (student)
26.	分配	fēnpèi	to assign; to allocate
27.	团队	tuánduì	team; group; crew
28.	幸运	xìngyùn	lucky; fortunate; luck
29.	为止	wéizhǐ	until
30.	职位	zhíwèi	position; post
31.	职责	zhízé	duty; obligation; responsibility
32.	涉及	shèjí	to involve; to touch upon
33.	发挥	fāhuī	to bring into play; to bring out (implicit or innate qualities)
34.	特长	tècháng	special aptitude; specialty
35.	职业	zhíyè	occupation; profession
36.	运营模式	yùnyíng móshì	operating mode
	运营	yùnyíng	to operate; operation
	模式	móshì	mode; model; method; pattern
37.	积累	jīlěi	to accumulate; accumulation

专有名词 / 特殊名词 Proper Nouns / Special Nouns

1.	人力资源部	rénlì zīyuán bù	human resources department
2.	浦东	Pǔdōng	Pudong District in Shanghai, China
3.	西雅图	Xīyǎtú	Seattle
4.	华盛顿大学	Huáshèngdùn Dàxué	University of Washington
5.	现代商贸公司	Xiàndài Shāngmào Gōngsī	Modern Commerce & Trading Co.

6.	自贸区	zìmàoqū	Free Trade Zone
7.	物流部	wùliúbù	logistics department
8.	亚马逊	Yàmǎxùn	Amazon
9.	客服部	kèfúbù	customer service department
10.	市场部	shìchǎngbù	marketing department

句型（一）　Sentence Patterns (1)

1. 对……有帮助／有利　　A is helpful to B; A is profitable to B; A benefits B

例：❶ 学好中文一定会对我将来的工作有帮助。

　　❷ 这份工作对我个人今后的职业发展更有利。

2. 到……为止　　up to; until...

例：❶ 到这个月为止，我在上海已经工作了快两年了。

　　❷ 今天的洽谈就到这儿为止。

3. 对于……来说　　as far as sb./sth. be concerned; as for sb./sth.

例：❶ 这个工作对于我来说是一个很好的挑战。

　　❷ 对于想进入中国市场的外商来说，这真是一个好机会。

4. 在……方面　　in terms of...; in respect of...

例：❶（我）在物流和客服方面也积累了一些经验。

　　❷ 如果您在价格方面有什么问题，可以随时跟市场部咨询。

（二）阅读短文 Reading Passage

在中国求职与招聘
Job Seeking and Hiring in China

课文英译

今天许多外国公司在中国开展业务并招聘人手。与此同时，越来越多的中国公司也开始从世界各地招聘专业人才。很多招聘单位都把双语能力视为录用的优先条件之一。

不管是你的公司计划在中国招聘新员工，还是你自己想在中国找工作，最简单有效的办法是首先上网搜一下儿。你可以从三大招聘网站开始。它们是"前程无忧（网）""智联招聘（网）"和"中华英才网"。这三大招聘网站都用中英文提供全国范围内求职与招聘的专业服务。在建立账户和登录之后，你就可以方便地使用网站提供的职位搜索、简历管理、求职指导以及招聘猎头等服务。

在中国找工作的另一个途径是参加招聘会。招聘会也叫人才市场。在中国，招聘会已经成为人们找工作和公司招聘新员工的热门场所。在经济增长和对专业人才需求的推动下，中国每年都举行许许多多类型和规模不同的招聘会。有的招聘会还办到了海外。近年来，有相当数量的外国公司也加入了中国人才市场的招聘活动。假如你有这方面的需要，不妨也来试一试。

词汇（二）　Vocabulary (2)

1.	求职	qiúzhí	to seek employment
2.	人手	rénshǒu	manpower; staff
3.	与此同时	yǔ cǐ tóng shí	at the same time; meanwhile
4.	人才	réncái	talented person
5.	视为	shìwéi	regard as; consider as
6.	录用	lùyòng	to employ; to hire
7.	优先	yōuxiān	preferential; preferred; priority
8.	不管	bùguǎn	no matter (what/how)
9.	搜	sōu	to search
	搜索	sōusuǒ	to search; to conduct a search
10.	网站	wǎngzhàn	website
11.	账户	zhànghù	account
12.	登录	dēnglù	to log in; to register
13.	简历	jiǎnlì	resume; curriculum vitae
14.	指导	zhǐdǎo	to guide; to direct; guidance
15.	以及	yǐjí	as well as; and
16.	猎头	liètóu	recruiting; headhunting
17.	人才市场	réncái shìchǎng	job fair; talent market
18.	热门	rèmén	popular; in great demand
19.	场所	chǎngsuǒ	place; location; arena
20.	需求	xūqiú	requirement; demand
21.	近年来	jìnnián lái	in recent years
22.	相当	xiāngdāng	quite; fairly
23.	假如	jiǎrú	if; supposing
24.	不妨	bùfáng	there is no harm in; might as well

专有名词 / 特殊名词 Proper Nouns / Special Nouns

1. 前程无忧（网）	Qiánchéng Wúyōu (Wǎng)	www.51job.com, an employment website
2. 智联招聘（网）	Zhìlián Zhāopìn (Wǎng)	www.zhaopin.com, an employment website
3. 中华英才网	Zhōnghuá Yīngcái Wǎng	www.chinahr.com, an employment website

句型（二）　Sentence Patterns (2)　

1. 把……视为……　　regard...as...; consider...as...

例：❶ 很多招聘单位都把双语能力视为录用的优先条件之一。

❷ 公司把参加这次交易会视为进入中国市场的机会。

2. 不管是……，还是……　　no matter A or B

例：❶ 不管是你的公司计划在中国招聘新员工，还是你自己想在中国找工作，最简单有效的办法是首先上网搜一下儿。

❷ 不管是白天还是晚上，这儿都堵车。

3. 在…… 推动下　　with the impetus of...; pushed forward by...; driven by...

例：❶ 在经济增长和对专业人才需求的推动下，中国每年都举行许多招聘会。

❷ 在新贸易合同的推动下，这种产品的出口增长得很快。

4. （……），不妨 + V. ……
(in case that...,) it might as well V. ...; (for the purpose of...,) it's no harm to V. ...

例：❶ 假如你有这方面的需要，不妨也来试一试。

❷ 为了招（聘）到有经验的优秀人才，我们不妨去今年的招聘会看一看。

（三）练习与活动　Exercises & Activities

I. 词汇练习　Vocabulary Exercises

1. 组词。你可以参考总附录中的词表。

Build upon the following words. You may refer to the Vocabulary List in the General Appendix.

例：（具）体　　（身）体

（1）职（　　　）　　职（　　　）　　职（　　　）

（2）分（　　　）　　分（　　　）　　分（　　　）

（3）客（　　　）　　客（　　　）　　客（　　　）

（4）发（　　　）　　发（　　　）　　发（　　　）

（5）面（　　　）　　面（　　　）　　面（　　　）

（6）经（　　　）　　经（　　　）　　经（　　　）

（7）特（　　　）　　特（　　　）　　特（　　　）

（8）人（　　　）　　人（　　　）　　人（　　　）

（9）简（　　　）　　简（　　　）　　简（　　　）

（10）优（　　　）　　优（　　　）　　优（　　　）

2. 字谜。Crossword puzzle.

请根据下面的提示，猜一猜是哪个生词，把它的拼音填进下面的空格里，在旁边写出汉字，最后找出谜底。

Read each clue first, and then fill in the boxes with *pinyin* of the word you guessed. You may write the characters next to each clue. Once you fill out all the boxes, find out what "the wonder word" is.

The wonder word ↑ ↑

* 提示 (Clues)：　　　　　　　　　　　　　　　　汉字

（1）公司需要更多的人来工作　　⟶

（2）能说两种语言　　⟶

（3）不上班也不上学的日子　　⟶

（4）工作的责任　　⟶

（5）在网上做生意的公司　　⟶

（6）为买东西的人提供服务　　⟶

3. 小测试：下面的这些词，哪些你能"过目不忘"？请写出它们的英文意思和拼音。

Pop quiz. can you memorize（"过目不忘"）the following words? Please write down the English equivalents and pronunciations (*pinyin*) for these words.

（1）　　a. 高铁　　b. 地铁　　c. 堵车　　d. 技能　　e. 能力　　f. 实习生

English equivalent　　　　　　Pronunciation (*pinyin*)

a._____　　_____

b._____　　_____

c._____   _____

d._____   _____

e._____   _____

f._____   _____

（2）　　g. 职业　　h. 筛选　　i. 招聘　　j. 面试　　k. 假期　　l. 物流

English equivalent	Pronunciation (*pinyin*)

g._____   _____

h._____   _____

i._____   _____

j._____   _____

k._____   _____

l._____   _____

（3）　　m. 求职　　n. 录用　　o. 人手　　p. 人才　　q. 热门　　r. 人才市场

English equivalent	Pronunciation (*pinyin*)

m._____   _____

n._____   _____

o._____   _____

p._____   _____

q._____   _____

r._____   _____

（4）　　　s. 搜索　　t. 网站　　u. 账户　　v. 登录　　w. 简历　　x. 猎头

English equivalent	Pronunciation (*pinyin*)
s.＿＿＿＿＿＿＿＿＿	＿＿＿＿＿＿＿＿＿
t.＿＿＿＿＿＿＿＿＿	＿＿＿＿＿＿＿＿＿
u.＿＿＿＿＿＿＿＿＿	＿＿＿＿＿＿＿＿＿
v.＿＿＿＿＿＿＿＿＿	＿＿＿＿＿＿＿＿＿
w.＿＿＿＿＿＿＿＿＿	＿＿＿＿＿＿＿＿＿
x.＿＿＿＿＿＿＿＿＿	＿＿＿＿＿＿＿＿＿

4. 用下列词汇填空。

Fill in the blanks by using the words given below. Each word can be used only once.

Ⓐ
参展　展示　幸运　荣幸　实习生　型号　多功能
积累　跨境　届　分配　筛选　团队　为止　模式

（1）市场部已经 ＿＿＿＿＿＿ 出几种新产品，准备在这一 ＿＿＿＿＿＿ 交易会 ＿＿＿＿＿＿。

（2）我很 ＿＿＿＿＿＿ 能为您 ＿＿＿＿＿＿ 我们的 ＿＿＿＿＿＿ 空调机。这是今年的新 ＿＿＿＿＿＿。

（3）到现在 ＿＿＿＿＿＿，李经理在这家 ＿＿＿＿＿＿ 电商公司已经工作了八年了。他对公司的运营 ＿＿＿＿＿＿ 非常熟悉。

（4）作为一个 ＿＿＿＿＿＿，我很 ＿＿＿＿＿＿ 被 ＿＿＿＿＿＿ 到一个很好很强的 ＿＿＿＿＿＿。通过这次实习，我一定能 ＿＿＿＿＿＿ 很多有用的经验。

Ⓑ
发挥　供应商　技能　职责　交流　涉及　人才
职位　双语　方面　优先　申请人　特长　经验

（1）这是一个派驻中国的 ＿＿＿＿＿＿，要求 ＿＿＿＿＿＿ 有两年的市场营销 ＿＿＿＿＿＿，还应该有双语的 ＿＿＿＿＿＿。

（2）他可以用中文和英文跟客户 _____。既然他有 _____ 能力，我们就应该 _____ 他的 _____。

（3）这个工作的 _____ 将 _____ 物流和销售两个 _____，还要和海外 _____ 打交道。

（4）我们会 _____ 录用有工作经验的 _____。

5. A. 你觉得哪些词汇在工作面谈的时候可能会被用到？请把它们写出来。

Please write down those words (in Chinese) that you think they might be used during a typical job interview.

_____

_____

B. 请问，用中文怎么说 "**I am much honored to meet you, sir**"？

_____

II. 句型练习（一）　Sentence Pattern Exercises (1)

1. 🎧 D07　请用"对……有帮助 / 有利"回答下面的问题。请注意，每个问题可以有一个以上的答案。

Please answer the following questions by using the pattern "对……有帮助 / 有利". Please note that there might be more than one proper answer for these questions.

（1）有双语能力可能会对什么有帮助（/ 有利）？

_____

（2）为什么很多商店都会采用"买一送一"的促销方法？

_____

（3）建立可靠的信用会对什么有帮助（/ 有利）？

_____

（4）为什么那家公司决定采用网上销售的运营模式？

_____

2. 请用"（直）到……为止"把下面的句子翻译成中文。请想一想，下面列出的词是否可以用到你的翻译里？

Please translate the following sentences into Chinese by using the pattern "（直）到……为止". In addition, can you use some of the listed words below into your translation too?

积累 / 供应商 / 面试 / 满意 / 电（子）商（务）/ 谈判 / 搜索 / 分配
职责 / 市场营销 / 涉及 / 招聘 / 职责 / 申请 / 面试 / 客服部 / 在……方面

（1）Until this year, I have worked at this e-commence company for 3 years. I have gained a lot of experience in marketing and sales.

_____

（2）Up until today's negotiation, our discussion has not yet touched on the issue about suppliers.

_____

（3）After work, he always goes online to search for hiring information. So far he has applied for over 10 different jobs, but has not had any interviews yet.

_____

_____

（4）As an intern, I have been assigned to the customer service department. My responsibility is to answer questions from the customers over the phone until they are satisfied.

_____

_____

3. 请用"对于……来说"回答下面的问题。请注意，每个问题可以有一个以上的答案。

Please answer the following questions by using the pattern "对于……来说". Please note that there might be more than one proper answer for these questions.

（1）对于招聘单位来说，录用（lùyòng / to hire）新人最重要的要求是什么？

_____

（2）你为什么决定申请这个职位？

_____

（3）你觉得一家外资企业在中国市场上可能面临哪些问题？

_____

（4）那家跨境电商公司正在招聘。可是为什么要求申请人必须有双语能力呢？

_____

4. 完成下面带"在……方面"的句子。
Please complete the following sentences with the pattern "在……方面".

（1）在 _____ 方面，我们的产品正面临新的竞争。

（2）在 _____ 方面，这家公司已经投资了五百万元。

（3）那家中国公司希望能够跟我们公司在 _____ 方面有进一步的合作。

（4）我的强项是在 _____ 方面，我对物流业务并不熟悉。

III. 句型练习（二）　Sentence Pattern Exercises (2)

1. 用"把……视为……"把下面的句子翻译成中文。
Translate the following sentences into Chinese by using the pattern of "把……视为……".

（1）New college graduates often regard a job fair as a good place to find a job.

_____

（2）You should regard next week's interview as the most important task, and must be well prepared.

_____

（3）I regard this job as a new challenge for me. I'll do my best to accomplish it!

_____

（4）Many businessmen consider e-commerce as a low-cost and high-profit business. What they don't know is that many e-commerce companies are sustaining losses due to very intense competition. (Hint: shēngyirén, péi běn, jīliè)

_____

_____

2. 用"不管是……，还是……"改写下面的句子。
Please rewrite the following sentences by using the pattern "不管是……，还是……".

（1）公司招聘新人和个人找工作都可以从招聘网站开始。

_____

（2）中英文双语能力是他的优势，所以他在中美两国工作都没有问题。

_____

（3）有问题的时候，他很善于跟客户沟通，所以老板和客户都很喜欢他。

_____

（4）在中国的大城市，交通总是非常繁忙，上午、下午和晚上都堵车。我觉得你最好坐地铁，又快又便宜，而且下雨下雪都不用担心。

_____

_____

3. 用"在……推动下"完成下面的句子。
Complete the following sentences by using the pattern of "在……推动下".

（1）在双方代表的努力推动下，_____

（2）近年来在经济增长的推动下，_____

（3）在市场竞争的推动下，_____

（4）在国有企业改革政策的推动下，_____

（5）在 _____ 的推动下，_____

4. 请根据下面的情况，用"不妨 + V. ……"说出你的建议。

Based on the situations described below, offer your suggestions by using the pattern "不妨 + V. ……".

（1）毕业以后，你的朋友想去中国工作两年。他问你怎样才能获得最新的招聘信息。你告诉他：

_____

（2）公司派你和一个同事（tóngshì / co-worker）从北京到上海出差。你的同事打算订飞机票，可是你有不同的想法。你说：

_____

（3）到达上海以后，你们要立刻去市中心见一位重要客户。你的同事很担心路上堵车。你说：

_____

_____

（4）收到供应商的报盘以后，李经理打算立刻进货。可是你觉得应该"货比三家"。你建议说：

_____

IV. 阅读、讨论和其他活动　　Reading, Discussion and Other Activities

1. 根据课文对话回答问题。

Answer the following questions according to the dialogues in this lesson.

（1）美国国际贸易公司为什么要招聘新人？

_____

（2）史强生和白琳面试的申请人叫什么名字？他今天是从哪儿来参加面试的？他是怎么来的？

_____

（3）在美国上大学的时候，马杰的专业是什么？他从什么时候开始学中文？

_____

（4）马杰目前在一家什么公司工作？他的工作职责是什么？他在这家公司工作了多久了？

_____

（5）马杰正在申请的这个工作有哪些职责？

_____

（6）这个职位对申请人有什么特别的要求？

_____

（7）马杰为什么要申请这个新工作？

_____

（8）申请做这个工作，马杰觉得他自己的强项是什么？

_____

（9）为什么这些是马杰的强项？

_____

（10）你觉得马杰能得到这个工作吗？为什么？

_____

2. 根据本课的阅读短文回答问题并跟你的同学交流、分享。

Answer the following questions based on the Reading Passage, and share the information and your opinions with your classmates.

（1）在中国求职或者招聘新员工，有哪些途径？你觉得这些途径会有效吗？

_____

（2）在你们国家，如果你要找工作，你会从哪儿开始？你会怎么做？

_____

3. 小任务。Tasks.

为你自己用中文做一份个人简历。你可以参考或者使用本课附录中的"个人简历模板"。

Use Chinese to make a curriculum vitae for yourself. You may refer to (or copy) the "Curriculum Vitae Template" in this lesson's Appendixes.

4. 角色扮演：工作面试。Role-playing: Job interview.

两到三人一组，用中文写一个短剧"工作面试"并表演。"面试"内容应该至少包括以下列出各项中的6项。

Please work with 1-2 classmates to write a skit of a "Job Interview" in Chinese and act it out. There are 8 items listed below, and your writing should cover at least 6 items.

（1）申请人的学历和背景。

（2）申请人的经历和工作经验。

（3）申请人为什么要申请这个工作。

（4）申请人有哪些特长和兴趣、爱好。

（5）为什么申请人觉得他 / 她是合适的人选？

（6）申请人的职业计划。

（7）这份工作的具体职责和待遇。

（8）申请人可以提出自己关心的其他问题。

5. 快速复习。Quick review.

Ⓐ 阅读下面的短文，复习学过的词汇和句型。

Read the following text and review vocabularies and sentence patterns that you have learned.

> 对于史先生和白小姐来说，今天又是很忙的一天。上午，他们在东方公司张红主任的陪同下，参观了今年的上海商品交易会。这次的交易会规模很大，有国内外一千多家厂商参展。史先生和白小姐在那里认识了好几位厂商代表，他们还交换了名片和联系方式。史先生对展出的一种新款空调机特别感兴趣。他还仔细地询问了这种空调的各种性能和市场销售价。白琳对服装展区更感兴趣。她参观了几乎每一个展位，比较了各家的设计、质量和价格。史先生和白小姐都觉得中国的消费者市场非常有潜力，但是竞争也很激烈。

下午，史先生和白小姐安排了一个面试。他们公司正在招聘一位派驻中国的业务代表。史先生和白小姐今天面试的申请人叫马杰，是个美国人。马杰从华盛顿大学毕业以后，就到中国来工作了。目前他在上海一家跨境电商公司工作，负责跟海外供应商的联系和沟通。一个多月前，马杰在网上看到了美国国际贸易公司的招聘信息，他立刻就申请了。马杰觉得这个职位可以让他更好地发挥自己的专业特长，也对他今后的职业发展更有利。

B 问答 Q & A：

（1）交易会有多少厂商参展？有外国公司参展吗？

_____

（2）史先生对什么最感兴趣？他问了什么问题？

_____

（3）白小姐对什么最感兴趣？她做了什么？

_____

（4）史先生和白小姐对中国市场有什么看法？

_____

（5）史先生和白小姐要面试的人是谁？（哪国人？学历？）

_____

（6）马杰现在做什么工作？

_____

（7）马杰怎么会知道美国国际贸易公司正在招聘？

_____

（8）为什么马杰决定申请这个新工作？

_____

（四）附录　　Appendix

1. 个人简历模板 Curriculum Vitae Template

个人简历
Curriculum Vitae

姓名 Full name：_____　　　性别 Gender：_____

出生年月 Date of birth：_____　　婚姻状况 Marital status：_____

国籍 Nationality：_____　　　身份证 / 护照号码 ID/Passport #：_____

家庭地址 Residential address：_____

通信地址 Mailing address：_____

联系电话 Contact phone：_____

电子邮件 Email address：_____

教育背景 Educational background：

_____ 年 (Y)___ 月 (M)— _____ 年 (Y)___ 月 (M)_____

_____ 年 (Y)___ 月 (M)— _____ 年 (Y)___ 月 (M)_____

_____ 年 (Y)___ 月 (M)— _____ 年 (Y)___ 月 (M)_____

工作经历 Work experience：

_____ 年 (Y)___ 月 (M)— _____ 年 (Y)___ 月 (M)_____

_____ 年 (Y)___ 月 (M)— _____ 年 (Y)___ 月 (M)_____

_____ 年 (Y)___ 月 (M)— _____ 年 (Y)___ 月 (M)_____

技能与专长 Skills & Specialties：

_____

_____

获奖与荣誉 Awards & Honors：

_____

_____

2. 招聘广告 Advertisement of Hiring

现代科技公司

加入我们
梦想起航

公司介绍：大型跨国公司位于上海浦东

主要业务：计算机与网络技术

招聘目的：公司发展需要

招聘岗位：研发部、营销部实习生（一年）

资历要求：本科、英语4、6级IT/营销专业优先

实习期待遇：带薪/不带薪　包食宿费和交通费

公司提供：三周免费培训

详情请查看：www.moderntechSH.com

14 工业园区
Industrial Park

深圳是史强生和白琳这次中国之行的最后一个城市。从上海到达深圳以后，张红陪他们参观了当地的一个工业园区，还考察了入驻园区的一家创业公司。园区的投资环境给他们留下了深刻的印象。

 （一）对 话 Dialogue

课文英译

1. 谈当地的发展 Discussing the Local Development

白　琳：真想不到这儿发展得这么快！

张　红：是啊，过去三十年来，深圳利用外资发展经济，已经从一个小镇变成了一个现代化的大城市。现在每年都有越来越多的外国厂商到这里来做生意，世界上很多有名的大公司在深圳都有投资。我们今天考察的这个工业园就是当地发展的一个缩影。

史强生：我很想知道深圳是依靠什么来吸引这么多外国投资的呢？

张　红：我想主要是靠良好的投资环境，尤其是完善的基础设施和当地政府对外商投资的积极支持。

史强生：这个工业园建立了多久了？

张　红：这是一年前刚刚建立的新园区。

史强生：那么，基础设施建设已经全部完成了吗？

张　红：是的。交通、通信和公共配套设施都已经投入使用了。到目前为止，已经有二十几家企业签约入驻了。

史强生：发展得真快。请问，入驻的企业中有多少家是外资企业？

张　红：据我所知，目前入驻的企业中，有二分之一是外资企业。

白　琳：哈，我的手机连上 Wi-Fi 了！信号很好！

张　红：是的。整个园区都可以免费使用无线网络。

课文英译

2. 考察创业公司 Visiting a Start-up Company

刘经理：张主任，你们来了！欢迎，欢迎！欢迎各位光临指导！

张　红：您好，刘经理。让您久等了。我来介绍一下儿，这位是东方新能源的刘总。刘经理，这位是美国国际贸易公司亚洲区总裁史强生先生，这位是白琳小姐——史先生的助理。

刘、史、白：您好！您好！（握手）

史强生：刘总，我对贵公司正在研发的家庭新能源项目很感兴趣，听说你们有意寻找合作伙伴。您可以为我们做一些介绍和说明吗？

刘经理：当然可以。我们是一家成立不久的科技创业公司，一半以上的研发人员都是海归。目前公司专门研发家庭新能源技术和配套产品。我们已经申请了多项专利。

史强生：很有意思。我认为家庭新能源的确有很大的发展潜力。请问，贵公司有哪些具体产品呢？

刘经理：是这样的。（打开电脑）请看，我们的产品将包括使用新能源的家用空调机、洗衣机、洗碗机和炉具等等。所有产品都将使用我们自己研发的技术。

史强生：如果我理解正确的话，贵公司到目前为止还没有产品正式投放市场，也没有任何盈利。请允许我冒昧地问一句，贵公司是怎样保持正常运营的呢？

刘经理：我们去年获得了第一笔风险投资。与此同时，在当地政府的积极支持下，公司还顺利获得了银行优惠贷款。为了保证我们的产品能在明年投放市场，公司正计划进行新的融资。不知道史先生有没有兴趣？

史强生：我个人看好你们的项目。我会在这次考察的基础上，向公司提交一份评估报告。如果有什么进展，我会及时跟您联系。

词汇 (一)　Vocabulary (1)　

1.	之行	zhī xíng	the trip of ...
2.	入驻	rùzhù	enter and stay
3.	镇	zhèn	small town
4.	现代化	xiàndàihuà	modern; modernized; modernization
5.	缩影	suōyǐng	miniature; epitome
6.	依靠	yīkào	to rely on; to depend on
7.	完善	wánshàn	complete and perfect
8.	基础设施	jīchǔ shèshī	infrastructure
9.	通信	tōngxìn	communication; to communicate
	通信设施	tōngxìn shèshī	communication facility
10.	公共配套设施	gōnggòng pèitào shèshī	public facilities
	配套	pèitào	compatible; to form a complete set
11.	投入	tóurù	to put into; to input; to invest
12.	据我所知	jù wǒ suǒ zhī	as far as I know; to my knowledge
13.	信号	xìnhào	signal
14.	无线网络	wúxiàn wǎngluò	wireless network; Wi-Fi
15.	久等	jiǔděng	to wait for a long time
16.	新能源	xīnnéngyuán	new energy
17.	研发	yánfā	research and development; to research and develop
18.	有意	yǒuyì	to intend; intentionally
19.	伙伴	huǒbàn	partner
20.	成立	chénglì	to found; to establish
21.	人员	rényuán	staff; personnel

22.	海归	hǎiguī	overseas returnee
23.	项	xiàng	a measure word for items/clauses/tasks/etc.
24.	专利	zhuānlì	patent; monopoly
25.	炉具	lújù	stoves; ovens
26.	盈利	yínglì	profit; to make a profit
27.	允许	yǔnxǔ	to allow
28.	冒昧	màomèi	(courteous/humble) presumptuous; to make bold
29.	保持	bǎochí	to keep; to maintain
30.	正常	zhèngcháng	normal(ly); regular(ly)
31.	风险投资	fēngxiǎn tóuzī	venture capital; VC
	风险	fēngxiǎn	risk; hazard
32.	贷款	dài kuǎn	loan; to loan
33.	融资	róngzī	financing; finance; fund-raising
34.	看好	kànhǎo	optimistic (about the outcome)
35.	提交	tíjiāo	to submit (a report etc.)
36.	评估	pínggū	to evaluate; evaluation
37.	进展	jìnzhǎn	progress; advance; to make progress

专有名词 / 特殊名词 Proper Nouns / Special Nouns

| 东方新能源（公司） | Dōngfāng Xīnnéngyuán (Gōngsī) | Eastern New Energy Company |

句型（一）　Sentence Patterns (1)

1. 从 A 变成（了）B　to change from A into B

例：❶ 深圳已经从一个小镇变成了一个现代化的大城市。

❷ 在过去的几年中，这家小公司从一家普通代理商变成了一家生产电脑的大公司。

2. （依）靠……（来）V.　to rely/depend on... to V.

例：❶ 这个工业园是依靠什么来吸引外国投资的呢？

❷ 这家工厂靠引进新技术来提高产品质量。

3. 据我所知　as far as I know...

例：❶ 据我所知，目前入驻的企业中，有三分之一是外资企业。

❷ 据我所知，那家公司只接受信用证付款方式。

4. 在……（的）基础上　based on...; on the basis of...

例：❶ 我会在这次考察的基础上，向公司提交一份评估报告。

❷ 在第一次面谈的基础上，公司筛选出三位申请人。

（二）阅读短文 Reading Passage

课文英译

中国的特区和新区
Special Zones and New Areas in China

经济特区、开发区、高新区、自贸区和新区，这些都是中国在改革开放过程中先后建立的特殊区域。

20世纪80年代改革开放初期，中国先后建立了深圳、珠海、汕头、厦门经济特区和海南（省）经济特区。它们都位于中国南部沿海地区。2010年，为了发展中国西部地区的经济，中国又建立了新疆喀什和霍尔果斯两个经济特区。中国在经济特区实行特殊的经济政策和灵活的管理措施，以便吸引外国投资和跨国企业入驻。

开发区和高新区分别是经济技术开发区和高新技术产业区的简称。20世纪90年代前后是开发区和高新区建立和发展的高峰期。开发区实际就是一种现代化的工业园区。高新区则是以打造知识密集型和技术密集型工业园区为目的。到现在为止，全国已经有超过200个以上的国家级经济技术开发区和超过100个以上的国家级高新技术产业开发区。入驻这两类园区的企业都享有一系列优惠政策和当地政府提供的许多便捷服务。

2005年以后，中国开始尝试建立规模更大的国家级新区。新区有政府职能部门的性质，区内实行国家特定优惠政策，是国家级的综合功能区。最早建立的是上海浦东新区。目前最新的是2017年建立的雄安新区。除此之外，2013年8月中国在浦东新区内建立了境内第一个自由贸易区——中国（上海）自由贸易试验区。上海自贸区享有更大的贸易自由和金融、投资便利。在经济全球化和"一带一路"倡议的双重推动下，中国正在建立更多的自由贸易区。

词汇（二） Vocabulary (2)

1.	先后	xiānhòu	early or late; one after another
2.	特殊	tèshū	special; exceptional; unusual
3.	区域	qūyù	zone; region; district; sector
4.	年代	niándài	decade; era
5.	初期	chūqī	beginning period
6.	位于	wèiyú	be located at/in
7.	沿海	yánhǎi	along the coast; coastal
8.	灵活	línghuó	flexible
9.	措施	cuòshī	measure; step
10.	以便	yǐbiàn	in order to; so that; with the aim of
11.	跨国企业	kuàguó qǐyè	multinational corporation
12.	分别	fēnbié	separately; individually
13.	前后	qiánhòu	around; about; front and rear
14.	高峰期	gāofēngqī	heyday; peak period; rush hour
15.	实际	shíjì	actual(ly); practical(ly)
16.	打造	dǎzào	to create; to build
17.	知识密集型	zhīshi mìjí xíng	knowledge-intensive model
	密集	mìjí	intensive; concentrated
18.	国家级	guójiājí	national/state level
19.	享有	xiǎngyǒu	to enjoy (rights, privileges, etc.)
20.	一系列	yíxìliè	a series of
21.	便捷	biànjié	convenient and fast
22.	职能部门	zhínéng bùmén	functional department
	职能	zhínéng	function

	部门	bùmén	department; branch
23.	性质	xìngzhì	quality; nature; character
24.	特定	tèdìng	specially designated; specific
25.	综合	zōnghé	multiple; comprehensive
26.	境内	jìngnèi	within a country's borders
27.	自由	zìyóu	free; freedom
28.	试验	shìyàn	experiment; test; experimental
29.	经济全球化	jīngjì quánqiúhuà	economic globalization
30.	倡议	chàngyì	to propose; initiative
31.	双重	shuāngchóng	double; dual

专有名词 / 特殊名词 Proper Nouns / Special Nouns

1.	经济特区	jīngjì tèqū	Special Economic Zone (SEZ)
2.	开发区	kāifāqū	Development Zone or ETDZ, a short form for Economic-Technological Development Zone（经济技术开发区）
3.	高新区	gāoxīnqū	HIDZ, a short form for High-Tech Industrial Development Zone（高新技术产业区）
4.	新区	xīnqū	new area
	国家级新区	guójiājí xīnqū	State-level New Area
5.	珠海	Zhūhǎi	*a city in Guangdong Province*
6.	汕头	Shàntóu	*a city in Guangdong Province*
7.	海南	Hǎinán	Hainan Province
8.	新疆	Xīnjiāng	Xinjiang Uygur Autonomous Region
9.	喀什	Kāshí	Kashgar, *a city in Xinjiang Uygur Autonomous Region*
10.	霍尔果斯	Huò'ěrguǒsī	Khorgos, *a city in Xinjiang Uygur Autonomous Region*
11.	浦东新区	Pǔdōng Xīnqū	Pudong New Area in Shanghai

12.	雄安新区	Xióng'ān Xīnqū	Xiongan New Area in Hebei Province
13.	中国（上海）自由贸易试验区	Zhōngguó (Shànghǎi) Zìyóu Màoyì Shìyànqū	China (Shanghai) Pilot Free Trade Zone
14.	一带一路	Yí Dài Yí Lù	the Belt and Road, a short form for the Silk Road Economic Belt and the 21st-Century Maritime Silk Road

句型（二）　Sentence Patterns (2)

1. 位于……　be located at/in...

例：❶ 最先建立的经济特区都位于中国南部沿海地区。

❷ 总裁办公室位于公司大楼的三楼。

2. ……，以便……　in order to; so that; with the aim of...

例：❶ 经济特区实行特殊的经济政策和灵活的管理措施，以便吸引外资和跨国企业入驻。

❷ 我们决定播出更多电视广告，以便打开市场销路。

3. 分别是……　be...respectively (*indicate a list of items)

例：❶ 开发区和高新区分别是经济技术开发区和高新技术产业区的简称。

❷ 本公司今年推出的新产品分别是节能空调机、洗衣机和洗碗机。

4. 以……为目的　with the aim of; be aimed at; for the purpose of

例：❶ 国家高新区以打造知识密集型和技术密集型工业园区为目的。

❷ 这次促销活动不以盈利为目的。

（三）练习与活动 Exercises & Activities

I. 词汇练习 Vocabulary Exercises

1. 根据英文的意思，填上正确的汉字。

Fill the blank with correct Chinese character according to English equivalent(s) provided.

汉字　　　　　　　　　　　　　　　　* 提示 (Clues)

A （1）进（　　）jìnzhǎn　←――――　progress; advance; to make progress

（2）融（　　）róngzī　←――――　financing; finance; fund-raising

（3）风（　　）fēngxiǎn　←――――　risk; hazard

（4）贷（　　）dàikuǎn　←――――　loan; to loan

（5）盈（　　）yínglì　←――――　profit; to make a profit

（6）（　　）估 pínggū　←――――　to evaluate; evaluation

（7）（　　）利 zhuānlì　←――――　patent; monopoly

（8）（　　）发 yánfā　←――――　research and development

（9）（　　）信 tōngxìn　←――――　communication; to communicate

（10）（　　）号 xìnhào　←――――　signal

B （1）打（　　）dǎzào　←――――　to create; to build

（2）密（　　）mìjí　←――――　intensive; concentrated

（3）措（　　）cuòshī　←――――　measure; step

（4）（　　）后 qiánhòu　←――――　around; about; front and rear

（5）（　　）后　xiānhòu　←——　early or late; one after another

（6）（　　）殊　tèshū　←——　special; exceptional; unusual

（7）（　　）定　tèdìng　←——　specially designated; specific

（8）（　　）议　chàngyì　←——　to propose; initiative

（9）（　　）捷　biànjié　←——　convenient and fast

2. 字谜。Crossword puzzle.

　　请根据下面的提示，猜一猜是哪个生词，把它的拼音填进下面的空格里，在旁边写出汉字，最后找出谜底。

Read each clue first, and then fill in the boxes with *pinyin* of the word you guessed. You may write the characters next to each clue. Once you fill out all the boxes, find out what "the wonder word" is.

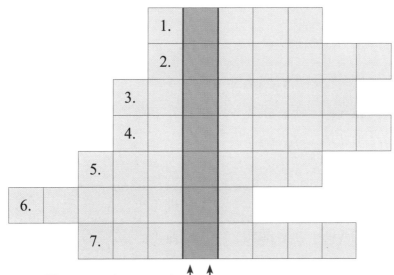

The wonder word ↑↑

＊提示 (Clues)		汉字
（1）很小的小城	→	
（2）在国外学习毕业以后回来的人	→	
（3）在生意上合作的人	→	
（4）很全很好	→	
（5）相信（结果）会很好	→	
（6）生意上赚了钱	→	
（7）从银行借钱	→	

3. 组词。你可以参考总附录中的词表。

Build upon the following words. You may refer to Vocabulary List in General Appendix.

例：成（ 本 ）；成（ 品 ）

（1）完（　　）；完（　　）；完（　　）

（2）投（　　）；投（　　）；投（　　）

（3）海（　　）；海（　　）；海（　　）

（4）保（　　）；保（　　）；保（　　）

（5）进（　　）；进（　　）；进（　　）；进（　　）

（6）通（　　）；通（　　）；通（　　）；通（　　）

（7）提（　　）；提（　　）；提（　　）；提（　　）

（8）特（　　）；特（　　）；特（　　）；特（　　）

4. 区分以下每组词汇在意义或用法上的不同并尝试造句。

Distinguish the meanings or usages of the words in each group below and then try to make a sentence for each of them.

（1）派驻 / 入驻：_____

_____

（2）完备 / 完善：_____

_____

（3）提交 / 提供：_____

_____

（4）发展 / 进展：_____

_____

（5）投资 / 融资：_____

_____

（6）投入 / 投放：_____

_____

（7）研究 / 研发：_____

_____

（8）看好 / 看起来：_____

_____

（9）区域 / 地区：_____

_____

（10）便捷 / 便利：_____

_____

（11）特殊 / 特定：_____

_____

（12）功能 / 职能：_____

_____

II. 句型练习（一）　Sentence Pattern Exercises (1)

1. 🎧 *007* 根据下面的要求，用 "从 A 变成（了）B" 造句。

Use the pattern of "从 A 变成（了）B" to accomplish the following tasks.

（1）说一说某一个人在过去十年中的变化。

_____

（2）说一说某一家公司在最近几年的发展和变化。

_____

（3）说一说某一个地区的发展和变化。

_____

（4）说一说世界的变化。

_____

2. 完成下面带 "（依）靠……（来）V." 的句子。

Complete the following sentences which contain the pattern "（依）靠……（来）V.".

（1）他靠 _____（来）赚钱上大学。

（2）这个地区决定依靠 _____来吸引外国投资。

（3）王总经理打算靠_____（来）提高企业的经济效益。

（4）这家新成立的创业公司一直依靠_____来保持公司正常运营。

3. 🎧 *008* 请用 "据我所知" 回答下面的问题。

Answer the following questions by using the pattern "据我所知".

（1）听说您认识这位申请人。您认为他的强项是什么？

_____

（2）我想了解一下儿那家国际贸易公司的资信情况。

_____

（3）为什么很多跨国企业都愿意签约入驻到这个工业园区？

　　_____

（4）听说这届交易会的规模很大。你觉得（我们）公司也应该参加吗？

　　_____

4. 完成下面带"在……（的）基础上"的句子。

Complete the following sentences which contain the pattern "在……（的）基础上".

（1）在 _____ 的基础上，老板
　　决定正式录用马杰。

（2）在 _____ 的基础上，我
　　们公司成功地申请到了三项新能源技术专利。

（3）这份评估报告是在 _____
　　的基础上完成的。

（4）我们是在 _____ 的基础上，做出
　　了向那家创业公司投资的决定。

III. 句型练习（二）　Sentence Pattern Exercises (2)

1. 🎧 009　请用"位于……"改写下面的句子。

Rewrite the following sentences by using the pattern of "位于……".

（1）国际商务中心在旅馆的二楼。

　　_____

（2）家用电器产品展览在交易会大厅入口的右边。

　　_____

（3）深圳、珠海和汕头都在广东省的沿海地区。

　　_____

（4）成品车间在工厂的东边，组装车间的后边。

_____

2. 用"分别是"回答下面的问题。

Answer the following questions by using the pattern of "分别是".

（1）贵公司今年推出了哪些新产品？

_____

（2）请问，贵公司常打交道的银行有哪几家？

_____

（3）销售代理商一般分为几种？哪几种？

_____

（4）这次中国之行，美国贸易代表团访问了哪几个城市？

_____

3. 请用"……，以便……"改写下面的句子。

Please rewrite the following sentences by using the pattern "……，以便……".

（1）为了赶在十月上旬交货，工厂调整了生产计划。

_____

（2）为了吸引更多的顾客，促销期间所有商品都打七折。

_____

（3）为了获得外资和吸引高新技术企业入驻，当地政府决定在（工业）园区实行特殊的经济政策和灵活的管理措施。

_____

（4）为了了解那个地区的投资环境，我去那儿考察了三天。

_____

4. 复习第3课的句型 "（sb. V.……的）目的是……" 和本课句型 "以……为目的"，并用这两个句型回答下面的问题。

Review the patterns of "(sb. V.……的) 目的是……" (L.3) and "以……为目的" (L.14), and use these two patterns to answer the following questions.

（1）请问，推出这次新广告的目的是什么？

_____

_____

（Hint: 建立品牌知名度）

（2）"买一送一"（的）策略当然能吸引大批顾客，可是公司不怕赔本吗？

_____

_____

（Hint: 薄利多销）

（3）中国改革开放的目的是什么？

_____

_____

（4）你认为中国为什么要建立经济特区、开发区、高新区等等特殊区域？

_____

_____

IV. 阅读、讨论和其他活动　Reading, Discussion and Other Activities

1. 根据课文对话回答问题。

Answer the following questions according to the dialogues in this lesson.

（1）深圳这些年有什么变化？

_____

（2）深圳依靠什么来吸引外资？

_____

（3）为什么史强生认为这个园区"发展得真快"？

_____

（4）史强生和白琳为什么参观这个创业公司？

_____

（5）这家创业公司目前在做什么？

_____

（6）这家创业公司目前盈利了吗？它依靠什么保持运营？

_____

（7）这家创业公司下一步的计划是什么？

_____

（8）史先生说他会向他的公司提交一份评估报告。你觉得史先生在报告里会说什么？

_____

2. 根据本课的阅读短文选出最合适的答案。

Choose the most appropriate answer for the following questions according to the Reading Passage in this lesson.

（1）下面的经济特区，哪几个建立得比较早？

a 厦门经济特区   b 海南（省）经济特区

c 喀什经济特区   d 珠海经济特区

e 深圳经济特区   f 汕头经济特区

g 霍尔果斯经济特区

（2）你觉得哪个经济特区最大？

a 厦门经济特区   b 海南（省）经济特区

c 喀什经济特区   d 珠海经济特区

e 深圳经济特区   f 汕头经济特区

g 霍尔果斯经济特区

（3）中国在经济特区实行特殊的经济政策和灵活的管理措施。这样做的目的是
什么？

　　a 吸引外资和跨国企业

　　b 发展南部沿海地区经济

　　c 发展西部地区经济

　　d 发展知识密集型和技术密集型产业

（4）中国建立国家级高新技术产业开发区的目的是什么？

　　a 吸引外资和跨国企业

　　b 发展南部沿海地区经济

　　c 发展西部地区经济

　　d 发展知识密集型和技术密集型产业

（5）上海自贸区的特点是：

　　a 在浦东新区内第一个自由贸易区

　　b 享有更大的贸易自由和金融、投资便利

　　c 在中国境内推动经济全球化和"一带一路"倡议

3. 小任务。Tasks.

请在中国的经济特区、国家高新区和自贸区中选择一个，写一篇短文介绍那里
的情况，然后在课堂上报告。你的文章（/报告）应该包括以下的信息：

Choose one of the Special Economic Zones, National High-Tech Industrial Development
Zones or Free Trade Zones in China, then write a short essay and present it in your class. Your
report should cover the following information:

（1）正式名称、地点、建立的时间和目的。
（2）投资环境。
（3）发展历史和目前情况。
（4）你对这个特殊经济区域的看法。

4. 🎧 014 **快速复习**。**Quick review.**

Ⓐ 阅读下面的短文，复习学过的词汇和句型。

Read the following text and review vocabularies and sentence patterns that you have learned.

今天史先生和白小姐在张红主任的陪同下，从上海飞到深圳。史强生在飞机上也没有休息。他在昨天面试的基础上，给公司人力资源部写了一封邮件，说明了他自己对这次招聘的意见。史先生认为公司派驻中国的这个职位很重要。申请人不但应该有一定的工作经验，而且需要有中英文双语能力。到目前为止，在已经面试过的几位申请人中，史强生最看好马杰。史先生要求人力资源部准备好有关资料，等他下星期返回美国以后，就会做出最后决定。

史强生和白琳到达深圳以后，立刻参观了一个新的工业园区。这个园区是一年前依靠当地政府贷款和商业融资建立的，目前已经有四十多家高新技术企业和创业公司入驻。其中有半数的企业都是外资企业。园区的环境很好，交通很方便，整个园区内都可以使用免费无线网络。园区的公共配套设施也非常完备。他们还专门考察了一家成立不久的创业公司。这家公司研发的是跟新能源配套的家用电器产品。史先生认为这家创业公司的产品很有发展潜力。他打算写一份评估报告，向自己的公司提出建议，考虑跟这家中国创业公司开展合作。

Ⓑ 是非题 True & False Questions:

（1）在去深圳的飞机上，史先生给公司人力资源部写了一封信。　对　不对

（2）史先生对这次招聘的意见是申请人要有工作经验和双语能力。　对　不对

（3）史先生的最后决定是把这个职位给马杰。　对　不对

（4）在当地政府贷款和商业融资的基础上，建立了这个工业园区。　对　不对

（5）目前已经有二十多家外资企业入驻了园区。　　对　　不对

（6）园区附近的公共配套设施完备，园区内外都有免费无线网络。　　对　　不对

（7）史先生和白琳考察的这家创业公司研究、生产新能源。　　对　　不对

（8）史强生看好这家创业公司，有意跟它合作。　　对　　不对

（四）附录　　Appendix

1. 经济特区位置示意图 Sketch Map of SEZs

中国地图

审图号：GS(2016)2923号
国家测绘地理信息局 监制

2. 2015 年国家高新区成果示意图 Graph of NHIDZs' Achievements in 2015

营业收入
25.37 万亿元

占全国货物和
服务出口的
20.9%

工业总产值
18.6 万亿元

2015 年
146 家国家高新区
共实现

出口创汇
4732.4 亿美元

净利润
1.6 万亿元

净利润率
63%

3. 一带一路经济走廊及其途经城市分布示意图
The Map of the Belt and Road Economic Corridor and Cities along Route

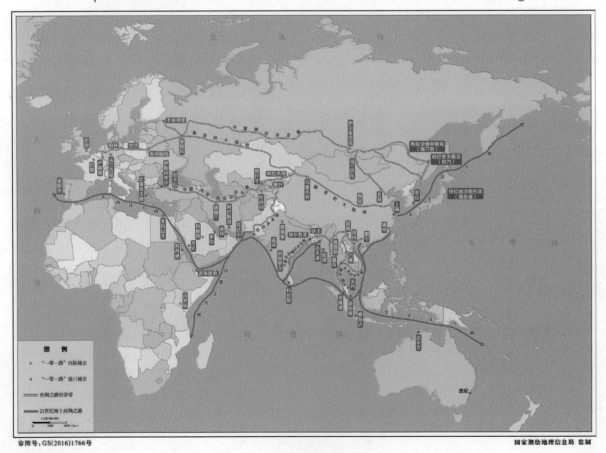

审图号：GS(2016)1766号

国家测绘地理信息局 监制

15 签订合同
Signing the Contract

今天是史强生和白琳在中国的最后一天。中美双方将要正式签订合同。一早，东方公司的副总经理李信文就从北京坐飞机到了深圳。他将代表东方公司参加今天的签字仪式。

（一）对话 Dialogue

1. 审核合同 Examining the Contracts

李信文：史先生、白小姐，这是我们今天将要签署的三份文件。每
　　　　份文件都有中英文对照。第一份是今年秋季的订货合同，
　　　　第二份是代理合同，第三份是长期合作意向书。请二位在
　　　　签字前对各项条款再审核一遍，尤其是订货合同上有关数

量、金额、包装要求、交货时间、验收标准和付款方式等项。如果还有任何遗漏或者不合适的地方，请立刻指出，以便修改。

史强生：好！白琳，我们一个人看一份。看完一遍以后，再交换看一遍。

（史强生、白琳审核合同）

白　琳：李先生，这儿有一句话我想再跟您确认一下儿。关于交货时间，文件上写的是"分两次在八月十日前和九月十日前交货"。这是不是说在十号以前贵公司就有可能交货呢？

李信文：（微笑）根据我们上一次洽谈的结果，双方商定的交货时间是八月上旬和九月上旬。"八月十日前和九月十日前交货"的意思是交货时间必须不晚于十号。当然，如果可能的话，我们会尽力提前交货。

白　琳：（笑）哦，我明白了。Johnson，你觉得还有别的问题吗？

史强生：我希望在合同中补充这样一条：如果因为卖方交货时间的延误，造成买方的经济损失，买方有权提出申诉和索赔。说实话，这份订单的交货时间对我们非常重要，我不想有任何差错。李先生，希望您能理解。

李信文：重合同、守信用是我们公司的原则，我们一定会按时交货。不过，我完全理解您的要求，我们马上把这一条写进去。

史强生：谢谢！另外，我建议在意向书中增加这样一句话：今后双方每季度应举行一次会谈，以便随时解决合同执行中可能发生的问题。

李信文：这一条很必要。我马上加进去。谢谢！

2. 正式签字 Formal Signing

课文英译

李信文: 史先生，这是合同的正本。凡是今天上午提出问题的地方，我们都按你们的意见做了修改。请您再看一遍。希望这次能让我们双方都满意。

史强生: （看合同）嗯，我认为所有条款都很详细清楚，看不出还有什么地方需要再修改、补充。白琳，你看呢？

白 琳: 我也觉得一切都很好。李先生，您费心了！

李信文: 不客气，这是我应该做的事。请问贵方需要几份副本？

史强生: 麻烦您每份文件给我两份副本。另外，如果方便的话，也请您给我发一份电子版的备份，以便保存。

李信文: 行！我马上就把它们发到您的邮箱。如果没有其他问题的话，我想我们可以签字了。史先生，请您在这儿签字吧！

史强生: 好。（签字）李先生，这次我们的合作非常成功。我非常高兴。希望今后跟您、跟贵公司能有更多的合作机会。

李信文: 一定，一定！现在我们有了长期协议，合作的机会一定会越来越多！（倒茶）来，让我们以茶代酒，为了庆祝我们这次合作的圆满成功和今后的更多合作干杯！

白 琳: （开玩笑）李先生，看起来今后我会常常来北京麻烦您了。您不会头疼吧？

词汇（一）　Vocabulary (1)

1.	签字	qiān zì	to sign or initial
2.	仪式	yíshì	ceremony; rite
3.	审核	shěnhé	to examine and verify
4.	签署	qiānshǔ	to sign (a document)
5.	文件	wénjiàn	document
6.	对照	duìzhào	contrast; comparison; to compare
7.	意向书	yìxiàngshū	letter of intent
8.	条款	tiáokuǎn	clause; article; provision
9.	金额	jīn'é	amount/sum of money
10.	包装	bāozhuāng	packing; packaging; to pack; dress up
11.	验收	yànshōu	check on delivery; inspection
12.	遗漏	yílòu	omission; to omit; to miss
13.	指出	zhǐchū	to point out
14.	确认	quèrèn	to confirm; to identify with certainty
15.	关于	guānyú	about; with regard to; concerning
16.	根据	gēnjù	on the basis of; according to
17.	不晚于	bù wǎn yú	no later than
18.	补充	bǔchōng	to add; to supplement; to replenish
19.	延误	yánwù	delay; to incur loss through delay
20.	造成	zàochéng	to create; to cause; to result in
21.	有权	yǒuquán	have the right to; to be entitled to
22.	申诉	shēnsù	appeal; to appeal
23.	索赔	suǒpéi	claim (for damages); to demand compensation

24.	差错	chācuò	mistake; error
25.	重合同，守信用	zhòng hétóng, shǒu xìnyòng	take one's contract seriously and keep one's word
26.	原则	yuánzé	principle
27.	按时	ànshí	on time
28.	季度	jìdù	season
29.	执行	zhíxíng	to carry out; to execute; to implement
30.	必要	bìyào	necessary; essential
31.	正本	zhèngběn	original (of document)
32.	凡是	fánshì	every; any; all
33.	副本	fùběn	duplicate; copy
34.	电子版	diànzǐbǎn	e-version; e-edition
35.	备份	bèifèn	backup (files, documents, etc.)
36.	邮箱	yóuxiāng	mailbox; email box
37.	以茶代酒	yǐ chá dài jiǔ	to have tea instead of liquor
38.	庆祝	qìngzhù	to celebrate
39.	头疼	tóuténg	to have a headache; headache

句型（一）　Sentence Patterns (1)

003

1. 关于……　about; with regard to; concerning

例：❶ 关于交货时间，我想再跟您确认一下儿。

　　❷ 昨天的洽谈讨论的是关于双方长期合作的问题。

2. 根据……　on the basis of; according to

例：❶ 根据我们上一次洽谈的结果，双方商定的交货时间是八月上旬和九月上旬。

　　❷ 我们可以根据客户的要求，对产品设计做出修改。

3. X 不晚于 Y　(the time of...) is not later than...; X is not later than Y

例：❶ 交货时间必须不晚于八月十号。

　　❷ 这批新产品投放市场的时间将不晚于三月上旬。

4. sb. 有权 do sth.　sb. has the right to do sth.

例：❶ 如果因为交货时间的延误造成买方的经济损失，买方有权提出索赔。

　　❷ 作为合作伙伴，我方有权获得更多的有关信息。

5. 凡是……都……　every; any; all (*an all-inclusive sentence structure)

例：❶ 凡是今天上午提出问题的地方，我们都按你们的意见做了修改。

　　❷ 凡是看了广告的客户，都对我们的产品很感兴趣。

（二）阅读短文 Reading Passage

中国的涉外经济法律、法规
Laws and Regulations of the PRC Regarding Foreign Economic Interests in China

课文英译

为了更好地利用外国资本和先进技术来帮助中国经济的发展，中国政府从 1979 年开始陆续制订了一系列的涉外经济法律、法规。其中，最重要是《中华人民共和国外资企业法》。《外资企业法》要求设立外资企业必须对中国国民经济的发展有利。它对外资企业的设立程序、组织形式、税务财会和外汇管理等各个方面都有清楚的说明。对于每一个打算到中国投资、做生意的外国人来说，了解这些法律、法规的内容是非常必要的。

中国的涉外经济法律、法规明确承诺保护外国投资者的合法权益，保证给予来中国投资的外国厂商、公司和个人以公平待遇。中国的涉外经济法律、法规强调平等互利的基本原则，同时也规定了解决争议的途径，即协商、调解、仲裁和诉讼等四种不同的方式。为了使争议得到公正合理的解决，中国也接受在第三国仲裁的要求。

全面、有效地实施中国涉外经济法律、法规明显地改善了中国的投资环境，起到了鼓励外国投资者的作用。今天的中国正在吸引着越来越多的外国投资者的关注。

词汇（二） Vocabulary (2)

1. 涉外	shèwài	involving foreign affairs/nationals
2. 法律	fǎlǜ	law
3. 法规	fǎguī	legislation; regulation

4.	陆续	lùxù	one after another; in succession
5.	其中	qízhōng	in/among
6.	设立程序	shèlì chéngxù	procedures for establishment
	设立	shèlì	to set up; to establish
	程序	chéngxù	order; procedure; program
7.	税务	shuìwù	taxation
8.	财会	cáikuài	financial affairs and accounting
9.	明确	míngquè	explicit(ly); clear and definite
10.	承诺	chéngnuò	to promise (to do sth.)
11.	保护	bǎohù	to protect; to safeguard
12.	合法	héfǎ	lawful; legal
13.	权益	quányì	rights and interests
14.	给予	jǐyǔ	to give; to grant
15.	公平	gōngpíng	fair; fairness
16.	待遇	dàiyù	treatment
17.	强调	qiángdiào	to stress; to emphasize
18.	平等互利	píngděng hùlì	equality and mutual benefit
19.	规定	guīdìng	to stipulate; to formulate; rule; stipulation
20.	争议	zhēngyì	dispute; controversy; to dispute
21.	协商	xiéshāng	to consult; to talk things over; consultation
22.	调解	tiáojiě	mediation; to mediate
23.	仲裁	zhòngcái	arbitration; to arbitrate
24.	诉讼	sùsòng	lawsuit; litigation
25.	公正	gōngzhèng	just; justice
26.	第三国	dì-sān guó	a third (and disinterested) country
27.	实施	shíshī	to put into effect; to implement
28.	改善	gǎishàn	to improve

29. 起作用	qǐ zuòyòng	have the effect of...
作用	zuòyòng	effect; function
30. 关注	guānzhù	attention; interest; to pay close attention to

专有名词 / 特殊名词 Proper Nouns / Special Nouns

中华人民共和国 外资企业法	Zhōnghuá Rénmín Gònghéguó Wàizī Qǐyè Fǎ	The Law of the People's Republic of China on Foreign Capital Enterprises

句型（二）　Sentence Patterns (2)　

1. 利用 A（来）V.　use A to V.

例：❶ 中国政府希望利用外国资本和先进技术来帮助中国经济的发展。

　　❷ 我想利用这个机会（来）跟贵公司讨论一下儿明年融资问题。

2. 从……开始　start from...

例：❶ 中国从 1979 年开始陆续制订了一系列的涉外经济法律、法规。

　　❷ 从去年开始，那家创业公司一直在研发、生产节能家用电器。

3. 给予 A 以 B　give B to A

例：❶ 外资企业法保证给予来中国投资的外国厂商、公司和个人以公平
　　　待遇。

　　❷ 作为合作伙伴，请贵公司给予我方以更多的支持和帮助。

4. 起到……作用　have the effect of...; play a part in...

例：❶ 全面、有效地实施中国涉外经济法规起到了鼓励外国投资者的作用。

　　❷ 我相信这次我们的宣传造势活动一定会起到推销产品的作用。

（三）练习与活动 Exercises & Activities

I. 词汇练习 Vocabulary Exercises

1. 连词比赛。Matching games.

按照拼音找出相应的英文并将标示该英文的字母填进"？"栏，再写出汉字。

Match each *pinyin* with its English equivalent by filling in the alphabet letter into the "?" box, and then write Chinese characters into the "汉字" box.

* 第一场 Game one:

	PINYIN	汉字	?
1	yíshì		
2	wénjiàn		
3	yìxiàngshū		
4	suǒpéi		
5	yóuxiāng		
6	yuánzé		
7	zhíxíng		
8	bāozhuāng		

	English equivalent
A	letter of intent
B	mailbox; email box
C	ceremony; rite
D	to implement
E	document
F	packing; packaging
G	claim (for damages)
H	principle

* 第二场 Game two:

	PINYIN	汉字	?
1	cáikuài		
2	guīdìng		
3	dàiyù		
4	fǎguī		
5	gǎishàn		
6	dì-sān guó		
7	shuìwù		
8	zhòngcái		

	English equivalent
A	rule; to stipulate
B	legislation; regulation
C	a third (/disinterested) country
D	financial affairs & accounting
E	arbitration
F	taxation
G	to improve
H	treatment

2. 字谜。**Crossword puzzle.**

请根据下面的提示，猜一猜是哪个生词，把它的拼音填进下面的空格里，在旁边写出汉字，最后找出谜底。

Read each clue first, and then fill in the boxes with *pinyin* of the word you guessed. You may write the characters next to each clue. Once you fill out all the boxes, find out what "the wonder word" is.

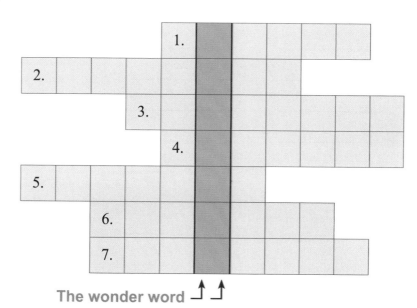

The wonder word

✱ 提示 (Clues)：　　　　　　　　　　　　　　　　汉字

（1）没有按时到达，晚了 ⟶

（2）不完善，需要再加一些 ⟶

（3）两份文件互相比较，看看有没有不同 ⟶

（4）为了保证没错，再问一次 ⟶

（5）出了问题，不对了 ⟶

（6）在文件上写下自己的名字 ⟶

（7）收到货物的时候，先检查一下儿 ⟶

3. 组词。 Build upon the following words.

例：涉外　→　　涉外法规　　　　　涉外活动

（1）签署　→ ＿＿＿＿＿＿　　＿＿＿＿＿＿

（2）审核　→ ＿＿＿＿＿＿　　＿＿＿＿＿＿

（3）执行　→ ＿＿＿＿＿＿　　＿＿＿＿＿＿

（4）验收　→ ＿＿＿＿＿＿　　＿＿＿＿＿＿

（5）补充　→ ＿＿＿＿＿＿　　＿＿＿＿＿＿

（6）造成　→ ＿＿＿＿＿＿　　＿＿＿＿＿＿

（7）按时　→ ＿＿＿＿＿＿　　＿＿＿＿＿＿

（8）保护　→ ＿＿＿＿＿＿　　＿＿＿＿＿＿

（9）确认　→ ＿＿＿＿＿＿　　＿＿＿＿＿＿

（10）指出　→ ＿＿＿＿＿＿　　＿＿＿＿＿＿

4. 用中文解释以下生词的意思并造句。

Explain the following in Chinese, then make a sentence for each of them.

例：周末： 一个星期的最后两天；星期六和星期天。

　　　　 这次促销从这个周末开始。

（1）季度：＿＿＿＿＿＿＿＿＿＿＿＿＿＿＿＿＿＿

　　　　　＿＿＿＿＿＿＿＿＿＿＿＿＿＿＿＿＿＿

（2）签字：＿＿＿＿＿＿＿＿＿＿＿＿＿＿＿＿＿＿

　　　　　＿＿＿＿＿＿＿＿＿＿＿＿＿＿＿＿＿＿

（3）遗漏：＿＿＿＿＿＿＿＿＿＿＿＿＿＿＿＿＿＿

　　　　　＿＿＿＿＿＿＿＿＿＿＿＿＿＿＿＿＿＿

（4）必要：＿＿＿＿＿＿＿＿＿＿＿＿＿＿＿＿＿＿

　　　　　＿＿＿＿＿＿＿＿＿＿＿＿＿＿＿＿＿＿

（5）关注：＿＿＿＿＿＿＿＿＿＿＿＿＿＿＿＿＿＿

　　　　　＿＿＿＿＿＿＿＿＿＿＿＿＿＿＿＿＿＿

（6）陆续：_____

_____

（7）承诺：_____

_____

（8）涉外：_____

_____

（9）改善：_____

_____

（10）平等互利：_____

_____

II. 句型练习（一）　Sentence Pattern Exercises (1)

1. 请用"关于……"回答下面的问题。

Answer the following questions by using the pattern of "关于……".

（1）请问，你拿的是一本什么小册子？

_____

（2）用中文怎么说"regarding to this issue, I have no opinion at all"？

_____

（3）明天要签署的是一份什么样的文件？

_____

（4）怎么用中文说"I have a question about the delivery time"？

_____

2. 用"根据……"回答下面的问题。

Use the pattern of "根据……" to answer the questions below.

（1）你认为厂商怎样决定商品的零售价？

_____

（2）你觉得为什么很多厂商都定期做市场调查？

_____

（3）你觉得风险投资公司怎样决定要不要给一家创业公司投资？

_____

（4）如果你打算自己创业，你怎样决定做什么？

_____

3. 🎧 008　用 "X 不晚于 Y" 回答下面的问题。

Use the pattern of "X 不晚于 Y" to answer the questions below.

（1）你：经理，我想跟您确认一下儿秋季订单的交货时间。

经理：_____

（Hint: No later than July 31.）

（2）你：经理，我想跟您再确认一下儿 101 号订单的付款时间。

经理：_____

（Hint: The first payment is due on April 15.）

（3）你：经理，请问新产品广告应该在什么时候推出？

经理：_____

（Hint: No later than next Friday.）

（4）你：经理，公司希望我们什么时候提交评估报告？

经理：_____

（Hint: The deadline is next Friday.）

4. 🎧 009　请用 "sb. 有权 do sth." 回答下面的问题。

Answer the following questions by using the pattern of "sb. 有权 do sth.".

（1）谁可以签署这份意向书？

_____

（2）谁可以代表厂家进行促销活动？

_____

（3）消费者买了质量有问题的商品应该怎么办？

_____

（4）如果延误了交货时间，买方可以跟卖方提出什么要求？

_____

5. 请用"凡是…… 都……"回答下面的问题。

Answer the following questions by using the pattern of "凡是…… 都……".

（1）你觉得什么样的产品受欢迎？

_____

（2）你认为什么样的生意伙伴不是好伙伴？

_____

（3）你认为做什么生意没有风险？

_____

（4）经理，这份合同上的哪些条款应该立刻执行？

_____

III. 句型练习（二）   Sentence Pattern Exercises (2)

1. 请用"利用 A 来 V."回答下面的问题。

Answer the following questions by using the pattern of "利用 A 来 V.".

（1）如果你是一个代理商，你怎样获得市场信息？

_____

（2）如果你是公司总裁，你打算怎样为你的产品打开中国市场？

_____

（3）如果一个企业长期亏损，有什么办法可以提高企业效益？

_____

（4）你和几个伙伴刚成立了一家创业公司，你打算怎样保证公司正常运营？

_____

2. 完成下面带"从……开始"的句子。

Complete the following sentences with the pattern of "从……开始".

（1）从到达中国的第一天开始，＿＿＿＿＿＿＿＿＿＿＿＿＿＿＿＿。

（2）从第一次洽谈开始，＿＿＿＿＿＿＿＿＿＿＿＿＿＿＿＿＿。

（3）从 1979 年改革开放开始，＿＿＿＿＿＿＿＿＿＿＿＿＿＿。

（4）从制订涉外经济法律、法规开始，＿＿＿＿＿＿＿＿＿＿＿。

3. 🎧 用"给予 A 以 B"回答下面的问题。

Answer the following questions with the pattern "给予 A 以 B".

（1）请问，作为合作伙伴，贵公司将为我方提供哪些支持或帮助？

＿＿＿＿＿＿＿＿＿＿＿＿＿＿＿＿＿＿＿＿＿＿＿＿＿＿＿

（Hint: 24-hour technical support）

（2）刘经理为什么决定去找那家民营银行谈贷款？

＿＿＿＿＿＿＿＿＿＿＿＿＿＿＿＿＿＿＿＿＿＿＿＿＿＿＿

（Hint: to give a concessional/preferential loan to us）

（3）我想了解一下儿，签约入驻园区的企业可以使用哪些公共设施和服务？

＿＿＿＿＿＿＿＿＿＿＿＿＿＿＿＿＿＿＿＿＿＿＿＿＿＿＿

（Hint: the privilege of using wireless network and the gym for free）

（4）我想了解一下儿，中国的涉外经济法律、法规将如何保护外国投资人的合法权益？

＿＿＿＿＿＿＿＿＿＿＿＿＿＿＿＿＿＿＿＿＿＿＿＿＿＿＿

（Hint: to grant foreign investors with fair treatment as well as legal protection）

4. 🎧 请用"起到……作用"回答下面的问题。

Answer the following questions by using the pattern of "起到……作用".

（1）销售旺季为什么还要降价、打折？

＿＿＿＿＿＿＿＿＿＿＿＿＿＿＿＿＿＿＿＿＿＿＿＿＿＿＿

（2）为什么要在广告宣传中突出品牌形象？

＿＿＿＿＿＿＿＿＿＿＿＿＿＿＿＿＿＿＿＿＿＿＿＿＿＿＿

（3）在国际贸易中，当买卖双方有了争议，找第三国调解或仲裁有什么好处？

_____

（4）改善投资环境有什么好处？

_____

IV. 阅读、讨论和其他活动　Reading, Discussion and Other Activities

1. 　　　根据课文对话回答问题。

Answer the following questions according to the dialogues in this lesson.

（1）中美双方将要签署什么文件？

_____

（2）白琳要求再次确认什么？

_____

（3）中方同意在合同中补充什么内容？

_____

（4）除了文件的正本以外，美方还需要什么？

_____

（5）谁代表中美双方签署文件？

_____

（6）为什么说今后双方一定会有更多的合作机会？

_____

（7）白琳问李先生："您不会头疼吧？"你觉得李先生会头疼还是会高兴？

　　　为什么？

_____

2. 根据本课课文对话的内容，写出谈判双方在签署合同时应该注意的事。

Based on the information in the dialogue, write a short paragraph talking about what issues buyers and sellers need to pay attention to when they are getting ready to sign a contract.

_____

_____

3. 根据本课的阅读短文回答下面的问题。

Please answer the following questions based on the Reading Passage in this lesson.

（1）中国的《外资企业法》涉及哪些方面的内容？

_____

（2）外资企业在中国遇到问题时，有哪些解决争议的途径？

_____

4. 小任务。Tasks.

Ⓐ 利用图书馆或者上网，查询你的国家制订的有关涉外经济和贸易的法律、法规。再从这些法律、法规中选择一个，在课堂上用中文做一个简单的介绍。

Using the Internet or the library, find out what kind of economic laws and regulations your country has with regard to foreign trade. Please choose one of these laws and regulations and share it with your class.

Ⓑ 课堂报告：介绍最近中国涉外贸易中成交的一笔生意或者达成的一项协议。你的报告中应该说明这是一笔什么样的生意，双方公司的名称，什么产品，成交或达成协议的时间、地点、金额，是否签署了什么合同，等等。请利用图书馆或者上网找到你需要的信息。

Class presentation: Using the Internet or the library, research a recent business deal or an agreement between China (or a Chinese company) and a foreign country（or a foreign company). Your presentation should provide some details about this deal, including the basic content of this deal, the names of companies involved, what kind of products, when and where this deal was made, the sum of the money involved, what kind of document was signed, etc.

5. 🎧 015 **快速复习**。**Quick review.**

Ⓐ 阅读下面的短文，复习学过的词汇和句型。
Read the following text and review vocabularies and sentence patterns that you have learned.

深圳是史先生和白小姐这次访问中国的最后一站。深圳的巨大变化和迅速发展给他们留下了深刻的印象。除了游览城市以外，昨天他们还参观了当地的一个工业园区，专门考察了入驻园区的一家创业公司。这家公司的研发人员有一半都是海归。他们目前的研发项目是家庭新能源技术和配套产品，并且已经申请了多项专利。史先生在考察过程中了解到，当地政府给予这家公司以很多支持，帮助他们获得优惠贷款和融资，保证了公司的正常运营。现在公司的产品很快就要正式投放市场了。史先生认为这家创业公司很有潜力。他非常看好这家公司。

今天上午，李信文副总经理从北京飞到深圳。中美双方将要正式签署三份文件。它们是订货合同、代理合同和长期合作意向书。双方代表在再次审核、确认文件内容以后，由李信文和史强生分别代表自己的公司在文件上签了字。最后，大家以茶代酒一起为签字仪式顺利完成而干杯。

Ⓑ 选择正确的答案　Choose the best answer based on the paragraphs above.

（1）史先生和白小姐在中国访问的最后一个地方是＿＿＿＿＿＿＿＿＿。

　　a 深圳的工业园区　　　b 创业公司　　　　　c 深圳

（2）这家创业公司生产的产品已经获得了专利。对吗？

　　a 对　　　　　　　　b 不对　　　　　　　c 可能

（3）这家创业公司有很多研发人员都是在国外学习过的。对吗？

　　a 对　　　　　　　　b 不对　　　　　　　c 可能

（4）史先生看好这家公司，因为＿＿＿＿＿＿＿＿＿＿＿＿。

　　a 公司有优惠贷款和很好的产品　　　b 公司有当地政府的支持
　　c 公司有资金也有很多海归　　　　　d 产品很快就要投放市场了
　　e 有政府的支持、也有很好的技术和专利产品

（5）李信文飞到深圳的目的是 _____。

　　a 陪史先生和白小姐参观　　　　　b 审核确认文件并代表中方签字
　　c 陪史先生和白小姐参加签字仪式　　d 以茶代酒参加签字仪式

（四）附录　Appendix

1. 合同实例 Example of Contract

广州市新禧科贸有限公司

购货合同

买方：广州市新禧科贸有限公司　　　　　　　　合同编号：GXX17-007891
卖方：杭州市伟文文教用品公司　　　　　　　　签约时间：2017-8-10

一、商品信息

货号	品名	商标	规格	产地	数量	单位	单价	金额 / 元
PC1091	套装彩色铅笔	光明	标准 A	杭州	8000	6 支 / 套	7.00	56,000
NB3062	笔记本	光明	标准 A	杭州	5000	本	8.00	40,000
总计人民币：（大写）玖万陆仟元整								96,000

二、验收方法：按样验收

三、包装、运输及费用：买方负责

四、交货时间及地点：2017.9.1 前于杭州市伟文文教用品公司仓库

五、货款结算：验收交货当日以电汇（T/T）付款结算。

六、提出异议的时间和规定：卖方应对其产品质量负责。买方在产品有效期内如发现质量问题，由
　　此产生的一切费用、损失由卖方负责。如发现数量 / 重量短少、包装破损，卖方有责任协助买
　　方及有关责任方解决赔偿。

七、合同的变更和解除：任何一方要求变更或解除合同时，应及时以书面形式通知对方。通知送达
　　时间不得晚于交货前一周。当事人一方在接到另一方要求变更或解除合同的要求后，应在三日
　　内做出答复。逾期不做答复，即视为默认接受。双方就合同变更或解除达成协议以前，原合同
　　依然有效。

八、合同争议的解决方式：本合同在履行过程中发生的争议，由双方当事人协商解决。协商无果，
　　可依法向需方所在地人民法院提出诉讼。

九、本合同正本一式两份。买方与卖方各一份，均具有同等法律效力。

十、违约责任：按照本合同上述各条执行。

买方（章）：广州新禧科贸有限公司　　　　　卖方（章）：杭州市伟文文教用品公司
单位地址：广州市珠江南路 123 号 36B　　　　单位地址：杭州市钱江路 765 号 11A
电话：020-28816166　　　　　　　　　　　　电话：0571-61522308
邮箱：xxkm@126.com　　　　　　　　　　　　邮箱：wwwj@yahoo.com
授权代理人签字：　　　　　　　　　　　　　授权代理人签字：

2. 意向书实例 Letter of Intent

意向书

中国东方进出口公司（英文名称：China Eastern Import & Export Corporation。以下简称甲方）与 US-Pacific Trading Company（中文名称：美国太平洋贸易公司。以下简称乙方）于二〇一七年六月十日经双方友好商谈，对合资经营服装工厂共同拟订意向如下：

1. 合资工厂设立于中国深圳，生产适销欧美市场的各类服装。

2. 甲方主要负责生产与管理，乙方主要负责产品设计与海外市场营销。

3. 合资工厂的投资金额初步商定为 9,000 万美元，投资比例为甲、乙双方各占百分之五十，盈利亦按双方投资比例分配。

4. 甲乙双方同意在意向书签订之日起 15 天之内组成项目工作组，负责该项目的各项前期准备工作。

5. 项目工作组成立后，必须在 60 天之内制定并完成设立合资工厂的详细实施计划。

6. 甲乙双方对合资工厂项目各自向上级有关主管部门报告，经获准后双方再进一步洽谈具体的合资协议。

甲方：中国东方进出口公司   乙方：US-Pacific Trading Company

    （签字、盖章）   （签字、盖章）

二〇一七年六月十日

16 饯行告别
Farewell Dinner

明天史强生和白琳就要回美国了。李信文以东方进出口公司的名义举行晚宴，庆祝中美两家公司这次成功的合作，同时也为史先生和白小姐饯行。

（一）对话 Dialogue

课文英译

1. 在告别晚宴上 At the Farewell Banquet

李信文：史先生、白小姐，今天的晚宴有两个目的。一是庆祝我们两家公司的成功合作，二是为你们二位饯行。请允许我代表东方进出口公司对你们表示衷心的感谢。来，让我先敬你们一杯！感谢你们为这次洽谈的圆满成功所做的努力。

（大家干杯）

史强生：李先生，这次我们来中国的收获很大。我们都非常高兴。我也想借这个机会代表我的公司对您和东方进出口公司表示感谢。感谢东方公司给予我们的热情接待，尤其是感谢您为我们这次访问所做的种种安排。

李信文：哪里，哪里。这次能跟您和白小姐合作，我感到非常愉快。你们这次来中国，不但加强了我们之间的业务联系，而且加深了我们之间的互相理解。我相信有了这样一个良好的基础，我们今后一定会有更多的生意往来。

史强生：我完全同意。这次来中国，我亲眼看到了中国的发展。中国已经成为一个重要的经济大国。难怪现在有这么多国家的厂商要到中国来做生意。我敢说在美国一定有很多公司羡慕我们有了东方公司和李先生这样可靠的"关系"。（笑）李先生，今后还要请您多多关照啊！

课文英译

2. 话别、赠送礼品 Parting Words and the Presentation of Gifts

白　琳：时间过得真快！我总觉得好像昨天我才刚到中国似的，可是明天一早我就要飞回美国了！

李信文：白小姐，如果您真想在中国多待一些日子，我们非常欢迎。

白　琳：想倒是想，不过这要看我的老板是不是愿意给我假期了。

李信文：我有一个办法。也许下一次我们可以把这个问题也列入我们的谈判。史先生，您看怎么样？

史强生：（笑）对不起，这件事可没有谈判的余地！白琳是我最得力的助手，少了她可不行！

李信文：（笑）史先生如果也打算来中国度假的话，我们更加欢迎！

史强生：我倒是想带太太一起来中国旅行，就是总是没有时间。她一直说要来看看长城和兵马俑。

李信文：好啊，您什么时候决定了，请通知我。我负责替您安排。史先生、白小姐，这是我们公司送给你们的礼物，算是你们这次中国之行的纪念吧！

史强生：谢谢！

白　琳：我现在就能打开看看吗？

李信文：当然，请！

白　琳：啊，景泰蓝花瓶，真漂亮！李先生，谢谢你。

李信文：不用谢，都是一些小礼物，留个纪念。

史强生：李先生，我也有一件礼物，想送给您。

李信文：不敢当，不敢当，您太客气了！

史强生：请您一定要收下。另外还有两件礼物，想麻烦您带给王总经理和张红女士。

李信文：好吧。那我就收下了。谢谢！史先生、白小姐，明天我还有一个重要的会，所以不能给你们送行了，很抱歉。不过，张红主任会陪你们去机场。

史强生：您陪了我们这么多天，又专程从北京赶到这儿来，我们已经非常感谢了！

李信文：哪里哪里，不必客气。祝你们一路平安！希望我们很快会再见！

史强生、白　琳：谢谢，再见！

词汇（一）　Vocabulary (1)

1.	饯行	jiànxíng	to give a farewell dinner
2.	告别	gàobié	to part from; to bid farewell
3.	名义	míngyì	name; nominal
4.	晚宴	wǎnyàn	evening banquet
5.	衷心	zhōngxīn	heartfelt; whole-hearted
6.	收获	shōuhuò	gains; results
7.	加强	jiāqiáng	to strengthen; to reinforce
8.	加深	jiāshēn	to deepen
9.	往来	wǎnglái	contact; dealings; intercourse
10.	难怪	nánguài	no wonder
11.	羡慕	xiànmù	to admire; to envy
12.	关系	guānxi	"connections"; relationship; ties
13.	话别	huàbié	to say a few parting words; to say goodbye
14.	赠送	zèngsòng	to present (as a gift); to give
15.	倒是	dàoshì	actually; really
16.	列入	lièrù	be included in; be placed on (an agenda, etc.)
17.	余地	yúdì	leeway; margin; room
18.	得力	délì	capable; competent
19.	度假	dù jià	to spend one's vacation
20.	更加	gèngjiā	(even) more
21.	太太	tàitai	wife; Mrs.
22.	花瓶	huāpíng	flower vase
23.	送行	sòngxíng	to see sb. off
24.	专程	zhuānchéng	special-purpose trip
25.	一路平安	yílù píng'ān	Have a safe journey!

专有名词 / 特殊名词 Proper Nouns / Special Nouns

| 1. 兵马俑 | bīngmǎyǒng | terra cotta figures of warriors and horses |
| 2. 景泰蓝 | jǐngtàilán | cloisonné |

句型（一） Sentence Patterns (1)

1. 以……的名义   in the name of...; on behalf of...

例：❶ 李经理以东方进出口公司的名义举行晚宴。

❷ 这次史先生和太太是以参加交易会的名义来中国的。

2. 所 + V. + 的   that which...

例：❶ 感谢你们为这次洽谈的圆满成功所做的努力。

❷ 这些都是本公司目前所代理销售的产品。

3. 难怪   no wonder

例：❶ 难怪现在有这么多国家的厂商要到中国来做生意。

❷ 史先生已经找到了更便宜的货源，难怪他不想再谈判了。

4. 好像…… 似的   seem; as if

例：❶ 我觉得好像昨天我才刚到中国似的。

❷ 陈厂长带来了很多货样，好像要开一个交易会似的。

5. 倒是……不过／就是……   actually/really...but/the only thing is...

例：❶ 想倒是想，不过这要看我的老板是不是愿意给我假期了。

❷ 我倒是想带太太一起来中国旅行，就是总是没有时间。

（二）阅读短文 Reading Passage

建立可靠的长期合作关系
Establishing a Long-term Cooperative Relationship

课文英译

　　说到"关系"这个词，许多在中国做生意的外国人都会立刻想到"走后门"。不可否认，"走后门"常常是能够解决一些问题的，可是"走后门"这种"关系"并不保险。有时候"走后门"不但不能帮你的忙，反而耽误了你的正经事，甚至让你上当受骗。对于每一位打算到中国做生意的人来说，与其想办法"走后门"，不如踏踏实实地建立起一种平等互利的合作关系更可靠。

　　中国人重视长期合作关系。如果你是一个有心人，就会利用各种场合，让他们知道你的公司也非常重视这种关系。跟中国人做生意、打交道，你不妨开诚布公，让对方清楚地了解你的立场。在激烈的谈判中，耐心、理解、尊重和友好的态度都是不可缺少的。不要让中国人觉得你是一个只顾眼前利益的生意人。有时候，为了解决双方的争议，你不妨做出适当的妥协。这样做不但让中国人觉得有面子，而且使他相信你是一个通情达理、值得交往的朋友。

　　签订合同以后，大功告成。这正是你趁热打铁、巩固双方关系的好机会。除了干杯以外，不要忘了代表你的公司表示对今后继续合作的期待。让你的中国朋友相信你的公司确实有保持长期合作关系的诚意。你也不妨借这个机会给你的中国朋友送上一两件有意义的小礼物。中国人常说："礼轻情义重。"这样做，既表示了你对他们的感谢，又说明了你对双方友谊的重视。

　　总之，多了解一些中国文化，多了解中国人，这对你在中国的生意一定会有帮助。

　　祝你成功！

词汇（二）　Vocabulary (2)

1. 走后门	zǒu hòumén	to get in by the back door; to secure advantages through pull or influence
2. 不可否认	bùkě fǒurèn	can't deny; undeniably
3. 保险	bǎoxiǎn	safe; secure; insurance
4. 反而	fǎn'ér	on the contrary; instead
5. 耽误	dānwù	to delay; to hold up; to hinder
6. 正经事	zhèngjingshì	serious matters; reputable affairs
7. 受骗	shòu piàn	be deceived/swindled
8. 与其……不如……	yǔqí……bùrú……	rather than..., it would be better to...
不如	bùrú	not as good as; inferior to; it would be better to
9. 踏实	tāshi	solidly; practical
10. 重视	zhòngshì	to value; to take sth. seriously; to consider important
11. 有心人	yǒuxīnrén	a person with a set purpose
12. 场合	chǎnghé	occasion; situation
13. 开诚布公	kāichéng-bùgōng	to speak friendly and sincerely
14. 立场	lìchǎng	position; stand; standpoint
15. 尊重	zūnzhòng	to respect; to value; to esteem
16. 缺少	quēshǎo	to lack; be short of
17. 只顾	zhǐgù	be absorbed in; to be concerned only with
18. 眼前	yǎnqián	at the moment; at present
19. 利益	lìyì	benefit; gain; interest
20. 妥协	tuǒxié	compromise; to compromise; to come to terms
21. 面子	miànzi	"face"; reputation; prestige

22.	通情达理	tōngqíng-dálǐ	sensible; reasonable
23.	大功告成	dàgōng-gàochéng	to have finally come to completion; to have been brought to a successful completion
24.	趁热打铁	chènrè-dǎtiě	to strike while the iron is hot
25.	巩固	gǒnggù	to consolidate; to strengthen; to solidify
26.	期待	qīdài	hope; expectation; to look forward to
27.	诚意	chéngyì	good faith; sincerity
28.	有意义	yǒu yìyi	significant; meaningful
29.	礼轻情义重	lǐqīng qíngyì zhòng	The gift is trifling, but feeling is profound; the thoughtfulness is worth far more than the gift itself.
30.	总之	zǒngzhī	in a word; in short

句型（二） Sentence Patterns (2) *006*

---

1. 不但不……，反而……   not only not... but instead...

例：❶ 有时候"走后门"不但不能帮你的忙，反而耽误了你的正经事。

❷ 王先生不但不肯跟我们合作，反而把销售代理权给了另一家公司。

---

2. 与其 A 不如 B   B is a better choice than A; rather than A, it would be better to B

例：❶ 与其想办法"走后门"，不如踏踏实实地建立起一种平等互利的合作关系更可靠。

❷ 与其每天自己上街推销产品，不如花一些钱在电视上做广告。

---

3. 借这个（/此）机会 do sth.   take this opportunity to do sth.

例：❶ 你不妨借这个机会给你的中国朋友送上一两件有意义的小礼物。

❷ 我想借此机会表示我的感谢。

---

4. 总之   in a word; in short

例：❶ 总之，多了解一些中国文化，这对你在中国的生意一定会有帮助。

❷ 总之，这次中国之行的收获很大。

（三）练习与活动 Exercises & Activities

I. 词汇练习 Vocabulary Exercises

1. 组词。你可以参考总附录中的词表。

Build upon the following words. You may refer to the Vocabulary List in the General Appendix.

例：成（ 本 ）；　　成（ 品 ）

（1）加（　　）；　　加（　　）；　　加（　　）；　　加（　　）；

（2）关（　　）；　　关（　　）；　　关（　　）；　　关（　　）；

（3）专（　　）；　　专（　　）；　　专（　　）；　　专（　　）；

（4）保（　　）；　　保（　　）；　　保（　　）；　　保（　　）；

（5）（　　）心；　　（　　）心；　　（　　）心；　　（　　）心；

（6）（　　）行；　　（　　）行；　　（　　）行；　　（　　）行；
　　　　　xíng　　　　　　xíng　　　　　　xíng　　　　　　xíng

2. 接龙。你可以参考总附录中的词表。

Build up word sequences. You may refer to the Vocabulary List in the General Appendix.

例：职业 →业（ 务 ）→务（ 必 ）→必（ 要 ）

Hint:　　business　　　　must　　　necessary

（1）立场→场（　　）→（　　）同→同（　　）→（　　）型→型（　　）

Hint:　　　　　　　　　contract　　the same kind

（2）尊重 →重（　　）→视（　　）→（　　）繁 →繁（　　）

Hint:　　　　　　　　　　　　　　frequently

（3）妥协→协（　　）→（　　）定 →定（　　）→（　　）待→待（　　）

Hint:　　　　to settle through discussion　　　　expectation

（4）提交 →交（　　）→（　　）收 →收（　　）→（　　）得→得（　　）

Hint:　　to pay taxes　　　　　　　gains/results

3. 用中文解释以下词汇的意思，然后造句。

Use Chinese to explain the meaning of the following words, then make a sentence.

例：频繁："很多很多次"的意思。

李经理频繁地给对方打电话，总算把事情安排好了。

（1）饯行：_____

_____

（2）专程：_____

_____

（3）难怪：_____

_____

（4）衷心：_____

_____

（5）得力：_____

_____

（6）收获：_____

4. 用中文回答下面的问题。

Answering the following questions in Chinese.

（1）"一路平安"有什么意思？什么时候你可以说"一路平安"？

What is the meaning of "一路平安"? When can one use this expression?

_____

（2）"礼轻情义重"有什么意思？什么时候可以说"礼轻情义重"？

What is the meaning of "礼轻情义重"? When can one use this expression?

_____

（3）什么样的人是"有心人"？

What kind of person is called "有心人" in Chinese?

_____

（4）什么是"通情达理"？在谈判中，什么样的态度是"通情达理"的态度？

What is "通情达理"? What attitude is considered "通情达理" during a negotiation?

_____

（5）"开诚布公"的意思是什么？什么时候应该"开诚布公"？

What is the meaning of "开诚布公"? When should one be "开诚布公"?

_____

（6）"趁热打铁"和"大功告成"的意思有什么不同？

What is the difference between the meanings of "趁热打铁"和"大功告成"?

_____

II. 句型练习（一） Sentence Pattern Exercises (1)

1. 🎧 用"以……的名义"改写下面的句子。
   Rewrite the following sentences by using the pattern of "以……的名义".

   （1）王总代表东方进出口公司给史强生先生写信，正式邀请他来访问。

   _____

   （2）马局长代表主办单位举行宴会，欢迎参加交易会的客商们。

   _____

   （3）公司为每位客人准备了小礼物，今天由公关部张主任向客人赠送。

   _____

   （4）借参加投资洽谈会的机会，美国商务代表团考察、访问了中国西部的几个城市。

   _____

2. 🎧 根据下面的要求，用"所 + V. + 的"造句。
   Use the pattern of "所 + V. + 的" to accomplish the following tasks.

   （1）指出哪种家用电器产品的牌子是你喜欢的。

   _____

（2）说一说哪些产品是你的公司希望立刻进货的。

_____

（3）说出一个你羡慕的成功企业家。

_____

（4）说出一个你想去度假的地方。

_____

3. 用"难怪"完成下面的句子。

Complete the following sentences by using the pattern of "难怪".

（1）这次的生意又赔本了，难怪 _____。

（2）白小姐刚刚跟好朋友话别，难怪 _____。

（3）交货日期已经到了，可是货还没有收到。难怪 _____。

（4）李经理刚度假回来，难怪 _____。

4. 🎧 *009* **根据下面的问题，用"好像……似的"造句。**

Use the pattern of "好像…… 似的" to accomplish the following tasks.

（1）怎么关心地提醒你的朋友，你觉得他应该注意身体？

_____

（2）怎么礼貌地告诉对方，你认为合同中的某一条条款需要修改补充？

_____

（3）怎么小心地（/礼貌地）让你的老板知道，你觉得你的佣金太低了？

_____

（4）怎么用开玩笑的办法提醒你的朋友，这次在中国他买的东西已经太多了、
不应该再买了？

_____

5. 🎧 *010* **用"倒是……不过/就是"改写下面的句子。**

Rewrite the following sentences by using the pattern of "倒是…… 不过/就是".

（1）昨天的饯行晚宴的确很丰盛，可是那家饭馆布置得不够漂亮。

_____

（2）这次谈判的收获很大，可是获得这些成功真不容易。

_____

（3）这件毛衣的式样张小姐很喜欢，可是价格她觉得贵了一点儿。

_____

（4）王总很愿意把销售电脑的独家代理权交给长城公司，可是他已经跟另一家公司有了合作协定。

_____

III. 句型练习（二）　Sentence Pattern Exercises (2)

1. 用"不但不……反而……"回答下面的问题。
   Answer the following questions by using the pattern of "不但不……反而……".

（1）为什么买了这种洗碗机的顾客都要求退货？

_____

（2）为什么你不要那家电视台为产品做广告了？

_____

（3）为什么你不愿意给总经理当助理了？

_____

（4）为什么你不想再跟那家公司合作了？

_____

2. 你和李经理在很多问题上都有不同的意见。请用"与其……不如……"完成下面的对话。
   You differ in opinion with Manager Li on many issues. Complete the following dialogues by using the pattern of "与其……不如……".

（1）李：为了打开市场销路，我打算在当地报纸上为我们的产品投放一个星期的广告。你觉得怎么样？

你：_____

（2）李：我打算赠送给每位客户一件小礼物，表示我们的感谢。你觉得怎么样？

你：_____

（3）李：你觉得我们应该先跟对方签订一份意向书还是签署一份长期合同？

你：_____

（4）李：这家公司的丝绸产品并不是最好的。不过他们的张经理是我们的老熟人。你说我们这次买不买他们的产品？

你：_____

3. 🎧 013 用"借这个（/此）机会 do sth."完成下面的对话。

Complete the following dialogues by using the pattern of "借这个（/此）机会 do sth.".

（1）甲：明天跟客户的洽谈您有什么打算？

乙：我想 _____

（2）甲：听说参加这个展销会的费用很高。公司决定要参展吗？

乙：费用的确比较高，不过 _____

（3）甲：王总，您最近这么忙，明天的饯行晚宴您一定要亲自参加吗？

王总：一定要参加！ _____

（4）白　琳：老板，这次访问中国为什么我们要增加三天的时间？

史强生：因为总公司希望我们 _____

4. 🎧 014 用"总之"说出你对以下问题的看法和结论（jiélùn / conclusion）。

Give your opinions and conclusions for the questions below. Please use the pattern of "总之" in your sentences.

（1）到了一个人地生疏的地方应该注意什么？

_____

（2）跟中国人做生意、打交道的时候应该注意什么？

_____

（3）找产品销售代理的时候应该注意什么？

_____

（4）只有怎样才能获得商务谈判的成功？

_____

IV. 阅读、讨论和其他活动　Reading, Discussion and Other Activities

1. 🎧 **根据课文对话回答问题。**

015

Answer the following questions according to the dialogues in this lesson.

（1）今天的晚宴是李信文以谁的名义举行的？

_____

（2）今天的晚宴有什么目的？

_____

（3）史先生为什么感谢李先生？

_____

（4）李先生提议"也许下一次我们可以把这个问题也列入我们的谈判"。他指的
是什么问题？真的吗？

_____

（5）谁想来中国度假？白小姐？史先生？还是史先生的太太？

_____

（6）谁给谁送了礼物？

_____

（7）白琳收到了李先生送的礼物。为什么她要问"我现在就能打开看看吗"？

_____

（8）谁会送史先生和白小姐去机场？

_____

2. 🎧 016 **根据本课的阅读短文回答下面的问题。**

Please answer the following questions based on Reading Passage in this lesson.

（1）什么是"走后门"？"走后门"是做生意的好办法吗？为什么？

What does "走后门" mean? Is it a good way to be successful in business? Why?

_____

_____

（2）怎样才能成功地跟一个中国企业建立起良好、可靠的关系？

What is the best way to establish a successful business relationship with a Chinese company?

_____

_____

（3）对中国人来说，什么是"面子"？你能举一个例子吗？在中国做生意遇到"面子"的问题的时候，你应该怎么办？

What does "面子" mean to the Chinese? Do you have any example of it? How can one prepare to deal with this subtle concept of the Chinese when doing business in China?

_____

_____

3. **思考与讨论。Points for Discussion.**

中方为史先生和白小姐举行宴会践行。请再读一遍本课的对话，说一说双方是怎样利用这个机会，趁热打铁，巩固双方的关系的。在这种情况下，你会怎么做？

The Chinese side has arranged a farewell dinner for Mr. Jonson Smith and Miss Lynn Petty. Please read the dialogues in this lesson again, and describe how both sides use this opportunity to further strengthen their relationship. What would you do under these circumstances?

_____

_____

4. 角色扮演。Role-playing.

你们公司跟中国商务代表团刚刚签署了一份很重要的合同。中国代表团明天就要回国了，所以公司总裁特别举行了一个正式的晚宴，庆祝这次的成功合作并给中国代表团饯行。请根据以上情境写一个对话并在课堂上表演。

Your company and a Chinese business delegation have just signed a major contract. The Chinese delegation is going to leave tomorrow. The CEO of your company will host a formal banquet to celebrate the signing of the contract and also to bid farewell to the Chinese delegation. Write a short dialogue for such a situation and act it out in class.

5. 🎧 017 快速复习。Quick review.

Ⓐ 阅读下面的短文，复习学过的词汇和句型。

Read the following text and review vocabularies and sentence patterns that you have learned.

史强生和白琳这次到中国的商务旅行很快就要结束了。今天上午双方正式签署了新的订货合同、东方公司代理销售美方产品的代理合同，以及两家公司的长期合作意向书。双方对这次访问和洽谈所取得的成果都非常满意，也都非常期待今后有更多这样的合作。

晚上，李经理以东方公司的名义为史先生和白小姐举行了饯行晚宴。在宴会上，李经理再一次对史先生、白小姐来中国访问表示感谢；史先生也对东方公司给予他们的热情接待表示了衷心感谢。双方互相赠送了小礼物和纪念品。美方代表还借此机会，向李经理询问了中国政府最新修改的《外资企业法》。

通过这次来中国访问，史强生和白琳再一次感觉到一件事。那就是在和中国人做生意的时候，建立并保持一种平等互利、互相尊重的友好关系是非常重要的。

Ⓑ 问答 Q & A：

（1）双方对什么成果非常满意？

_____

（2）在饯行晚宴上，双方有哪些交流和互动（hùdòng / interaction）？

（3）除了签订了合同以外，史先生和白小姐还有别的收获吗？

（四）附录　Appendix

1. 出境登记卡 Departure Card

外国人出境卡
DEPARTURE CARD

请交边防检查官员查验
For Immigration clearence

姓
Family name

名
Given names

护照号码
Passport No.

出生日期　　　　年 Year　　月 Month　　日 Day
Date of birth

男 □ Male　　女 □ Female

航班号 / 船名 / 车次　　　　　　　　　　　国籍
Flight No./ Ship's name/Train No.　　　　　　Nationality

以上申明真实准确。
I hereby declare that the statement given above is true and accurate.

签名 Signature

妥善保留此卡，如遗失将会对出境造成不便。
Retain this card in your possession, failure to do so may delay your departure from China.
请注意背面重要提示。See the back →

2. 感谢信 A Letter of Thanks

尊敬的张经理：

　　您好！

　　我已于本月 10 日回国。这次在贵国洽谈业务期间，承蒙您的热情帮助，使我顺利地完成了任务。为此，谨向您表示最真诚的感谢。

　　我在贵国期间，您除了在业务上给予我很大的支持与帮助以外，在生活上还给予我很多的关心和照顾。特别是您在百忙中陪同我参观了工厂、游览了北京的名胜古迹。临行前，尊夫人又为我准备了丰盛的晚餐。为此，我再次向您及尊夫人表示衷心的感谢。

　　希望以后加强联系。欢迎您有机会到我们国家来。盼望有一天能在这儿接待您。

　　此致

敬礼！

布莱恩

1994 年 10 月 21 日

（摘引自赵洪琴，吕文珍编《外贸写作》，北京语言学院出版社 1994 年。有删改）

总附录
General Appendix

课文英译（第9–16课）
English Translation of the Text (Lesson 9–16)

Lesson 9

Delivery and Payment

The Chinese and American [representatives] have already tentatively worked out the new order over the last couple days of negotiations. Now they're most concerned about the delivery schedule and method of payment, and this morning they are going to hold further talks to address these issues.

Dialogue

1. Delivery Schedule

Johnson Smith:	I suppose today we should discuss the delivery schedule for this order.
Li Xinwen:	Okay. Do you have any specific requirements concerning the time of delivery?
Johnson Smith:	You understand the strong seasonal nature of the clothing [business]. The sweaters and jeans in this order will all go on the market this fall. Mr. Li, can you make the delivery sometime during the first ten days of August?
Li Xinwen:	The first ten days of August? Mr. Smith, you aren't joking, are you? Last year we didn't deliver until September. Our current production schedule is already full.
Johnson Smith:	(earnestly) I'm not joking. The peak sales period for sweaters is in September and October. Last year our merchandise went on the market two weeks later than that of other [companies], and it put us at a disadvantage. This year I definitely don't want to let the opportunity slip by again.
Li Xinwen:	But it would indeed be difficult for us to adjust our production schedule and increase output immediately.
Lynn Petty:	Mr. Li, I realize this delivery schedule is rather tight, but we also have our difficulties. Mr. Li, we're old friends... please think of a way to help us out.

Li Xinwen:	Miss Petty, I do want to help you and to help myself as well. But to make the delivery over a month ahead of time would truly not be easy.
Lynn Petty:	I have an idea. Could we divide the garments into two separate shipments... half of the order to be delivered during the first ten days of August and the other half during the first ten days of September? Do you think this would work, Johnson?
Johnson Smith:	Hmm. That's a solution. What do you say, Mr. Li?
Li Xinwen:	Let me think it over... I need to call President Wang. Why don't we take a break first?
Johnson Smith、Lynn Petty:	Okay!

2. Method of Payment

Li Xinwen:	I'm sorry for keeping you waiting so long. I just talked with President Wang. We can accept the two shipments arrangement...
Johnson Smith:	That's great! Thank you!
Li Xinwen:	However, I must explain our requirements concerning the method of payment.
Johnson Smith:	Of course. I'm also concerned about this matter. May I ask what type of method you have in mind?
Li Xinwen:	We generally take payment by letter of credit, but your requesting an early delivery this time will have a definite impact on our flow of funds. Therefore, we are asking that your company make 30% of the payment in advance and use a letter of credit at sight for the remainder of the payment.
Johnson Smith:	We can have Citibank wire you the 30% advance payment. Can we pay the rest with a document against acceptance or another [type of] installment plan?
Li Xinwen:	I'm sorry, but we don't accept these payment methods at present. So as not to influence the time of delivery, please be sure to [have the bank] issue a letter of credit thirty days before loading and transport.
Lynn Petty:	Mr. Li, you're tough! When it comes to money, you show no mercy!
Li Xinwen:	(laughing) Haven't you heard the Chinese saying, "Even blood brothers keep careful accounts"?
Lynn Petty:	(laughing) No, this is more like, "no dough, no go"!

Chinese Banks and Renminbi

China's central bank is the People's Bank of China. The national commercial banks can be divided into two big categories. The so-called "Big 4 Banks" are state-owned banks. They are the Industrial and Commercial Bank of China, the China Construction Bank, Agricultural Bank of China and the Bank of China. Other mega banks including Bank of Communications, China Merchants Bank and SPD Bank are shareholding banks. Foreigners who come to China for business will often deal with one of those banks.

China's legal currency is the renminbi (RMB). It has three units: *yuan*, *jiao* and *fen*. One *yuan* equals ten *jiao*; and one *jiao* equals ten *fen*. There are a total of thirteen denominations of RMB: 100 *yuan*, 50 *yuan*, 20 *yuan*, 10 *yuan*, 5 *yuan*, 2 *yuan*, 1 *yuan*, 5 *jiao*, 2 *jiao*, 1 *jiao*, 5 *fen*, 2 *fen* and 1 *fen*. However, certain denominations of RMB are barely in circulation now. At present, the circulation and use of RMB is limited to within China only. In foreign trade, China and its trade partners normally settle accounts using the more internationally prevalent hard currencies, such as the U.S. dollar, Japanese yen, euro and pound sterling, using internationally prevalent methods such as remittance, collection, and letter of credit to make the payment. In 2001, China joined the World Trade Organization. Along with the rapid expansion of the Chinese economy and the financial reforms in progress, China is trying to use RMB to settle accounts in international trade. Many Chinese commercial banks have now already entered the finance market overseas. In 2015, the International Monetary Fund (IMF) approved global reserve-currency status for China's yuan. China is speeding up the pace of RMB internationalization.

Lesson 10

Sales Agents

The Chinese and American [representatives] just reached an agreement on the delivery schedule and method of payment, and Johnson Smith and Lynn Petty are both very satisfied. Now the two parties are going to continue their negotiations; the issue at hand is that the Eastern Corporation acts as the American International Trading Company's sales agent in China.

Dialogue

1. Sole Agency

Wang Guo'an:	Mr. Smith, Miss Petty, Vice President Li told me that you reached an agreement on this fall's new order this morning. I'm very happy. May I ask if your company is satisfied?
Johnson Smith:	We're very satisfied, especially since we were able to smoothly resolve the issue of the delivery schedule. That's very important for us. President Wang, thank you for looking after us.
Wang Guo'an:	Not at all! Your company is a longtime client... We should do our best to satisfy your requests.
Lynn Petty:	(smiling) President Wang, our company purchased over four million U.S. dollars'(!) worth of your products this time. Are you planning to buy a little something from us?
Li Xinwen:	(laughing) Miss Petty, I think that the really tough one here is you. For your information, President Wang has come this afternoon precisely to talk over this matter of distributing your company's products in China.
Wang Guo'an:	It's like this. This was the Eastern Corporation's first year distributing your company's energy-saving air conditioners, environment-friendly washing machines and other household appliances, and sales were very good. We would like to further expand our cooperation in this area.
Johnson Smith:	Good. That's another reason we've made this trip to China. What particularly do you have in mind, Mr. Wang?
Wang Guo'an:	We hope to become your company's sole agent in China.
Johnson Smith:	As you know, we also have an agreement in place allowing a company in Guangdong to distribute our air conditioners. I'm afraid that giving you the right of sole agency might influence other business that we have with that company.

189

Li Xinwen:	Mr. Smith, our company has excellent commercial networks all over the country. If we had the right of sole agency, we would surely do even better!
Johnson Smith:	How's this... we can give you the right of sole agency for our washing machines. Besides that, we have a new type of energy-saving household dishwasher that we plan to try out on the Chinese market, and if you're willing, we'd like you to be the sole agent. Mr. Wang, Mr. Li, what do you think?
Wang Guo'an、Li Xinwen:	Okay! It's settled!

2. Credit Check and Commission

Johnson Smith:	Mr. Wang, seeing that your company is about to become our sole agent, we need to understand your credit situation a little better.
Wang Guo'an:	You can inquire about our credit at the Beijing branch of the Bank of China.
Johnson Smith:	I'm sure you also know that as sole agent, the Eastern Corporation must consent not to take on any similar products of other companies while our agreement is in effect.
Wang Guo'an:	Yes, we're very clear on this point.
Johnson Smith:	How much do you want to take as commission?
Wang Guo'an:	When distributing foreign products, we normally draw a 10% commission.
Johnson Smith:	10% is too much! I think that 8% is more reasonable.
Wang Guo'an:	If your company is willing to share half of the advertising expenses, we can reduce the commission to 8%.
Johnson Smith:	How much can you guarantee for our yearly export value?
Wang Guo'an:	Last year the gross sales for the washing machines [totaled] 2,500,000 [U.S. dollars]. As sole agent, we can import at least 5,000,000 U.S. dollars' worth of your washing machines every year. However, this is the first time the dishwashers will be tried out in China, and it's not yet clear how they will sell. We need to do a market survey before we can decide.
Johnson Smith:	How about this... we can sign a sole agency agreement for one year first and see how our products are received.
Lynn Petty:	I'm sure Chinese women will like using a dishwasher.
Li Xinwen:	(smiling) You're mistaken, Miss Petty! These days it's the men who do the dishes in China!

Foreign Goods in China

As China's trade with other countries has grown rapidly, more and more foreign products have come into China. From the basic necessities of life to high-tech products, Chinese interest in foreign goods is becoming stronger and stronger. Without a doubt, populous China is a huge market with immense potential, and foreign firms are now faced with an extraordinary business opportunity. However, for foreign companies unfamiliar with China, doing business there is by no means an easy matter. Foreign goods entering the Chinese market have different fates: some make a profit and some sell at a loss; still others sustain economic losses because of illegal imitations. In order to succeed in Chinese market competition, many foreign firms are commissioning Chinese companies with reliable credit as agents to sell their products. Generally speaking, there are three types of agency: general agency, sole agency and commission agency. General agents are fully authorized to represent foreign firms in all kinds of business dealings in the region as well as to appoint sub-agents. Sole agents enjoy the exclusive right to sell a specific type of product in their area. Commission agents have the permission from manufacturers to sell a specific type of product and to draw a commission, but they don't have exclusive selling rights. Therefore a manufacturer can assign several commission agents to sell the same products at the same time. Sales agency not only can provide convenient commercial networks and lower the cost of product sales for foreign firms, it can also help in opening the market and establishing a good product reputation. It is a type of business operations beneficial to both parties.

Lesson 11

Advertising and Sales Promotion

During the negotiation yesterday, the Chinese and American [representatives] reached an agreement and decided to share the expenses of advertisements in China. Because Mr. Smith and Miss Petty will leave Beijing for Shanghai this noon by high-speed train, today's negotiation starts quite early. Representatives from the two sides are having discussions on the issues about advertisement planning and sales strategies.

Dialogue

1. Advertisement Planning

(In a small meeting room at the Great Wall Hotel)

Lynn Petty:	Mr. Li, you came so early! Have you had your breakfast?
Li Xinwen:	Thank you, I had breakfast already. Since you will go to Shanghai by the high-speed train this noon, I wanted to come a little bit early. [So] we could have a little more time to exchange opinions on how to advertise [our] products and promote sales, then make a preliminary plan. Mr. Smith, do you have anything on your mind?
Johnson Smith:	This time the advertisement is for building up publicity for our household appliances officially entering China's market. I think that it should give prominence to brand image first.
Li Xinwen:	I agree completely. Energy savings and environmental friendliness are the advantages and selling points of this brand's products. Our advertisement must deliver this information effectively.
Lynn Petty:	Mr. Li, you are more familiar with China's market situation than us, and advertisement planning is your specialty as well. What specific suggestions do you have?
Li Xinwen:	I am thinking that we could invite a famous movie star serving as spokesperson of the brand image.
Johnson Smith:	Uh, it ought to be a good approach to take advantage of the celebrity effect, but [I guess] the cost may be quite a lot.
Li Xinwen:	Let's do this: I will first consult with an experienced advertising agency regarding

the cost, and then make a decision after a further discussion. Unless the cost is within a reasonable range, we will use other approaches.

2. Sales Strategy

Johnson Smith: I would like to know that, besides the advertisement we just discussed, are there more specific plans that your company has? Is there anything your company needs us to cooperate with?

Li Xinwen: In order to open up the market quickly, we plan to have a large-scale sales promotion, and it will increase the effect of the advertisement as well as building up the brand recognition.

Johnson Smith: How big in scale do you think this sales promotion should be?

Li Xinwen: I propose that [we] divide this sales promotion into two phases: first, the sales promotion is conducted in big cities nationwide. If the sale goes well, then we will extend the sales promotion to medium and small cities; if the sales doesn't go well, we can adjust and change the sales strategies promptly.

Lynn Petty: Excuse me. May I ask something? Will your company's official website also put out a sales promotion at the same time correspondingly?

Li Xinwen: Yes. We will put out even more preferential activities online. For example, free home-delivery, extending the warranty period of the products, "buy one and get one free" and so on.

Lynn Petty: (smiling) It sounds very appealing! I do love "buy one and get one free"!

Reading Passage

Advertisements and the Chinese Mentality

Advertising is an essential part of doing business. Good advertisements can not only help firms break into the market; they also help in building up a product's name recognition. Generally speaking, young people like new trends and fashions, while those of middle and old age value good quality and reasonable prices. This seems to be a common pattern. However, [when] advertising in China, one definitely should understand the Chinese cultural tradition and value system. The Great Wall, the Yellow River, the Chinese dragon, Confucius, Tian'anmen and so on are symbols of China and Chinese culture. Chinese consumers usually cannot accept using these images to make funny jokes or do weird things. On the contrary, some foreign commercials deliver the information about their products in a form that Chinese consumers love, and often can see very good effects. For instance, [The Chinese names for] Coca-Cola and Pepsi are immediately pleasing to the ear of the Chinese, a people keen on seeking good fortune. A Toyota Auto advertisement in China is: "When the carriage reaches the mountain, there will surely be a road; and where there's a road, there will surely be a Toyota." It has skillfully borrowed from a Chinese old saying to advertise the [Toyota Auto] products, so that it is unforgettable to Chinese consumers. Additionally, it's worth noting that the Chinese have traditionally felt that the best advertisement is the product itself. "If your wine really tastes good, you don't need to worry that your wine shop is located at the end of a narrow lane."... If you have an excellent product, you don't need to worry that nobody will buy it. In the eyes of Chinese consumers, overly exaggerated or overly beautiful advertisements are often untrustworthy. "When old lady Wang sold melons, she was always overstating her goods." What person doesn't like to say that his products are the best?

Lesson 12

At a Trade Fair

Accompanied by Zhang Hong, the director of the Department of Public Relations for the Eastern Corporation, Johnson Smith and Lynn Petty arrived at Shanghai from Beijing by high-speed train. Today, they visited Shanghai Trade Fair.

Dialogue

1. At the Exhibition Zone of Household Appliances

Lynn Petty: Oh, this is huge! Director Zhang, I've heard that more than one thousand firms are taking part in this trade fair. Is that so?

Zhang Hong: Yes, this is one of the largest trade fairs in the country this year. There are not only firms from all over the country, but quite a few foreign companies as well. Mr. Smith, Miss Petty, these two booklets introduce the firms taking part in the fair.

Johnson Smith: (looking at the booklets) Hmm...textiles, clothing, household articles, cellular phones, bicycles, toys... There are so many firms and goods on display! However, what I am most interested in is household appliances, textiles and clothing. Aha, the exhibition zone of household appliances is right there! Let's go and take a look! (Walking to an exhibition booth)

M. Rep. A: Hello, sir! This is a multifunctional air conditioner that we newly introduced to the market this year. May I show it to you with an explanation?

Johnson Smith: There are so many air conditioners on the market now. What special [features] does your product have?

M. Rep. A: Please take a look, the external design of our product is simple, neat and fashionable, with 5 colors for consumers to choose from. The size of the product is small, (but) the cooling efficiency is very good. In addition to cooling, it can also dehumidify, heat and purify air. It is excellent in energy-savings too.

Johnson Smith: So many functions, what is your price?

M. Rep. A: We have total 3 models, retail prices are all below the price of the same type of products on the market. The wholesale price is even more favorable. Please give me a second, I will get you a packet of the product information for your reference.

Johnson Smith: Thank you! (to Lynn Petty) It seems that business competition is very intense in China!

2. At the Exhibition Zone of Textile and Clothing

M. Rep. B: Hello, Director Zhang! It's been a long time. Are you also here to take part in the fair?

Zhang Hong: No, I'm escorting these two guests. This is the CEO of Asia Region for the American International Trading Company, Mr. Smith. This is Miss Petty. They are very interested in your products.

M. Rep. B: Mr. Smith, Miss Petty, it's a pleasure to meet you! We welcome your patronage!

Lynn Petty: We just looked at the silk products of several companies, but you have the largest and most beautiful selection here.

M. Rep. B: Thank you for the compliment! The truth is that our silks won the gold medal several times for top quality product in the country. If you're interested in Chinese silks, you've come to the right place! Those cheap imitating reproductions on the market have no way to compare with ours! (taking out two booklets) This is our product catalogue. You see, (we) not only have traditional style products, but also have fashion designs with new trends. Please take a look!

Johnson Smith: (looking at the catalogue) You're right—these products really are appealing. The styles are trendy, the prices are very competitive. May I ask if you have all of these products in stock?

M. Rep. B: That's guaranteed. Mr. Smith, if you intend to order right now, I can give you a special discount of 5%.

Johnson Smith: I'm afraid that I can't [decide] today. I need to think it over some more. Perhaps we'll come and confer with you again tomorrow.

M. Rep: That's okay. When doing business, friendly relations should be more important even if we fail to clinch a deal. [In that case,] If we don't have a deal this time, then we will have it next time! Here is my business card. You're welcome to get in touch with me anytime.

Zhang Hong: (jokingly) Hey, you're not trying to steal my clients, are you?

M. Rep: (laughing) How could that be? Everyone is here to do business!

Chinese Trade Fairs

Commodity fairs, also called commodity exhibitions, are one of the major ways for Chinese firms to exhibit and sell products, exchange information, expand foreign trade, and attract foreign investments. In order to promote economic growth, China holds a certain number of international commodity fairs at regular intervals throughout the year. Some of these fairs are large, and some are small; and there is some variation in the type of fairs. The oldest and largest one is the China (Guangzhou) Import and Export Commodities Fair. It is held twice a year, once in the spring and once in the fall. It is called "*Guangjiaohui*" for short. Many Chinese firms consider it an honor to be able to exhibit their products at the Guangzhou Import and Export Commodities Fair, and it could be said that this fair is one window through which we can understand Chinese economic growth. The China International Fair for Investment and Trade, held in Xiamen in September every year, is China's most important investment exhibition at the international level. Taking investment as its theme, the Xiamen Fair provides a complete list of all kinds of investment projects of the current year and is a bridge to investing in China. Additionally, other important fairs also include China Beijing International Fair for Trade in Services (*Jingjiaohui* for short) and China Hi-Tech Fair (in Shenzhen, *Gaojiaohui* for short).

As for foreign firms that would like to do business in China, taking part in a Chinese commodity fair is undoubtedly an effective way to know China's market as well as to gain the latest business information. And if you want to import goods from China, a trade fair is an ideal place to get quality products at reasonable prices. As a large number of firms take part in the exhibitions, fierce competition is inevitable. Many firms [try to] attract buyers by lowering prices and offering all kinds of favorable terms. You don't want to miss such a great opportunity!

Job Interview

In order to expand (their) business in China, the American International Trading Company has decided to hire a business representative dispatched to China. After initial telephone interviews, three excellent candidates have been selected by the company's Human Resources Department. One of these selected candidates, Jack Martin, is in Shanghai at present. Johnson Smith and Lynn Petty have arranged a formal interview with him as soon as they arrived in Shanghai.

Dialogue

1. Introducing Personal Background

(In the suite's living room of the hotel. Lynn Petty opens the door when the doorbell rings)

Jack Martin:	Hello, I am Jack Martin.
Lynn Petty:	Hello, Jack. Please come in!
Jack Martin:	Thank you!
Lynn Petty:	Allow me make an introduction. This is the CEO of the Asia Region of our company, Mr. Johnson Smith. Johnson, this is Jack Martin.
Jack Martin:	I am much honored to meet you, sir.
Johnson Smith:	(shaking hands) Hello. Please have a seat. Thank you for coming over from Pudong for the interview. Was there much traffic on your way here?
Jack Martin:	I took the metro. It's very convenient. I feel very lucky to have such opportunity for the interview.
Johnson Smith:	Well, let's get started. First, please tell us your background and experiences.
Jack Martin:	Should I speak in Chinese?
Johnson Smith:	Yes. This is a job position in China. It requires that the applicant has bilingual ability, especially the communication capability in Chinese with Chinese clients.
Jack Martin:	Ok. My name is Jack Martin, my Chinese name is Ma Jie. I am American. I graduated from the University of Washington in Seattle two years ago. My major was Marketing. Currently I work at the Modern Commerce & Trading Company in Shanghai.
Johnson Smith:	What kind of company is it? What does your job do specifically?
Jack Martin:	That is a cross-border e-commerce company. It is located in the Shanghai Free

	Trade Zone. I work in the logistics department and my [job] responsibility is to contact and communicate with overseas suppliers.
Lynn Petty:	Your Chinese is fluent. May I ask how many years you have been learning Chinese?
Jack Martin:	Probably 6-7 years. I began to learn Chinese when I was in high school. I have kept learning Chinese through my college period. It's because I believe that learning Chinese will be definitely helpful in my future career.
Johnson Smith:	(smile) It seems that you have made a very good decision in your language learning. Well then, will you tell us more details about what other experiences you have?

2. Experiences and Skills

Jack Martin:	From my sophomore year to my graduation, I had been working at Amazon during school breaks. At the beginning, I worked in the customer service department and later in the marketing department. I participated in my school's study abroad program when I was a junior, and studied for one semester in Peking University. During that period, I also had an intern job at an e-commerce company in Beijing.
Johnson Smith:	As a foreign intern, what did you do specifically?
Jack Martin:	I was assigned to the market department and took part in a project to promote new products. We had a team for the project. The job details included market surveys, making sales promotion plans, contacting customers, and so on. I gained a lot of useful experiences from this intern job. When I graduated [from college], I decided to come back to China to work for a while. Luckily, I got this job. Up until this month, I have worked in Shanghai for almost 2 years.
Johnson Smith:	Well then, why do you [want] apply for this position?
Jack Martin:	I carefully looked at the job requirements and description of this position online. My understanding is that the duty of this job involves several fields, including marketing, logistics and customer service. As for me, this is not only a true challenge but also a good opportunity to enhance [my] professional knowledge and capability. I feel that this job will allow me to bring out my specialty in a better way. Moreover, it will benefit my personal career in the future.
Johnson Smith:	In doing this job, what would you consider to be your strengths?
Jack Martin:	I think that I'm more familiar with the operating mode of e-commerce, and have accumulated some experience in the fields of logistics and customer service.

199

	Since I have been working in China for 2 years, I also have certain knowledge on Chinese market and its consumers.
Johnson Smith:	Very well. The last question: are you willing to work in China for the long term?
Jack Martin:	Hmm, this question is not easy to answer. Let's put in this way: I love to work in China very much, I hope that I can work and live here at least 3 to 5 years.
Johnson Smith:	Good! That's all for today's interview. We will notify you of the final decision within 2 weeks. Thank you!
Jack Martin:	Thank you! See you!

Reading Passage

Job Seeking and Hiring in China

Today many foreign companies are recruiting people in China while they set up business there. On the other hand, more and more Chinese companies have started to recruit professionals from all over the world. Many companies have considered bilingual ability as one of the preferential conditions of hiring.

No matter whether your company plans to recruit new employees in China, or you want to find a job in China, the most simple and effective way is to search on the internet. You can start with these top-three recruitment websites. They are *Qiánchéng-wúyōu* (www.51job.com), *Zhìlián-zhāopìn* (www.zhaopin.com) and *Zhōnghuá-yīngcái-wǎng* (www.chinahr.com). These three websites use both Chinese and English and provide professional services in job seeking and hiring nationwide. Once you have registered an account and logged in, you are able to use services such as job-searching, resume-managing (profile management), job-hunting guidance and headhunters (namely employment recruiters) etc. provided by the website.

Another way to finding jobs in China is to attend job fairs. A job fair is also called a human resources market (HR market). In China, the job fair has become a popular place for people to find a job and for companies to recruit new employees. Driven by the growing economy and demand for professionals, each year there are numerous job fairs of different types and scales taking place in China. Some job fairs are even held overseas. A notable number of foreign companies have also joined the Chinese HR market in recent years. You may want to give it a try if you need an employment solution in China.

Industrial Park

Shenzhen is the last stop for Johnson Smith and Lynn Petty on this trip to China. After arriving in Shenzhen from Shanghai, Zhang Hong accompanied them as they toured a local industrial park as well as visiting a start-up company at the industrial park. They were deeply impressed by the industrial park's investment environment.

1. Discussing the Local Development

Lynn Petty: I can't believe how fast [Shenzhen] has grown!

Zhang Hong: I know. Shenzhen has been utilizing foreign capital to develop its economy over the last several decades, and it has already gone from being a small town to a large and modern city. More and more foreign firms are coming here to do business every year now, and many large and well-known companies from all over the world have investments in Shenzhen. The industrial park that we are visiting today is the epitome of the local development.

Johnson Smith: I really want to know what Shenzhen has that draws in foreign investment.

Zhang Hong: I think it's primarily the desirable investment environment, particularly the excellent infrastructure and the positive support for foreign investment by the local government.

Johnson Smith: How long has this industrial park been established?

Zhang Hong: This is a new industrial park which was established a year ago.

Johnson Smith: If so, has the infrastructure been completed yet?

Zhang Hong: Yes. (Infrastructure) including transportation, communication facilities and public facilities has been put into use already. Up to now, there are about 20 more companies that have signed the contracts and set up here.

Johnson Smith: That is really a fast development! May I ask how many foreign-capital enterprises are among those companies setting up here?

Zhang Hong: According to what I know, among the companies setting up here, half of them are foreign-capital enterprises.

Lynn Petty: Ha, my cellphone has connected to Wi-Fi now! The signal is very strong!

| Zhang Hong: | Yes. The entire park is equipped with free Wi-Fi network. |

2. Visiting a Start-up Company

Manager Liu:	Director Zhang, you are here! Welcome, welcome to inspect our work!
Zhang Hong:	Hello, Manager Liu! I am sorry for keeping you waiting. Let me make an introduction: this is Manager Liu of Eastern New Energy, this is Mr. Johnson Smith, the CEO of Asia Region for the American International Trading Company. This is his assistant, Miss Lynn Petty.
Liu, Smith, Petty:	Hello, hello! (Shake hands)
Johnson Smith:	Mr. Liu, I am very interested in the household new energy project that your company has been working on. I have been also told that you are intentionally looking for partners for working together. Could you provide us with some details along with an introduction?
Manager Liu:	Of course. We are a newly established start-up technology company. More than half of our research and development personnel are overseas returnees. Currently, the company focuses on developing new energy technologies for household as well as related products. We have applied for several patents.
Johnson Smith:	Very interesting! I believe that this area has a great potential indeed. May I ask what relevant products your company produce?
Manager Liu:	Here they are. (turns on the computer) Please take a look, our products will include household air-conditioners, washing machines, dishwashers, stoves and so on, powered by new energy. All of these products will use the technology developed by ourselves.
Johnson Smith:	If I understood correctly, your company hasn't put any products into market officially or made any profits yet at this point. Would you mind me asking how your company maintains normal operation?
Manger Liu:	We received the first venture capital investment last year. At the same time, with positive support from the local government, the company had received a concessional loan from the bank smoothly. In order to ensure that our products can be placed on the market next year, the company is planning a new financing. Would you be interested in it?
Johnson Smith:	I am personally optimistic about your project. I will submit an evaluation report to my company based on this visit. If there is any progress [regarding this], I will contact you promptly.

Special Zones and New Areas in China

In the course of reforming and opening-up to the outside world, China has established some (different) special zones, which are Special Economic Zones (SEZs), Economic-Technological Development Zones (ETDZs), High-Tech Industrial Development Zones (HIDZs), Free Trade Zone (FTZs) and State-level New Areas.

During the 1980s when the Reforming and Opening policy had just begun, China established several special economic zones one after another. They are the Shenzhen SEZ, Zhuhai SEZ, Shantou SEZ, Xiamen SEZ and Hainan (province) SEZ. These SEZs are located in the southern coastal area of China. In 2010, China again established the Kashgar SEZ and Khorgos SEZ in Uygur Autonomous Region in order to develop the economy of Western China. The Chinese government implements special economic policies as well as flexible management measures in SEZs for appealing to foreign capital and multinational corporations.

ETDZ and HIDZ are abbreviations for Economic-Technological Development Zone and High-Tech Industrial Development Zone, separately. The peak period of establishment of ETDZ and HIDZ was around the 1990s. ETDZ is actually a type of modern industrial park, while the purpose of HIDZ is to create knowledge-intensive and technology-intensive industrial parks. Up to the present, there are more than 200 National Economic-Technological Development Zones and over 100 National High-Tech Industrial Development Zones nationwide. Companies located in these two special zones enjoy a series of preferential policies and many other convenient services provided by local governments.

Starting from 2005, China has attempted to create some state-level New Areas on even larger scales. A New Area has functional departments like a government, and implements preferential policies which are specially designated. It is state-level area with comprehensive functions. Pudong New Area is the first one established. Xiongan New Area, established in 2017, is the most recent one (so far). Additionally, the first free trade zone (FTZ) within China's borders, China (Shanghai) Pilot Free Trade Zone, was established in August of 2013 and located in Pudong New Area. The China (Shanghai) Pilot Free Trade Zone has been given much greater freedom in trade and enjoys more conveniences in banking and investment. With the double-impetus of economic globalization and the initiative of "the Belt and Road," China is in the process of setting up more FTZs.

Lesson 15

Signing the Contract

Today is Johnson Smith and Lynn Petty's last day in China, and the Chinese and American [companies] are going to formally sign the contracts. Vice President Li Xinwen of the Eastern Corporation flew from Beijing to Shenzhen early this morning, and he will represent the Eastern Corporation in today's signing ceremony.

Dialogue

1. Examining the Contracts

Li Xinwen: Mr. Smith, Miss Petty, these are the three contracts we will sign today. Each one has both Chinese and English for comparison. The first one is the contract for this fall's order, the second one is the agency agreement, and the third one is a letter of intent for a long-term corporation agreement. Please examine every article one more time before signing, especially [paying attention to] items regarding quantity, amount of money, packing, delivery schedule, [inspection and] acceptance standard and payment method, etc. If there are any oversights or objectionable points, please point them out immediately so that we can make corrections.

Johnson Smith: Okay! Lynn, let's each read through one contract, and when we're finished we can switch.

(Johnson Smith and Lynn Petty examine the contracts)

Lynn Petty: Mr. Li, there is a sentence I would like confirm with you. Regarding the delivery schedule, the contract says that two deliveries will be made—one is before August 10 and one is before September 10. Does this mean that your company might be able to make a delivery before the 10th [of August and September]?

Li Xinwen: (smile) According to the agreement from our last discussion, both parties agreed that delivery would be made during the first ten days of August and the first ten days of September. That "the deliveries will be made before August 10 and September 10" means the deliveries definitely will be no later than the 10th [of the given month]. Of course, if it's possible, we will do our best to make an earlier delivery.

Lynn Petty:	(smile) Ok, I got it. Johnson, do you have other questions?
Johnson Smith:	I would like to add a clause like this in the contract: if a delay in delivery on the part of the seller leads to economic losses for the buyer, the buyer has the right to lodge an appeal and a claim for damages. To be honest with you, the delivery dates for this order are extremely important to us, and I don't want there to be any mistakes. I hope you can understand, Mr. Li.
Li Xinwen:	Our company [strongly believes in] taking our contracts seriously and honoring our word. We will definitely deliver on schedule. However, I completely understand your request, and we can write this clause in right away.
Johnson Smith:	Thank you! In addition, I suggest that we add something like this in the letter of intent: the two parties should henceforth hold talks once every three months in order to resolve any problems that might come up in the execution of the contract as necessary.
Li Xinwen:	This clause is a necessity. I'll put it in at once. Thank you!

2. Formal Signing

Li Xinwen:	Mr. Smith, here are the contract originals. We revised each problem area that you brought up this morning according to your suggestions. Please read through them once more. I hope that both parties will be satisfied this time.
Johnson Smith:	(reading the contracts) Hmm, I think that all of the clauses are detailed and clear, and I don't see anything else that needs to be changed or added. What do you think, Lynn?
Lynn Petty:	I think everything [looks] great, too. Mr. Li, you've gone to a lot of trouble!
Li Xinwen:	Not at all—it's my job. May I ask how many copies you need?
Johnson Smith:	Please give me two copies of each contract. In addition, if it's not too much trouble, please send me an e-copy so that I can save it.
Li Xinwen:	Sure! I will send them to your email immediately. If there aren't any other problems, I guess we can sign now. Mr. Smith, please sign here!
Johnson Smith:	Okay. (signing) Mr. Li, this has been a very successful cooperation, and I'm delighted. I hope we'll have more opportunities to work with you and your company in the future.
Li Xinwen:	Certainly! Certainly! Now that we have a long-term agreement, we will surely have more and more opportunities to work together! (pouring tea) Come, let's toast with tea instead of wine in celebration of our satisfactory and successful

cooperation and to more [opportunities to] work together in the future!

Lynn Petty: (jokingly) Mr. Li, it looks like I'll be coming to bother you in Beijing a lot from now on. It won't be a headache for you, will it?

Laws and Regulations of the PRC Regarding Foreign Economic Interests in China

In order to better utilize foreign capital and advanced technology to help develop the Chinese economy, the Chinese government began in 1979 to successively draft a series of laws and regulations regarding foreign economic interests. Among these laws and regulations, the most important one is The Law of the People's Republic of China on Foreign Capital Enterprises. The Law of Foreign Capital Enterprises involves various aspects of a foreign company, which includes procedures for establishment, corporate structure, taxation and accounting, foreign exchange regulation, and so on. Understanding the content of these laws and regulations is of great benefit to every foreigner who plans to invest or do business in China.

These laws and regulations regarding foreign economic interests explicitly promise to protect the legal rights and interests of foreign investors, and guarantee a fair and equal treatment for foreign manufacturers, companies and individuals who invest in China. China's laws and regulations regarding foreign economic interests emphasize the fundamental principles of equality and mutual benefit, and at the same time stipulate four different channels of conflict resolution, namely, consultation, mediation, arbitration and litigation. In order to [ensure] that disputes are resolved in a fair and reasonable manner, China is also amenable to arbitration in a third country.

The full and effective implementation of China's laws and regulations regarding foreign economic interests has clearly improved China's investment environment, [thus] serving to encourage foreign investors. Present-day China is now attracting the interest of more and more foreign investors.

Lesson 16

Farewell Dinner

Johnson Smith and Lynn Petty are about to return to America tomorrow. Li Xinwen is hosting an evening banquet on behalf of the Eastern Import & Export Corporation to celebrate the successful cooperation between the Chinese and American companies. It's also a farewell dinner for Mr. Smith and Miss Petty.

Dialogue

1. At the Farewell Banquet

Li Xinwen: Mr. Smith, Miss Petty, there are two reasons for tonight's banquet: one, to celebrate the successful cooperation between our two companies; and two, to bid farewell to the two of you. Please allow me to sincerely thank you on behalf of the Eastern Import & Export Corporation. Let me propose a toast to you! Thank you for all you did to ensure a satisfactory and successful conclusion to our negotiations. (everyone toasts)

Johnson Smith: Mr. Li, this has been a very fruitful trip, and we are very happy. I would also like to take this opportunity to thank you and the Eastern Import & Export Corporation on behalf of my company. We're thankful for the warm reception the Eastern Corporation has given us, and especially for all the arrangements you made for us during this trip.

Li Xinwen: Not at all. I was very happy to be able to work with you and Miss Petty. This trip has not only strengthened our business ties; it has also deepened our mutual understanding. I believe that with such a good foundation, we will definitely have even more business intercourse from this time forward.

Johnson Smith: I agree completely. During this trip I have seen China's development with my own eyes. China has already become a significant economic power. No wonder firms from so many countries want to do business here now. I dare say that many companies in America envy us for having such reliable "connections" as you and the Eastern Corporation. (smiling) Mr. Li, we hope you'll continue to look after us in the future!

2. Parting Words and the Presentation of Gifts

Lynn Petty:	Time sure flies! It seems like I just arrived in China yesterday, but I'm already returning to the U.S. tomorrow morning!
Li Xinwen:	Miss Petty, if you'd really like to stay in China a little longer, you would be more than welcome.
Lynn Petty:	I would like to, but it depends on whether or not my boss is willing to give me a vacation.
Li Xinwen:	I have a solution... perhaps we can include this issue in our next negotiations. What do you think, Mr. Smith?
Johnson Smith:	(laughing) I'm sorry. There's absolutely no room for negotiation on this matter! Lynn Petty is my most capable assistant, and I couldn't get along without her!
Li Xinwen:	(smiling) We'd be even more delighted if Mr. Smith planned a vacation in China, too!
Johnson Smith:	I am actually thinking of bringing my wife along next time to do some traveling, it's just that I can't find time to do it. She is always saying that she'd like to come see the Great Wall and the terra cotta soldiers.
Li Xinwen:	Good. Please let me know when you decide, and I'll take care of the arrangements for you. Mr. Smith, Miss Petty, these are presents for you from our company. You can think of them as mementos from this trip!
Johnson Smith:	Thank you!
Lynn Petty:	Can I open it right now?
Li Xinwen:	Of course. Go ahead!
Lynn Petty:	Oh, a cloisonné vase. It's just beautiful! Thank you, Mr. Li.
Li Xinwen:	Not at all. They're just a little something to keep as souvenirs.
Johnson Smith:	Mr. Li, I also have a present for you.
Li Xinwen:	You really shouldn't have! You're too kind!
Johnson Smith:	Please accept it. I also have two gifts that I'd like to ask you to give to President Wang and Ms. Zhang Hong.
Li Xinwen:	Okay. I'll take them, then. Thank you! Mr. Smith, Miss Petty, I have an important meeting tomorrow, so I won't be able to see you off. I'm very sorry. However, Director Zhang Hong will take you to the airport.
Johnson Smith:	We're already very grateful that you accompanied us for so many days and [even] made this special trip here from Beijing!
Li Xinwen:	It was nothing. You needn't be so polite. I wish you a pleasant trip! I hope we will meet again soon!
Johnson Smith, Lynn Petty:	Thanks! Good-bye!

Establishing a Long-term Cooperative Relationship

When the word, "connections" is mentioned, many foreigners doing business in China immediately think of "going through the back door." It cannot be denied that "going through the back door" can often solve problems, but these kinds of "connections" are by no means safe. Sometimes "going through the back door" is not only unhelpful; on the contrary, it [can] hold up your reputable business, and you might even [end up] being swindled. For foreigners planning to do business in China, making a solid effort to establish a working relationship based on equality and mutual benefit is more dependable than thinking of ways to "go through the back door."

Chinese value long-term cooperative relationships. If you are shrewd, you will make use of various occasions to let them know that your company also places great value on this kind of relationship. [When] doing business or interacting with Chinese people, there is no harm in speaking with frankness and sincerity [so that] the other party clearly understands your position. During intense negotiations, patience, understanding, respect and a friendly attitude are all essential. Don't let the Chinese think that you are a business person only concerned with present gains. In some cases, it doesn't hurt to make [reasonable] compromises in order to resolve a dispute. This way, the Chinese will not only feel like they have [kept] face; they will also be convinced that you are a reasonable friend with whom it is worthwhile to associate.

After the contract has been signed, the business transaction has been brought to a successful conclusion, and you have a great opportunity to solidify the relationship by striking while the iron is hot. Besides toasting, don't forget to express your company's hope to continue working together in the future [so that] your Chinese friends will be assured that your company is truly sincere about maintaining a long-term cooperative relationship. It's also a good idea to take advantage of this opportunity to give your Chinese friends a few meaningful little gifts. Chinese often say, "The gift is trifling, but the feeling is profound." Giving gifts both communicates your gratitude and shows that you value the friendship.

In short, gaining a better understanding of Chinese culture and the Chinese people will definitely help you as you do business in China.

I wish you success.

总词汇表（全二册）
Vocabulary Index (Volume I & II)

A

0001	按时	ànshí	on time	L.15a
0002	按照	ànzhào	according to; on the basis of	L.6a

B

0003	白琳	Bái Lín	*a name*	L.1a
0004	白云宾馆	Báiyún Bīnguǎn	Baiyun Hotel	L.2b
0005	百分之……	bǎifēnzhī……	… percent	L.6a
0006	百事可乐	Bǎishì Kělè	Pepsi	L.11b
0007	百万	bǎiwàn	Million	L.10a
0008	办事情	bàn shìqing	to attend to matters; to handle affairs	L.1b
0009	办手续	bàn shǒuxù	to go through formalities/procedures	L.1a
0010	帮忙	bāng máng	to help; to give a hand	L.2b
0011	磅	bàng	Pound	L.4a
0012	包括	bāokuò	to include	L.3b
0013	包装	bāozhuāng	packing; packaging; to pack; dress up	L.15a
0014	薄利多销	bólì-duōxiāo	small profits but high volume	L.8a
0015	保持	bǎochí	to keep; to maintain	L.14a
0016	保护	bǎohù	to protect; to safeguard	L.15b
0017	保留	bǎoliú	to retain; to continue to have	L.6a
0018	保险	bǎoxiǎn	safe; secure; insurance	L.16b
0019	保修期	bǎoxiūqī	warranty period	L.11a
0020	报价	bào jià	quoted price; offer; to quote (a price)	L.8a
0021	报盘	bào pán	offer; quoted price; to make an offer	L.8a
0022	抱歉	bàoqiàn	be apologetic; to feel sorry about	L.9a
0023	北京烤鸭	Běijīng Kǎoyā	Beijing roast duck	L.4a
0024	备份	bèifèn	backup (files, documents, etc.)	L.15a
0025	背景	bèijǐng	background	L.13a
0026	本厂	běn chǎng	one's own factory; this factory	L.7a
0027	本领	běnlǐng	ability; skills; talent	L.8b
0028	本身	běnshēn	itself; oneself	L.11b
0029	比如	bǐrú	for instance; for example	L.11a

0030	必要	bìyào	necessary; essential	L.15a
0031	变得	biànde	have become; to turn (into)	L.1b
0032	便捷	biànjié	convenient and fast	L.14b
0033	便利	biànlì	convenient	L.10b
0034	便于	biànyú	easy to; convenient for	L.3b
0035	标准	biāozhǔn	standard; typical	L.2a
0036	标准间	biāozhǔnjiān	standard room	L.2a
0037	宾馆	bīnguǎn	hotel; guesthouse	L.2b
0038	宾主	bīnzhǔ	guest and host	L.3b
0039	兵马俑	bīngmǎyǒng	terra cotta figures of warriors and horses	L.16a
0040	并	bìng	and; besides; moreover	L.7b
0041	并不	bìng bù	not at all, by no means	L.10b
0042	博览会	bólǎnhuì	exhibition; fair	L.12b
0043	补充	bǔchōng	to add; to supplement; to replenish	L.15a
0044	不得不	bùdébù	have no choice but to; to have to	L.8a
0045	不妨	bùfáng	there is no harm in; might as well	L.13b
0046	不敢当	bùgǎndāng	I don't deserve your compliment; you flatter me.	L.3a
0047	不管	bùguǎn	no matter (what/how)	L.13b
0048	不行	bùxíng	won't do/work; be no good	L.8a
0049	不好意思	bù hǎoyìsi	to feel embarrassed; sorry	L.2a
0050	不讲情面	bùjiǎng qíngmiàn	to have no consideration for sb.'s feelings	L.9a
0051	不可否认	bùkě fǒurèn	can't deny; undeniably	L.16b
0052	不可信	bù kě xìn	cannot be trusted; untrustworthy	L.11b
0053	不如	bù rú	not as good as; inferior to; it would be better to	L.16b
0054	不善	búshàn	not good; bad; not good at	L.7b
0055	不少	bùshǎo	not few; many	L.7b
0056	不晚于	bù wǎn yú	no later than	L.15a
0057	布置	bùzhì	to decorate; to arrange	L.5a
0058	步伐	bùfá	pace	L.9b
0059	部门	bùmén	department; branch	L.14b

C

0060	财会	cáikuài	financial affairs and accounting	L.15b
0061	采用	cǎiyòng	to select for use; to employ; to adopt	L.9a
0062	参考	cānkǎo	to consult; to refer to	L.12a

0063	参展	cān zhǎn	a short form for 参加展览 (i.e., take part in an exhibition)	L.12a
0064	参照	cānzhào	to refer to; to consult	L.6a
0065	策划	cèhuà	planning; to plan	L.11a
0066	策略	cèlüè	tactics; strategy	L.11a
0067	查询	cháxún	to inquire about	L.10a
0068	差不多	chàbuduō	about the same; similar	L.8a
0069	差错	chācuò	mistake; error	L.15a
0070	产量	chǎnliàng	output; yield	L.7a
0071	产品	chǎnpǐn	product	L.1a
0072	产业	chǎnyè	industry; estate; property	L.4a
0073	尝	cháng	to taste	L.5a
0074	长城	Chángchéng	the Great Wall	L.4a
0075	长期	chángqī	over a long period of time; long-term	L.7b
0076	尝试	chángshì	to attempt; to try	L.9b
0077	厂家	chǎngjiā	manufacturer	L.6a
0078	厂商	chǎngshāng	manufacturer; firm; commercial corporation	L.10b
0079	厂长	chǎngzhǎng	factory director/manager	L.4a
0080	场合	chǎnghé	occasion; situation	L.16b
0081	场所	chǎngsuǒ	place; location; arena	L.13b
0082	倡议	chàngyì	to propose; initiative	L.14b
0083	超过	chāoguò	to exceed; to surpass	L.1a
0084	车到山前必有路	chē dào shān qián bì yǒu lù	When the carriage reaches the mountain, there will surely be a road.	L.11b
0085	车间	chējiān	workshop	L.7a
0086	趁热打铁	chènrè-dǎtiě	to strike while the iron is hot	L.16b
0087	称	chēng	to call; to name	L.9b
0088	成本	chéngběn	cost	L.7a
0089	成功	chénggōng	succeed; success; successful	L.5a
0090	成果	chéngguǒ	achievement; positive result	L.12b
0091	成立	chénglì	to found; to establish	L.14a
0092	成品	chéngpǐn	finished products	L.7a
0093	成为	chéngwéi	to become; to turn into;	L.4b
0094	诚意	chéngyì	good faith; sincerity	L.16b
0095	承包	chéngbāo	to contract	L.7b
0096	承兑交单	chéngduì jiāodān	documents against acceptance bill (D/A)	L.9a

0097	承诺	chéngnuò	to promise (to do sth.)	L.15b
0098	程序	chéngxù	order; procedure; program	L.15b
0099	吃亏	chī kuī	to suffer loss; to come to grief; to be at a disadvantage	L.6b
0100	充分	chōngfèn	full; fully	L.6b
0101	出差	chū chāi	be away on official business or on a business trip	L.4b
0102	出口	chūkǒu	export; to export; exit	L.1a
0103	出口额	chūkǒu'é	value of exports; export quota	L.10a
0104	出售	chūshòu	to offer for sale; to sell	L.8a
0105	出席	chūxí	to attend; be present (at a banquet, etc.)	L.5a
0106	初步	chūbù	initial; preliminary	L.6a
0107	初次	chūcì	the first time	L.3b
0108	初期	chūqī	beginning period	L.14b
0109	除此之外	chú cǐ zhī wài	other than this; in addition to this	L.12b
0110	除非	chúfēi	unless	L11.a
0111	除湿	chúshī	to dehumidify	L.12a
0112	储备	chǔbèi	reserve; to reserve	L.9b
0113	储备货币	chǔbèi huòbì	reserve currency	L.9b
0114	传达	chuándá	to pass on; to convey; to deliver	L.11a
0115	传统	chuántǒng	traditional; tradition	L.6a
0116	窗口	chuāngkǒu	window	L.12b
0117	创业	chuàngyè	to start an undertaking	L.4a
0118	创业公司	chuàngyè gōngsī	start-up company	L.4a
0119	吹	chuī	to blow; to play (a wind instrument); to break up (with boyfriend/girlfriend); to fall through (of plans)	L.4a
0120	春季	chūnjì	spring	L.12b
0121	次序	cìxù	order; sequence	L.5b
0122	促销	cùxiāo	to promote sales; sales promotion	L.11a
0123	促销价	cùxiāojià	sale price	L.6a
0124	催	cuī	to urge; to hasten; to press	L.7a
0125	措施	cuòshī	measure; step	L.14b
0126	错过	cuòguò	to miss; to let slip by	L.9a

D

| 0127 | 达成 | dáchéng | to reach (an agreement, etc.) | L.10a |

0128	打	dá	dozen	L.8a
0129	打交道	dǎ jiāodào	have dealings with; come into contact with	L.9b
0130	打印机	dǎyìnjī	printer	L.2b
0131	打造	dǎzào	to create; to build	L.14b
0132	打折	dǎ zhé	to make a discount	L.12a
0133	大菜	dàcài	main dish	L.5a
0134	大功告成	dàgōng gàochéng	to have finally come to completion	L.16b
0135	大厅	dàtīng	lobby	L.2a
0136	大型	dàxíng	large-scale	L.11a
0137	大致	dàzhì	roughly; approximately; in general	L.7a
0138	待	dāi	to stay	L.4a
0139	代表	dàibiǎo	representative; to represent	L.1a
0140	代理	dàilǐ	agency; representation; to act as agent; agent	L.3a
0141	代言人	dàiyánrén	spokesperson	L.11a
0142	贷款	dài kuǎn	loan; to loan	L.14a
0143	待遇	dàiyù	treatment	L.15b
0144	袋	dài	bag	L.2a
0145	担任	dānrèn	to serve as; to take charge of	L.11a
0146	担心	dān xīn	to worry; to feel anxious	L.1b
0147	单	dān	list; form; voucher	L.1a
0148	单位	dānwèi	unit in measurement	L.9b
0149	单位	dānwèi	unit; organization; place of work	L.4b
0150	耽误	dānwù	to delay; to hold up; to hinder	L.16b
0151	当地	dāngdì	local	L.2b
0152	当年	dāngnián	the same year; that very year	L.12b
0153	倒	dào	to pour (tea, etc.)	L.3a
0154	倒是	dàoshì	actually; really	L.16a
0155	到达	dàodá	to arrive	L.1a
0156	盗版	dàobǎn	piracy; pirated edition	L.10b
0157	盗版产品	dàobǎn chǎnpǐn	illegal copy; pirated products	L.10b
0158	道	dào	a measure word for dishes; courses	L.5b
0159	得力	délì	capable; competent	L.16a
0160	的确	díquè	indeed; really; certainly	L.8b
0161	登记	dēng jì	registration; to register; to check in	L.1a
0162	登记卡	dēngjìkǎ	registration card	L.1a

0163	登录	dēnglù	to log in; to register	L.13b
0164	等等	děngděng	etcetera; and so on	L.2b
0165	等于	děngyú	be equal to; the same as	L.9b
0166	迪士尼	Díshìní	Disney	L.7a
0167	底价	dǐjià	bottom price	L.8a
0168	地点	dìdiǎn	place; site; location	L.2a
0169	地区	dìqū	region; area; district	L.3a
0170	地铁	dìtiě	subway; metro	L.13a
0171	第三国	dì-sān guó	a third (and disinterested) country	L.15b
0172	电汇	diànhuì	to wire money; telegraphic transfer (T/T)	L.9a
0173	电器	diànqì	electrical equipment/appliance	L.10a
0174	电商	diànshāng	e-business; e-commerce (a short form for 电子商务)	L.13a
0175	电梯	diàntī	elevator;	L.2a
0176	电子版	diànzǐbǎn	e-version; e-edition	L.15a
0177	调查	diàochá	to investigate	L.8b
0178	顶楼	dǐnglóu	top floor; attic	L.2a
0179	订单	dìngdān	order sheet; order	L.3a
0180	订购	dìnggòu	to order (goods)	L.7a
0181	订货	dìng huò	to order goods	L.12a
0182	订票	dìngpiào	to book tickets; ticket booking	L.2b
0183	定期	dìngqī	at regular intervals; periodically; regular; periodic	L.12b
0184	东方进出口（公司）	Dōngfāng Jìnchūkǒu (Gōngsī)	Eastern Import & Export Corporation	L.1a
0185	东方新能源公司	Dōngfāng Xīnnéngyuán Gōngsī	Eastern New Energy Company	L.14a
0186	逗留	dòuliú	to stay; to stop	L.4a
0187	独家代理	dújiā dàilǐ	sole/exclusive (sales) agent/agency	L.10a
0188	独家代理权	dújiā dàilǐquán	right of the sole agency	L.10a
0189	独资企业	dúzī qǐyè	single venture enterprise	L.7b
0190	堵车	dǔ chē	traffic jam	L.13a
0191	度假	dù jià	to spend one's vacation	L.16a
0192	对方	duìfāng	the opposite side; the other party	L.3b
0193	对手	duìshǒu	opponent; adversary	L.7b
0194	对外	duìwài	foreign; external	L.9b

0195	对照	duìzhào	contrast; comparison; to compare	L.15a
0196	兑换	duìhuàn	to exchange; to convert	L.2a
0197	顿	dùn	a measure word for meals	L.4b
0198	多功能	duōgōngnéng	multifunction	L.12a

E

0199	额	é	a specified quantity	L.10a

F

0200	发挥	fāhuī	to bring into play; to bring out (implicit or innate qualities)	L.13a
0201	发展	fāzhǎn	development; to develop	L.4a
0202	法定	fǎdìng	legal; stipulated by law	L.9b
0203	法规	fǎguī	legislation; regulation	L.15b
0204	法律	fǎlǜ	law	L.15b
0205	凡是	fánshì	every; any; all	L.15a
0206	繁忙	fánmáng	(very) busy; hectic	L.4b
0207	反而	fǎn'ér	on the contrary; instead	L.16b
0208	反正	fǎnzhèng	anyway; anyhow; in any case	L.4a
0209	范围	fànwéi	scope; range; area	L.11a
0210	方案	fāng'àn	scheme; plan; project	L.11a
0211	方式	fāngshì	manner; mode; way; method	L.9a
0212	房卡	fángkǎ	key card; room card	L.2a
0213	纺织	fǎngzhī	textiles	L.12a
0214	非……不可	fēi……bùkě	must...	L.8b
0215	费心	fèixīn	to give a lot of care; to take a lot of trouble	L.4a
0216	费用	fèiyòng	cost; expenses	L.10a
0217	分别	fēnbié	separately; individually	L.14b
0218	分成	fēnchéng	divide into; split up into	L.9a
0219	分代理	fēndàilǐ	sub-agent	L.10b
0220	分担	fēndān	to share responsibility for (a task/duty/etc.)	L.10a
0221	分配	fēnpèi	to assign; to allocate	L.13a
0222	分期付款	fēn qī fù kuǎn	to pay in installments; payment in installments	L.9a
0223	分为	fènwéi	to divide (into)	L.7b
0224	丰盛	fēngshèng	rich; sumptuous	L.4b
0225	丰田	Fēngtián	Toyota	L.11b
0226	风险	fēngxiǎn	risk; hazard	L.14a

0227	风险投资	fēngxiǎn tóuzī	venture capital; VC	L.14a
0228	否则	fǒuzé	otherwise	L.11a
0229	服务台	fúwùtái	service desk; front desk	L.2a
0230	服装	fúzhuāng	dress; clothing	L.4a
0231	服装厂	fúzhuāngchǎng	clothing factory	L.4a
0232	付	fù	to pay	L.2a
0233	付款	fù kuǎn	to make payment; payment	L.9a
0234	负担	fùdān	burden	L.4b
0235	赴宴	fù yàn	to attend a banquet	L.4b
0236	复印机	fùyìnjī	copy machine; duplicator	L.2b
0237	副	fù	vice; associate	L.1a
0238	副本	fùběn	duplicate; copy	L.15a
0239	副总经理	fù zǒngjīnglǐ	vice president; vice general manager	L.1a

G

0240	改革	gǎigé	reform; to reform	L.6b
0241	改革开放政策	Gǎigé Kāifàng Zhèngcè	Reform and Opening-up to the Outside World policy (first implemented in 1979)	L.6b
0242	改进	gǎijìn	to improve; improvement	L.8a
0243	改善	gǎishàn	to improve	L.15b
0244	赶	gǎn	to rush; to hurry; to make a dash for	L.7a
0245	干杯	gān bēi	to drink a toast; Cheers!; Bottoms up!	L.5a
0246	高峰期	gāofēngqī	heyday; peak period; rush hour	L.14b
0247	高铁	gāotiě	high-speed rail	L.11a
0248	高新科技	gāoxīn kējì	high and new technology	L.4a
0249	高新区	gāoxīnqū	High-Tech Industrial Development Zone	L.14b
0250	搞怪	gǎoguài	to do weird things; to make funny jokes	L.11b
0251	告别	gàobié	to part from; to bid farewell	L.16a
0252	个人	gèrén	individual; oneself	L.7b
0253	各地	gèdì	various places/localities	L.10a
0254	各类	gèlèi	various kinds; various categories	L.12b
0255	根据	gēnjù	on the basis of; according to	L.15a
0256	更加	gèngjiā	(even) more	L.16a
0257	工厂	gōngchǎng	factory	L.4a
0258	工业园区	gōngyè yuánqū	industrial park	L.4a
0259	公共关系部	Gōnggòng Guānxì Bù	Department of Public Relations	L.3b

0260	公共配套设施	gōnggòng pèitào shèshī	public facilities	L.14a
0261	公筷	gōng kuài	serving-chopsticks; chopsticks for serving food	L.5a
0262	公平	gōngpíng	fair; fairness	L.15b
0263	公认	gōngrèn	generally recognized; universally acknowledged	L.8a
0264	公司	gōngsī	company	L.1a
0265	公正	gōngzhèng	just; justice	L.15b
0266	功能	gōngnéng	function	L.12a
0267	巩固	gǒnggù	to consolidate; to strengthen; to solidify	L.16b
0268	供	gōng	to supply; provide; to be for (the use/convenience of)	L.12a
0269	供应	gōngyìng	to supply (goods/merchandise / materials); supply	L.12a
0270	供应商	gōngyìngshāng	supplier	L.13a
0271	沟通	gōutōng	to communicate	L.8b
0272	购买	gòumǎi	to purchase; to buy	L.7b
0273	股份制	gǔfènzhì	shareholding system; joint-stock system	L.9b
0274	鼓励	gǔlì	to encourage; to urge	L.7b
0275	固然	gùrán	no doubt; it is true; admittedly	L.8b
0276	故宫	Gùgōng	the Imperial Palace	L.4a
0277	顾客	gùkè	customer	L.6b
0278	关键	guānjiàn	key; key point; crux	L.8a
0279	关系	guānxì	"connections"; relationship; ties	L.16a
0280	关于	guānyú	about; with regard to; concerning	L.15a
0281	关照	guānzhào	to look after; concern and care	L.10a
0282	关注	guānzhù	attention; interest; to pay close attention to	L.15b
0283	官网	guānwǎng	official website	L.11a
0284	官员	guānyuán	officer; official	L.1a
0285	管理	guǎnlǐ	to manage; to run; to administer; management	L.7a
0286	光临	guānglín	presence (of a guest, etc.); be present	L.3a
0287	广东	Guǎngdōng	a province in southeast China	L.10a
0288	广告	guǎnggào	advertisement; commercial	L.1a
0289	广州	Guǎngzhōu	*a city name*	L.2b
0290	规定	guīdìng	to stipulate; to formulate; rule; stipulation	L.15b
0291	规律	guīlǜ	law; regular pattern	L.11b
0292	规模	guīmó	scale; scope	L.11a

0293	贵宾	guìbīn	honored/distinguished guest	L.5a
0294	国际	guójì	international	L.1a
0295	国际化	guójìhuà	internationalization	L.9b
0296	国际货币基金组织	Guójì Huòbì Jījīn Zǔzhī	International Monetary Fund; IMF	L.9b
0297	国家级	guójiājí	national/state level	L.14b
0298	国家级新区	guójiājí xīnqū	National/State level New Area	L.14b
0299	国内	guónèi	interior (of a country); domestic	L.9b
0300	国外	guówài	overseas; abroad	L.7a
0301	国有	guóyǒu	state-owned	L.7b
0302	过程	guòchéng	course (of events); process	L.7b
0303	过份	guòfèn	excessive(ly); over(ly)	L.11b
0304	过目	guò mù	to look over (a paper/list/etc.); so as to check or approve; to go over	L.6a
0305	过目不忘	guò mù bú wàng	to have a photographic memory; very impressive	L.11b

H

0306	海关	hǎiguān	customs	L.1a
0307	海归	hǎiguī	overseas returnee	L.14a
0308	海南	hǎinán	Hainan Province	L.14b
0309	海外	hǎiwài	overseas	L.9b
0310	行情	hángqíng	business conditions; market conditions; quotation	L.6b
0311	毫无疑问	háowú yíwèn	without a doubt; undoubtedly	L.10b
0312	好好儿	hǎohāor	carefully; to the best of one's ability	L.4a
0313	好客	hàokè	hospitable	L.5b
0314	好手	hǎoshǒu	expert; ace; old pro	L.8b
0315	合法	héfǎ	lawful; legal	L.15b
0316	合理	hélǐ	reasonable; rational	L.4a
0317	合同	hétóng	contract; agreement	L.3a
0318	合资企业	hézī qǐyè	joint venture enterprise	L.7b
0319	合作	hézuò	to cooperate; to work together; cooperation	L.3a
0320	后天	hòutiān	day after tomorrow	L.4a
0321	互联网	hùliánwǎng	internet	L.2a
0322	护照	hùzhào	passport	L.1a
0323	花瓶	huāpíng	flower vase	L.16a

0324	花旗银行	Huāqí Yínháng	Citibank	L.9a
0325	华盛顿大学	Huáshèngdùn Dàxué	University of Washinton	L.13a
0326	话别	huàbié	to say a few parting words; to say goodbye	L.16a
0327	还盘	huán pán	counter offer; to make a counter offer	L.8a
0328	环保	huánbǎo	environment (al) protection (*the short form for "环境保护huánjìng bǎohù")	L.10a
0329	环境	huánjìng	environment	L.3a
0330	黄河	Huáng Hé	Yellow River	L.11b
0331	汇付	huìfù	remittance (e.g. 电汇 T/T, 信汇 M/T, 票汇 D/D)	L.9b
0332	会客室	huìkèshì	reception room	L.7a
0333	会谈	huìtán	talks; to talk	L.3a
0334	伙伴	huǒbàn	partner	L.14a
0335	货	huò	goods; commodities	L.6b
0336	货币	huòbì	currency; money	L.9b
0337	货款	huòkuǎn	payment for goods	L.9a
0338	货样	huòyàng	merchandise/product sample	L.1a
0339	货源	huòyuán	source of goods; supply of goods	L.8a
0340	获得	huòdé	to gain; to win; to achieve	L.12a
0341	霍尔果斯	Huò'ěrguǒsī	Khorgos, *a city in Xinjiang Uygur Autonomous Region*	L.14b

J

0342	积极	jījí	positive(ly); active(ly)	L.7b
0343	积累	jīlěi	to accumulate; accumulation	L.13a
0344	基础设施	jīchǔ shèshī	infrastructure	L.14a
0345	激烈	jīliè	intense; sharp; fierce	L.8a
0346	及时	jíshí	in time; promptly	L.11a
0347	吉利	jílì	good luck/fortune; auspicious; lucky	L.11b
0348	级	jí	rank; level; grade	L.2a
0349	即	jí	namely; to be (with emphasis)	L.10b
0350	即期信用证	jíqī xìnyòngzhèng	letter of credit at sight	L.9a
0351	即使	jìshǐ	even; even if	L.3b
0352	几乎	jǐhū	almost; nearly	L.8a
0353	给予	jǐyǔ	to give; to grant	L.15b
0354	记得	jìdé	to remember; to recall	L.7a

0355	技能	jìnéng	skill; technical ability	L.13a
0356	季度	jìdù	season	L.15a
0357	季节	jìjié	season	L.9a
0358	季节性	jìjiéxìng	seasonal	L.9a
0359	既然	jìrán	since; given the fact that	L.5a
0360	加快	jiākuài	to speed up; to accelerate	L.9b
0361	加强	jiāqiáng	to strengthen; to reinforce	L.16a
0362	加入	jiārù	to join; accede to	L.9b
0363	加深	jiāshēn	to deepen	L.16a
0364	家用电器	jiāyòng diànqì	household appliances	L.10a
0365	夹菜	jiā cài	to pick up food with chopsticks	L.5a
0366	假期	jiàqī	vacation	L.13a
0367	假如	jiǎrú	if; supposing	L.13b
0368	价格	jiàgé	price	L.6a
0369	价钱	jiàqián	price	L.6b
0370	价值	jiàzhí	value; worth	L.1a
0371	价值观	jiàzhíguān	value system	L.11b
0372	兼并	jiānbìng	to merge; to annex; merger	L.7b
0373	检验	jiǎnyàn	inspection; to inspect	L.7a
0374	简称	jiǎnchēng	be called sth. for short; abbreviation	L.12b
0375	简洁	jiǎnjié	succinct; simple and neat; to-the-point	L.12a
0376	简历	jiǎnlì	resume; curriculum vitae	L.13b
0377	饯行	jiànxíng	to give farewell dinner	L.16a
0378	建立	jiànlì	to establish; to build	L.4b
0379	建议	jiànyì	suggestion; to suggest	L.6a
0380	健身房	jiànshēnfáng	gym	L.2a
0381	将（要）	jiāng (yào)	be about to; will	L.10a
0382	降低	jiàngdī	to reduce; to lower; to cut down	L.7a
0383	降价	jiàng jià	to lower prices	L.8a
0384	交换	jiāohuàn	to exchange; to swap	L.3b
0385	交货	jiāo huò	to deliver goods	L.7a
0386	交流	jiāoliú	to exchange (ideas/information/etc.)	L.8b
0387	交朋友	jiāo péngyou	to make friends	L.1b
0388	交税	jiāoshuì	to pay taxes/customs duties	L.1a
0389	交通	jiāotōng	traffic; transportation; communications	L.4b

0390	交易	jiāoyì	deal; trade; transaction; to deal; to trade	L.4a
0391	交易会	jiāoyìhuì	trade fair	L.4a
0392	叫醒	jiàoxǐng	to wake sb. up (For instance: 叫醒服务 wake-up call)	L.2a
0393	阶段	jiēduàn	phase; stage; period	L.11a
0394	接待	jiēdài	to receive/admit a guest	L.4b
0395	接待单位	jiēdài dānwèi	host organization	L.4b
0396	接风	jiēfēng	to give a welcome reception for visitors from afar	L.5a
0397	接受	jiēshòu	to accept	L.8a
0398	接下来	jiē xialai	then; next	L.13a
0399	节能	jiénéng	energy-saving	L.10a
0400	结算	jiésuàn	to settle/close an account	L.9b
0401	届	jiè	a measure word for periodic terms or events.	L.12a
0402	借用	jièyòng	to borrow; to use sth. for another purpose	L.11b
0403	今后	jīnhòu	from now on; henceforth; in the future	L.3b
0404	金额	jīn'é	amount/sum of money	L.15a
0405	金奖	jīnjiǎng	gold medal	L.12a
0406	金融	jīnróng	banking; finance	L.9b
0407	仅	jǐn	only	L.9b
0408	紧张	jǐnzhāng	nervous; tense	L.1b
0409	锦江饭店	Jǐnjiāng Fàndiàn	Jinjiang Hotel	L.2b
0410	尽力	jìnlì	to do all one can; to do one's best	L.10a
0411	进出口	jìnchūkǒu	import and export	L.1a
0412	进货	jìnhuò	to purchase merchandise; to replenish stocks	L.8a
0413	进口	jìnkǒu	import; to import; entrance	L.1a
0414	进入	jìnrù	to enter; to get into	L.7b
0415	进一步	jìnyíbù	go a step further	L.9a
0416	进展	jìnzhǎn	progress; advance; to make progress	L.14a
0417	近年来	jìnnián lái	in recent years	L.13b
0418	经济全球化	jīngjì quánqiúhuà	economic globalization	L.14b
0419	经济特区	jīngjì tèqū	Special Economic Zone (SEZ)	L.14b
0420	经历	jīnglì	to go through; to experience; experience	L.13a
0421	经销	jīngxiāo	to sell/distribute on commission	L.10a
0422	经验	jīngyàn	experience	L.13a
0423	景泰蓝	jǐngtàilán	cloisonné	L.16a

0424	净化	jìnghuà	to purify	L.12a
0425	竞争	jìngzhēng	competition; to compete	L.6b
0426	竞争力	jìngzhēnglì	competitiveness	L.8a
0427	敬	jìng	to offer politely	L.5a
0428	境内	jìngnèi	within a country's borders	L.14b
0429	九五折	jiǔwǔ zhé	5 % discount	L.12a
0430	久等	jiǔděng	to wait for a long time	L.14a
0431	久仰	jiǔyǎng	a short form of "久仰大名" which means "I have heard your illustrious name for a long time."	L.3b
0432	酒店	jiǔdiàn	hotel; wine shop	L.1a
0433	酒香不怕巷子深	jiǔ xiāng bú pà xiàngzi shēn	If your wine really tastes good, you don't need to worry that your wine shop is located at the end of a narrow lane; Good wine needs no bush ... No matter where you are, people will find you if your product is good.	L.11b
0434	局长	júzhǎng	director (of a government office or bureau)	L.5a
0435	举办	jǔbàn	to conduct; to hold; to run	L.12b
0436	举行	jǔxíng	to hold (a meeting, etc.)	L.5a
0437	巨大	jùdà	huge; tremendous	L.10b
0438	具体	jùtǐ	specific; particular; concrete	L.3a
0439	据说	jùshuō	it is said...	L.5b
0440	据我所知	jù wǒ suǒ zhī	as far as I know; to my knowledge	L.14a

K

0441	喀什	Kāshí	Kashgar, *a city in Xinjiang Uygur Autonomous Region*	L.14b
0442	卡	kǎ	card	L.1a
0443	卡通	kǎtōng	cartoon	L.7a
0444	开诚布公	kāichéng-bùgōng	to speak friendly and sincerely	L.16b
0445	开出	kāichū	to write out; to make out (a check, etc.)	L.9a
0446	开发区	kāifāqū	Development Zone	L.14b
0447	开放	kāifàng	to open (to trade/to the public/etc.); to lift a ban or restriction	L.6b
0448	开玩笑	kāi wánxiào	to joke; to make fun of	L.9a
0449	开展	kāizhǎn	to develop; to launch; to expand	L.12b
0450	看好	kànhǎo	optimistic (about the outcome)	L.14a
0451	看起来	kàn qilai	it seems; it looks as if	L.12a

0452	考察	kǎochá	make on-the-spot investigation; observe and study	L.3a
0453	考虑	kǎolǜ	to consider; to think over	L.8a
0454	科技	kējì	science and technology	L.4a
0455	可爱	kě'ài	cute; lovable	L.7a
0456	可靠	kěkào	reliable; dependable; trustworthy	L.10b
0457	可口可乐	Kěkǒu-Kělè	Coca-Cola	L.11b
0458	客服	kèfú	customer service (a short form for 顾客服务)	L.13a
0459	客服部	kèfúbù	customer service department	L.13a
0460	客户	kèhù	client; customer	L.6a
0461	客人	kèrén	guest; visitor	L.2a
0462	客套	kètào	polite formula; civilities	L.3b
0463	空调	kōngtiáo	air conditioner	L.10a
0464	孔子	Kǒngzǐ	Confucius (551 BC – 479 BC)	L.5a
0465	恐怕	kǒngpà	I am afraid; perhaps	L.8a
0466	夸奖	kuājiǎng	praise; to praise; to commend	L.12a
0467	夸张	kuāzhāng	to exaggerate; exaggeration	L.8b
0468	跨国企业	kuàguó qǐyè	multinational corporation	L.14b
0469	跨境	kuàjìng	cross-border	L.13a
0470	跨境电商	kuàjìng diànshāng	cross-border e-commerce	L.13a
0471	筷子	kuàizi	chopsticks	L.5a
0472	款	kuǎn	a measure word for the design of certain things (especially clothing); item/clause (in document)	L.6a
0473	亏损	kuīsǔn	financial loss; deficit; to suffer a loss	L.7b
0474	扩大	kuòdà	to expand; to enlarge; to extend	L.10a

L

0475	老板	lǎobǎn	boss	L.1a
0476	老话	lǎohuà	old saying; adage	L.6b
0477	老年	lǎonián	old age	L.11b
0478	老一辈	lǎoyíbèi	older generation	L.5b
0479	乐意	lèyì	to be willing/happy to	L.1b
0480	类	lèi	type; kind	L.9b
0481	类型	lèixíng	type; category	L.7b
0482	冷盘	lěngpán	cold dish; hors d'oeuvres	L.5a
0483	离不开	líbukāi	cannot do without; unable to separate from	L.11b

0484	礼貌	lǐmào	courtesy; politeness	L.3b
0485	礼品部	lǐpǐnbù	gift shop	L.2b
0486	礼轻情义重	lǐqīng qíngyì zhòng	The gift is trifling, but feeling is profound	L.16b
0487	礼仪	lǐyí	etiquette; rite; protocol	L.3b
0488	李信文	Lǐ Xìnwén	*a name*	L.1a
0489	理解	lǐjiě	to understand	L.8b
0490	厉害	lìhai	tough; sharp; formidable	L.9a
0491	立场	lìchǎng	position; stand; standpoint	L.16b
0492	利润	lìrùn	profit;	L.8a
0493	利益	lìyì	benefit; gain; interest	L.16b
0494	廉价	liánjià	low-priced; cheap	L.12a
0495	廉价货	liánjiàhuò	cheap goods	L.12a
0496	良好	liánghǎo	good; well	L.2a
0497	列	liè	to list	L.3b
0498	列入	lièrù	be included in; be placed on (an agenda, etc.)	L.16a
0499	猎头	liètóu	recruiting; headhunting	L.13b
0500	灵活	línghuó	flexible	L.14b
0501	零售价	língshòujià	retail price	L.6a
0502	领导	lǐngdǎo	leader; leadership	L.5a
0503	另外	lìngwài	in addition; besides	L.4a
0504	另议	lìngyì	be discussed/negotiated separately	L.6a
0505	流通	liútōng	to circulate	L.9b
0506	龙	lóng	dragon	L.11b
0507	炉具	lújù	stoves; ovens	L.14a
0508	陆续	lùxù	one after another; in succession	L.15b
0509	录用	lùyòng	to employ; to hire	L.13b
0510	旅馆	lǚguǎn	hotel	L.2b
0511	旅行社	lǚxíngshè	travel agency	L.2b
0512	旅客	lǚkè	hotel guest; traveler; passenger	L2.a

M

0513	买卖	mǎimai	buying and selling; business	L.8b
0514	买一送一	mǎi yī sòng yī	buy one and get one free	L.11a
0515	买主	mǎizhǔ	buyer	L.6b
0516	卖点	màidiǎn	selling point	L.11a
0517	卖主	màizhǔ	seller; vendor	L.6b

0518	满汉全席	Mǎn-Hàn Quánxí	the complete Manchu and Chinese banquet	L.5b
0519	满足	mǎnzú	to satisfy; to meet (a demand/request, etc.)	L.10a
0520	漫天要价	màntiān-yàojià	to quote an exorbitant price in anticipation of haggling	L.8b
0521	茅台酒	Máotái Jiǔ	Maotai (liquor)	L.5a
0522	冒昧	màomèi	(courteous/humble) presumptuous; to make bold	L.14a
0523	贸易	màoyì	trade	L.1a
0524	没法（儿）	méifǎ(r)	no way; can do nothing about it	L.12a
0525	没什么	méishénme	it's nothing; it doesn't matter	L.4a
0526	美国国际贸易公司	Měiguó Guójì Màoyì Gōngsī	American International Trading Company	L.1a
0527	美容沙龙	měiróng shālóng	beauty salon	L.2b
0528	门铃	ménlíng	doorbell	L.13a
0529	密集	mìjí	intensive; concentrated	L.14b
0530	密码	mìmǎ	password; secret code	L.2a
0531	免费	miǎn fèi	to be free of charge	L.2a
0532	免税	miǎn shuì	to exempt from taxation; tax-free; duty-free	L.1a
0533	面对	miànduì	to face	L.5b
0534	面临	miànlín	to face; be faced with; be up against	L.10b
0435	面试	miànshì	interview; to interview	L.13a
0536	面值	miànzhí	face value; denomination	L.9b
0537	面子	miànzi	"face"; reputation; prestige	L.16b
0538	民营	mínyíng	privately-run	L.7b
0539	名牌	míngpái	famous brand	L.8a
0540	名片	míngpiàn	business card; name card	L.3a
0541	名人	míngrén	famous person; celebrity	L.11a
0542	名人效应	míngrén xiàoyìng	celebrity effect	L.11a
0543	名义	míngyì	name; nominal	L.16a
0544	明确	míngquè	explicit(ly); clear and definite	L.15b
0545	命运	mìngyùn	fate; destiny	L.10b
0546	模式	móshì	mode; model; method; pattern	L.13a
0547	某	mǒu	certain; some	L.8a
0548	某些	mǒuxiē	certain (people/things/etc.); some	L.8a
0549	目的	mùdì	purpose; objective; goal	L.3a

0550	目录	mùlù	catalogue; list	L.6a

N

0551	嗯	ǹg	"mmm" (express an agreement or satisfaction)	L.5a
0552	耐心	nàixīn	patience; patient	L.8b
0553	难处	nánchù	difficulty; problem	L.9a
0554	难得	nándé	rare; hard to come by; seldom	L.10b
0555	难怪	nánguài	no wonder	L.16a
0556	难免	nánmiǎn	hard to avoid	L.12b
0557	能力	nénglì	ability; capability	L.13a
0558	年代	niándài	decade; era	L.14b
0559	牛仔裤	niúzǎikù	jeans	L.6a
0560	浓	nóng	strong; dense	L.10b
0561	女士	nǚshì	woman; lady; Ms.; Miss	L.3a

O

0562	欧元	ōuyuán	euro	L.9b

P

0563	派驻	pàizhù	to dispatch; to accredit	L.13a
0564	陪	péi	to accompany; to keep sb. company	L.5a
0565	陪同	péitóng	to accompany	L.12a
0566	赔本	péi běn	to sustain losses in business	L.8a
0567	配合	pèihé	to coordinate with; to cooperate and support;	L.11a
0568	配套	pèitào	compatible; to form a complete set	L.14a
0569	批	pī	a measure word for goods; batch; lot;	L.7a
0570	批发价	pīfājià	wholesale price	L6a
0571	皮夹克	píjiákè	leather jacket	L.8a
0572	频繁	pínfán	frequently; incessant	L.4b
0573	品尝	pǐncháng	to taste; to sample	L.4a
0574	品牌	pǐnpái	brand name; trademark	L.6a
0575	品种	pǐnzhǒng	variety; assortment; kind	L.6b
0576	平等互利	píngděng hùlì	equality and mutual benefit	L.15b
0577	评估	pínggū	to evaluate; evaluation	L.14a
0578	葡萄酒	pútáojiǔ	wine	L.5a
0579	浦东	Pǔdōng	Pudong District in Shanghai, China	L.13a
0580	浦东新区	Pǔdōng Xīnqū	Pudong New Area in Shanghai	L.14b

0581	浦发银行	Pǔfā Yínháng	SPD Bank, a short form for Shanghai Pudong Development Bank (上海浦东发展银行)	L.9b
0582	普通	pǔtōng	ordinary; common; average	L.5b
0583	普通代理	pǔtōng dàilǐ	commission agent/agency	L.10b

Q

0584	期待	qīdài	hope; expectation; to look forward to	L.16b
0585	期间	qījiān	duration; period; time	L.3a
0586	其余	qíyú	the rest; the remainder	L.9a
0587	其中	qízhōng	among; of which	L.15b
0588	企业	qǐyè	enterprise; business	L.7b
0589	起作用	qǐ zuòyòng	have the effect of ...	L.15b
0590	洽谈	qiàtán	to talk over with; to negotiate; negotiation	L.3a
0591	签订	qiāndìng	to conclude and sign (a contract, etc.)	L.3a
0592	签署	qiānshǔ	to sign (a document)	L.15a
0593	签约	qiān yuē	to sign a contract	L.10b
0594	签字	qiān zì	to sign or initial	L.15a
0595	前程无忧网	Qiánchéng Wúyōu Wǎng	www.51job.com, an employment website	L.13b
0596	前后	qiánhòu	around; about; front and rear	L.14b
0597	潜力	qiánlì	potential	L.10b
0598	强	qiáng	strong	L.9a
0599	强调	qiángdiào	to stress; to emphasize	L.15b
0600	强项	qiángxiàng	key strength; specialty	L.11a
0601	桥梁	qiáoliáng	bridge	L.12b
0602	巧妙	qiǎomiào	ingenious; skillful; clever	L.11b
0603	亲兄弟，明算账	qīn xiōngdì, míng suàn zhàng	Even blood brothers keep careful accounts.	L.9a
0604	亲眼	qīnyǎn	with one's own eyes; personally	L.4a
0605	轻松	qīngsōng	relaxed; light	L.1b
0606	情面	qíngmiàn	feelings; sensibilities; "face"	L.9a
0607	请客	qǐng kè	invite/entertain guests; treat sb. (to a meal)	L.4b
0608	庆祝	qìngzhù	to celebrate	L.15a
0609	秋季	qiūjì	autumn	L.3a
0610	求职	qiúzhí	to seek employment	L.13b
0611	区域	qūyù	zone; region; district; sector	L.14b
0612	取决	qǔjué	be decided by; to depend on	L.8b

0613	权益	quányì	rights and interests	L.15b
0614	全国性	quánguóxìng	national; nationwide	L.9b
0615	全面	quánmiàn	overall; comprehensive	L.12b
0616	全权	quánquán	with full authority; full/plenary powers	L.10b
0617	缺少	quēshǎo	to lack; be short of	L.16b
0618	确定	quèdìng	to define; to determine; to settle; to decide firmly	L.3a
0619	确认	quèrèn	to confirm; to identify with certainty	L.15a

R

0620	让价	ràng jià	to better one's price	L.8a
0621	热炒	rèchǎo	a fried dish (stir-fried, etc.)	L.5b
0622	热门	rèmén	popular; in great demand	L.13b
0623	人才	réncái	talented person	L.13b
0624	人才市场	réncái shìchǎng	job fair; talent market	L.13b
0625	人地生疏	rén dì shēngshū	be unfamiliar with the place and the people	L.10b
0626	人口	rénkǒu	population	L.10b
0627	人口众多	rénkǒu zhòngduō	have a very large population	L.10b
0628	人力资源部	rénlì zīyuán bù	human resource department	L.13a
0629	人民币	rénmínbì	RMB (Chinese currency)	L.2a
0630	人手	rénshǒu	manpower; staff	L.13b
0631	人员	rényuán	staff; personnel	L.14a
0632	日程	rìchéng	schedule; itinerary	L.3a
0633	日程表	rìchéngbiǎo	schedule; agenda; itinerary	L.4b
0634	元	rìyuán	Japanese yen	L.9b
0635	荣幸	róngxìng	honored (to have the privilege of...)	L.13a
0636	融资	róngzī	financing; finance; fund-raising	L.14a
0637	入境	rù jìng	to enter a country	L.1a
0638	入口	rùkǒu	entrance	L.5b
0639	入席	rù xí	to take one's seat (at a ceremony, etc.)	L.5a
0640	入驻	rùzhù	enter and stay	L.14a
0641	若干	ruògān	a certain number/amount	L.10b

S

0642	筛选	shāixuǎn	to filter; to screen out; to select	L.13a
0643	山寨	shānzhài	knockoff; to make knockoff products; (literally, mountain stockade/stronghold)	L.10b
0644	山寨产品	shānzhài chǎnpǐn	imitating reproduction	L.10b

0645	汕头	Shàntóu	*a city in Guangdong Province*	L.14b
0646	善于	shànyú	be good at; be adept in	L.8b
0647	商定	shāngdìng	to settle through discussion	L.9a
0648	商品	shāngpǐn	merchandise; goods; commodity	L.4a
0649	商务	shāngwù	business, business affairs	L.2a
0650	商务中心	shāngwù zhōngxīn	business center	L.2a
0651	商业	shāngyè	commerce; trade; business	L.1a
0652	商业价值	shāngyè jiàzhí	commercial value	L.1a
0653	上菜	shàng cài	to serve (food); to place dishes on the table	L.5a
0654	上当	shàng dàng	to be fooled/taken in;	L.6b
0655	上网	shàng wǎng	to access the internet	L.2a
0656	上旬	shàngxún	the first ten days of the month	L.9a
0657	上座	shàngzuò	the seat of honor	L.5a
0658	稍	shāo	a little; a bit; slightly	L.3a
0659	稍等	shāoděng	to wait a moment	L.12a
0660	稍后	shāohòu	later	L.3a
0661	少不了	shǎobuliǎo	cannot do without; indispensable	L.4b
0662	少数	shǎoshù	a few; a small number	L.9b
0663	设备	shèbèi	equipment; facilities	L.7a
0664	设计	shèjì	design; to design	L.6a
0665	设立	shèlì	to set up; to establish	L.15b
0666	设立程序	shèlì chéngxù	procedures for establishment	L.15b
0667	设施	shèshī	facilities; amenities	L.2a
0668	设有	shèyǒu	to have; to include within	L.2b
0669	涉及	shèjí	to involve; to touch upon	L.13a
0670	涉外	shèwài	involving foreign affairs/nationals	L.15b
0671	申报	shēnbào	declaration; to declare (dutiable goods)	L.1a
0672	申报单	shēnbàodān	declaration form	L.1a
0673	申请	shēnqǐng	to apply; application	L.13a
0674	申请人	shēnqǐngrén	applicant	L.13a
0675	申诉	shēnsù	appeal; to appeal	L.15a
0676	深刻	shēnkè	deep; profound	L.7a
0677	深圳	Shēnzhèn	*a city name*	L.3b
0678	审核	shěnhé	to examine and verify	L.15a

0679	甚至	shènzhì	even (to the extent that ...); to go so far as	L.4b
0680	生产区	shēngchǎnqū	production area	L.7a
0681	生产效率	shēngchǎn xiàolǜ	productivity	L.7a
0682	生意	shēngyi	business; trade	L.1a
0683	生意不成情义在	shēngyi bù chéng qíngyì zài	Be friendly even if the Business fails	L.12a
0684	圣诞节	Shèngdàn Jié	Christmas	L.7a
0685	失败	shībài	to fail; failure	L.8a
0686	时差	shíchā	time difference; jet lag	L.5a
0687	时尚	shíshàng	fashion; fashionable; stylish	L.11b
0688	实行	shíxíng	to implement; to put into practice; to carry out	L.6b
0689	实话	shíhuà	(the) truth	L.12a
0690	实际	shíjì	actual(ly); practical(ly)	L.14b
0691	实施	shíshī	to put into effect; to implement	L.15b
0692	实习	shíxí	to intern; to practice; internship	L.13a
0693	实习生	shíxíshēng	trainee; intern (student)	L.13a
0694	实在	shízài	really; indeed; truly	L.9a
0695	史强生	Shǐ Qiángshēng	*a name*	L.1a
0696	使	shǐ	to make; to cause	L.1b
0697	使用	shǐyòng	to use	L.2b
0698	世界贸易组织	Shìjiè Màoyì Zǔzhī	World Trade Organization; WTO (世贸组织)	L.9b
0699	世界五百强（企业）	Shìjiè Wǔbǎi Qiáng (qǐyè)	Fortune Global 500 (companies)	L.7b
0700	市场	shìchǎng	market	L.6a
0701	市场部	shìchǎngbù	marketing department	L.13a
0702	市场价	shìchǎngjià	market price	L.6a
0703	市场经济	shìchǎng jīngjì	market economy; market-directed economy	L.6b
0704	市场调查	shìchǎng diàochá	market survey	L.10a
0705	市场营销	shìchǎng yíngxiāo	marketing	L.13a
0706	式样	shìyàng	style	L.6a
0707	事先	shìxiān	in advance; beforehand	L.4b
0708	试生产	shìshēngchǎn	to manufacture on a trial basis; trial production	L.6a
0709	试销品	shìxiāopǐn	trial item/products	L.6a

0710	视频	shìpín	video	L.6a
0711	视为	shìwéi	regard as; consider as	L.13b
0712	适当	shìdàng	proper(ly)	L.8a
0713	收获	shōuhuò	gains; results	L.16a
0714	手续	shǒuxù	procedure; formalities	L.1a
0715	首先	shǒuxiān	in the first place; first of all	L.3b
0716	受欢迎	shòu huānyíng	be well-received; popular	L.10a
0717	受骗	shòu piàn	be deceived/swindled	L.16b
0718	熟悉	shúxi	be familiar with	L.11a
0719	数	shǔ	to count; to be reckoned as exceptionally (good/bad/etc.)	L.12a
0720	数量	shùliàng	quantity	L.8a
0721	刷卡	shuā kǎ	to swipe card; to use a credit card	L.2a
0722	双方	shuāngfāng	both sides/parties (in negotiations, etc.)	L.3a
0723	双语	shuāngyǔ	bilingual	L.13a
0724	双重	shuāngchóng	double; dual	L.14b
0725	税务	shuìwù	taxation	L.15b
0726	顺便	shùnbiàn	conveniently	L.3b
0727	顺便说一句	shùnbiàn shuō yí jù	by the way; incidentally	L.3b
0728	顺利	shùnlì	smooth(ly)	L.1a
0729	说到	shuōdào	to speak of; to mention; when it comes to...	L.9a
0730	说法	shuōfǎ	way of saying sth.; wording	L.8b
0731	丝绸	sīchóu	silk; silk cloth	L.12a
0732	私人	sīrén	private; personal	L.4b
0733	私有	sīyǒu	privately-owned	L.7b
0734	送行	sòngxíng	to see sb. off	L.16a
0735	送货上门	sòng huò shàng mén	home delivery	L.11a
0736	搜	sōu	to search	L.13b
0737	搜索	sōusuǒ	to search; to conduct a search	L.13b
0738	俗语	súyǔ	common saying; slang	L.11b
0739	诉讼	sùsòng	lawsuit; litigation	L.15b
0740	算是	suànshì	considered to be	L.12a
0741	随便	suíbiàn	as you like; do as one pleases	L.5a
0742	随时	suíshí	at any time	L.3a
0743	随着	suízhe	along with; in pace with	L.9b

0744	孙子兵法	Sūnzǐ Bīngfǎ	*The Art of War* by Sun Wu, ancient Chinese philosopher during the Chunqiu period (777- 476 B.C.).	L.6b
0745	损失	sǔnshī	loss; to lose	l.10b
0746	缩影	suōyǐng	miniature; epitome	L.14a
0747	索赔	suǒpéi	claim (for damages); to demand compensation	L.15a

T

0748	踏实	tāshí	solidly; practical	L.16b
0749	台湾	Táiwān	Taiwan	L.1a
0750	太太	tàitai	wife; Mrs.	L.16a
0751	谈判	tánpàn	negotiations; talks; to negotiate	L.1b
0752	讨	tǎo	to demand; to ask for; to seek	L.11b
0753	讨吉利	tǎo jílì	to seek good fortune (through auspicious sayings)	L.11b
0754	讨价还价	tǎojià-huánjià	to bargain; to haggle	L.8b
0755	套房	tàofáng	suite	L.2a
0756	特点	tèdiǎn	characteristic; peculiarity	L.12a
0757	特定	tèdìng	specially designated; specific	L.14b
0758	特价	tèjià	special/bargain price	L.8a
0759	特色菜	tèsècài	special dish; chef's special	L.5a
0760	特殊	tèshū	special; exceptional; unusual	L.14b
0761	特长	tècháng	special aptitude; specialty	L.13a
0762	提出（来）	tí chū (lái)	to pose (questions); to raise (an issue)	L.7a
0763	提供	tígōng	to provide; to supply; to offer	L.2b
0764	提交	tíjiāo	to submit (a report etc.)	L.14a
0765	提前	tíqián	in advance; beforehand	L.9a
0766	提取	tíqǔ	to draw; to collect	L.10a
0767	体积	tǐjī	bulk; size; volume	L.12a
0768	天安门	Tiān'ānmén	Tian'anmen (i.e. Gate of Heavenly Peace)	L.11b
0769	甜点	tiándiǎn	dessert	L.5b
0770	填	tián	to fill out	L.1a
0771	挑战	tiǎozhàn	challenge; to challenge	L.6b
0772	条款	tiáokuǎn	clause; article; provision	L.15a
0773	调解	tiáojiě	mediation; to mediate	L.15b
0774	调整	tiáozhěng	to adjust	L.7b
0775	听起来	tīng qǐlái	to sound like; to sound as if	L.4a

0776	通常	tōngcháng	normal(ly); usual(ly)	L.2b
0777	通过	tōngguò	by means of; through	L.9a
0778	通行	tōngxíng	prevalent; of general use; current	L.9b
0779	通情达理	tōngqíng-dálǐ	sensible; reasonable	L.16b
0780	通信	tōngxìn	communication; to communicate	L.14a
0781	通信设施	tōngxìn shèshī	communication facility	L.14a
0782	同类	tónglèi	the same kind; similar	L.6a
0783	同一	tóngyī	same; identical	L.10b
0784	头疼	tóuténg	to have a headache; headache	L.15a
0785	头衔	tóuxián	official title	L.3b
0786	投放	tóufàng	to throw in; to put (sth. on the market)	L.7a
0787	投入	tóurù	to put into; to input; to invest	L.14a
0788	投资	tóuzī	to invest; investment	L.3a
0789	投资环境	tóuzī huánjìng	investment environment	L.3a
0790	突出	tūchū	to give prominence to; to protrude	L.11a
0791	途径	tújìng	way; channel	L.12b
0792	团队	tuánduì	team; group; crew	L.13a
0793	推出	tuīchū	to present (to the public); to put out	L.6a
0794	推动	tuīdòng	to push forward; to promote; to give impetus to; to spur	L.7b
0795	托收	tuōshōu	collection; to collect (e.g. 承兑交单 D/A, 付款交单 D/P)	L.9b
0796	妥协	tuǒxié	compromise; to compromise; to come to terms	L.16b

W

0797	挖	wā	to dig; to scoop	L.12a
0798	挖走	wāzǒu	to dig out and take away	L.12a
0799	哇	wa	wow; (expresses surprise)	L.2a
0800	外币	wàibì	foreign currency	L.2a
0801	外币兑换	wàibì duìhuàn	foreign currency exchange	L.2a
0802	外汇	wàihuì	foreign exchange	L.9b
0803	外贸局	wàimàojú	Foreign Trade Bureau	L.5a
0804	外形	wàixíng	appearance; external form; outside type	L.12a
0805	外资	wàizī	foreign investment	L.7b
0806	外资企业	wàizī qǐyè	foreign-capital enterprises	L.7b
0807	完备	wánbèi	well provided; complete with everything	L.2a
0808	完善	wánshàn	complete and perfect	L.14a

0809	玩具	wánjù	toy	L.4a
0810	晚宴	wǎnyàn	evening banquet	L.16a
0811	王府井希尔顿酒店	Wángfǔjǐng Xī'ěrdùn Jiǔdiàn	Hilton Beijing Wangfujing Hotel	L.2b
0812	王国安	Wáng Guó'ān	*a name*	L.3b
0813	王婆卖瓜，自卖自夸	Wángpó mài guā, zì mài zì kuā	When old lady Wang sold melons, she was always overstating her goods.	L.11b
0814	王总	Wáng zǒng	a short form for President Wang	L.3b
0815	网站	wǎngzhàn	website	L.13b
0816	往来	wǎnglái	contact; dealings; intercourse	L.16a
0817	往往	wǎngwǎng	often; frequently; more often than not	L.11b
0818	旺季	wàngjì	peak sales period; busy season	L.9a
0819	微笑	wēixiào	to smile; smile	L.1b
0820	为止	wéizhǐ	until	L.13a
0821	委托	wěituō	to entrust	L.10b
0822	位于	wèiyú	be located at/in	L.14b
0823	文件	wénjiàn	document	L.15a
0824	闻名	wénmíng	famous; well-known;	L.5b
0825	问候	wènhòu	greeting	L.3a
0826	无论	wúlùn	no matter; regardless	L.4b
0827	无线网络	wúxiàn wǎngluò	wireless network; Wi-Fi	L.14a
0828	无疑	wúyí	beyond a doubt; undoubtedly	L.12b
0829	五星级	wǔxīngjí	five star ranking; five star	L.2a
0830	务必	wùbì	must; should	L.9a
0831	物流	wùliú	logistics	L.13a
0832	物流部	wùliúbù	logistics department	L.13a
0833	物美价廉 / 价廉物美	wùměi-jiàlián / jiàlián-wùměi	excellent quality and reasonable price	L.11b

X

0834	厦门	Xiàmén	*a city name*	L.12b
0835	西雅图	Xīyǎtú	Seattle	L.13a
0836	西装	xīzhuāng	Western-style clothes; suit	L.6a
0837	吸引	xīyǐn	to attract; to draw	L.6a
0838	吸引力	xīyǐnlì	appeal	L.6a
0839	洗碗	xǐ wǎn	to wash dishes	L.10a

0840	洗碗机	xǐwǎnjī	dishwasher	L.10a
0841	洗衣袋	xǐyīdài	laundry bag	L.2a
0842	洗衣房	xǐyīfáng	laundry room	L.2a
0843	洗衣机	xǐyījī	washing machine	L.10a
0844	喜闻乐见	xǐwén-lèjiàn	love to see and hear	L.11b
0845	细心	xìxīn	carefulness; thoroughness; careful(ly)	L.8b
0846	先后	xiānhòu	early or late; one after another	L.14b
0847	先进	xiānjìn	advanced; state-of-the-art	L.7a
0848	现代化	xiàndàihuà	modern; modernized; modernization	L.14a
0849	现代商贸公司	Xiàndài Shāngmào Gōngsī	Modern Commerce & Trading Co.	L.13a
0850	现货	xiànhuò	merchandise on hand; goods in stock	L.12a
0851	现金	xiànjīn	cash	L.2a
0852	限于	xiànyú	be limited/confined to	L.9b
0853	羡慕	xiànmù	to admire; to envy	L.16a
0854	相当	xiāngdāng	quite; fairly	L.13b
0855	相反	xiāngfǎn	opposite; contrary; on the contrary	L.11b
0856	相应	xiāngyìng	relevant; corresponding;	L.11a
0857	香	xiāng	fragrant; aroma	L.11b
0858	箱子	xiāngzi	Suitcase; box	L.1a
0859	详细	xiángxì	detailed; thorough(ly)	L.13a
0860	享有	xiǎngyǒu	to enjoy (rights, privileges, etc.)	L.14b
0861	想不到	xiǎngbudào	unexpected	L.4b
0862	想法	xiǎngfǎ	idea; opinion; view	L.9a
0863	项	xiàng	a measure word for items/clauses/tasks/etc.	L.14a
0864	项目	xiàngmù	item; project; program	L.12b
0865	巷子	xiàngzi	lane; narrow road	L.11b
0866	象征	xiàngzhēng	symbol; to symbolize	L.11b
0867	消费	xiāofèi	to consume	L.11b
0868	消费者	xiāofèizhě	consumer	L.11b
0869	销路	xiāolù	sales; market	L.8a
0870	销售	xiāoshòu	sales; marketing; to sell; to market	L.7b
0871	销售网点	xiāoshòu wǎngdiǎn	commercial networks	L.10a
0872	销售总额	xiāoshòu zǒng'é	gross sales	L.10a
0873	小册子	xiǎocèzi	booklet	L.12a

0874	效果	xiàoguǒ	effect; result	L.11a
0875	效率	xiàolǜ	efficiency	L.7a
0876	效益	xiàoyì	beneficial result; benefit	L.7b
0877	效应	xiàoyìng	effect	L.11a
0878	协商	xiéshāng	to consult; to talk things over; consultation	L.15b
0879	协议	xiéyì	agreement	L.10a
0880	心理	xīnlǐ	mentality	L.11b
0881	新潮	xīncháo	new trend; trendy	L.11b
0882	新疆	xīnjiāng	Xinjiang Uygur Autonomous Region	L.14b
0883	新能源	xīnnéngyuán	new energy	L.14a
0884	新区	xīnqū	new area	L.14b
0885	信号	xìnhào	single	L.14a
0886	信息	xìnxi	information	L.6b
0887	信用	xìnyòng	credit	L.9a
0888	信用卡	xìnyòngkǎ	credit card	L.2a
0889	信用证	xìnyòngzhèng	letter of credit (L/C)	L.9a
0890	形式	xíngshì	form; shape	L.11b
0891	形象	xíngxiàng	image	L.11a
0892	型	xíng	model; type	L.12a
0893	型号	xínghào	model; type	L.12a
0894	行李	xíngli	luggage; baggage	L.1a
0895	兴趣	xìngqù	interest；hobby	L.6a
0896	幸会	xìnghuì	to be honored to meet (sb.)	L.3a
0897	幸运	xìngyùn	lucky; fortunate; luck	L.13a
0898	性质	xìngzhì	quality; nature; character	L.14b
0899	姓名	xìngmíng	full name	L.3b
0900	雄安新区	Xióng'ān Xīnqū	Xiongan New Area in Hebei Province	L.14b
0901	修改	xiūgǎi	to revise; to modify; revision	L.4a
0902	需求	xūqiú	requirement; demand	L.13b
0903	许可	xǔkě	permission; to permit; to allow	L.10b
0904	宣布	xuānbù	to announce; to declare	L.9b
0905	宣传	xuānchuán	propaganda; to propaganda; to give publicity to	L.11a
0906	选择	xuǎnzé	choice; to choose	L.6b
0907	旬	xún	a period of ten days	L.9a
0908	寻求	xúnqiú	to seek; to pursue	L.7b

0909	询问	xúnwèn	to ask about; to inquire	L.6a
0910	迅速	xùnsù	rapid; speedy; prompt	L.4a

Y

0911	押金	yājīn	deposit; cash pledge	L.2a
0912	亚马逊	Yàmǎxùn	Amazon	L.13a
0913	亚洲	Yàzhōu	Asia	L.3b
0914	延误	yánwù	delay; to incur loss through delay	L.15a
0915	延长	yáncháng	to extend	L.11a
0916	严肃	yánsù	serious; solemn; stern	L.1b
0917	沿海	yánhǎi	along the coast; coastal	L.14b
0918	研发	yánfā	research and development; to research and develop	L.14a
0919	眼前	yǎnqián	at the moment; at present	L.16b
0920	验收	yànshōu	check on delivery; inspection	L.15a
0921	邀请	yāoqǐng	to invite; invitation	L.4a
0922	业务	yèwù	business; professional work;	L.4a
0923	一般	yìbān	general(ly); common(ly)	L.2b
0924	一般来说	yìbān láishuō	generally speaking	L.2b
0925	一带一路	Yí Dài Yí Lù	the Belt and Road	L.14b
0926	一方面	yì fāngmiàn	one side; on the one hand	L.6b
0927	一口气	yìkǒuqì	in one breath; at one go; without a break; in one stretch	L.5b
0928	一路平安	yílù píng'ān	Have a safe journey!	L.16a
0929	一手交钱，一手交货	yì shǒu jiāo qián, yì shǒu jiāo huò	to deliver (only) when the cash is in hand	L.9a
0930	一系列	yíxìliè	a series of	L.14b
0931	一言为定	yìyán-wéidìng	that's settled then	L.8a
0932	衣食住行	yī shí zhù xíng	clothing, food, shelter and transportation; basic necessities for life	L.10b
0933	依靠	yīkào	to rely on; to depend on	L.14a
0934	仪式	yíshì	ceremony; rite	L.15a
0935	遗憾	yíhàn	regrettable; to regret; to feel sorry	L.8a
0936	遗漏	yílòu	omission; to omit; to miss	L.15a
0937	以……为荣	yǐ……wéi róng	consider/regard...as an honor	L.12b
0938	以便	yǐbiàn	in order to; so that; with the aim of	L.14b
0939	以茶代酒	yǐ chá dài jiǔ	to have tea instead of liquor	L.15a

0940	以及	yǐjí	as well as; and	L.13b
0941	以上	yǐshàng	over...; above...; more than	L.8a
0942	以下	yǐxià	below; under	L.12a
0943	意向书	yìxiàngshū	letter of intent	L.15a
0944	引进	yǐnjìn	to introduce from elsewhere; to import	L.7a
0945	印象	yìnxiàng	impression	L.7a
0946	英镑	yīngbàng	pound	L.9b
0947	盈利	yínglì	profit; to make a profit	L.14a
0948	影星	yǐngxīng	movie star	L.11a
0949	硬通货	yìngtōnghuò	hard currency	L.9b
0950	佣金	yòngjīn	commission	L.10a
0951	拥抱	yōngbào	to hug; to embrace	L.3b
0952	拥有	yōngyǒu	to possess; to have; to own	L.10b
0953	优惠	yōuhuì	preferential; favorable	L.11a
0954	优惠活动	yōuhuì huódòng	promotions; favorable offers	L.11a
0955	优势	yōushì	advantage; superiority; dominant position	L.7b
0956	优先	yōuxiān	preferential; preferred; priority	L.13b
0957	优质	yōuzhì	high quality; top quality	L.12a
0958	尤其	yóuqí	especially	L.2b
0959	由	yóu	by; through; via; from	L.6a
0960	由于	yóuyú	due to; as a result of; because of	L.12b
0961	邮件	yóujiàn	mail; email	L.2a
0962	邮箱	yóuxiāng	mailbox; email box	L.15a
0963	游览	yóulǎn	tour; to tour; to go sight-seeing	L.2b
0964	有关	yǒuguān	concerning; related to; to relate; to have sth. to do with	L.6b
0965	有力	yǒulì	strong; powerful	L.7b
0966	有利	yǒulì	beneficial; advantageous	L.10b
0967	有朋自远方来，不亦乐乎	yǒu péng zì yuǎn-fāng lái, bú yì lè hū	Isn't it a joy to have friends coming from distant places?	L.5a
0968	有权	yǒuquán	have the right to; to be entitled to	L.15a
0969	有效	yǒuxiào	effective(ly); valid	L.11a
0970	有效期	yǒuxiàoqī	duration/term of validity	L.10a
0971	有心人	yǒuxīnrén	a person with a set purpose	L.16b
0972	有意	yǒuyì	to intend; intentionally	L.14a

0973	有意义	yǒu yìyi	significant; meaningful	L.16b
0974	有助于	yǒuzhùyú	be conductive/helpful to	L.4b
0975	余地	yúdì	leeway; margin; room	L.16a
0976	与此同时	yǔ cǐ tóng shí	at the same time; meanwhile	L.13b
0977	与其…… 不如……	yǔqí……bùrú……	rather than..., it would be better to...	L.16b
0978	预订	yùdìng	to reserve; to book	L.2a
0979	预付	yùfù	to pay in advance	L.9a
0980	预祝	yùzhù	to congratulate beforehand	L.5a
0981	原料	yuánliào	raw material	L.7b
0982	原则	yuánzé	principle	L.15a
0983	圆满	yuánmǎn	satisfactory; satisfactorily	L.5a
0984	越来越	yuèláiyuè	more and more	L.1b
0985	允许	yǔnxǔ	to allow	L.14a
0986	运费	yùnfèi	transport fees; freight charge	L.8a
0987	运营	yùnyíng	to operate; operation	L.13a
0988	运营模式	yùnyíng móshì	operating mode	L.13a

Z

0989	遭受	zāoshòu	to incur (losses, etc.); to sustain; to suffer	L.10b
0990	造成	zàochéng	to create; to cause; to result in	L.15a
0991	造势	zào shì	to put spin on sth.; to build up publicity	L.11a
0992	则是	zéshì	then; and so (*used in formal writing)	L.12b
0993	赠送	zèngsòng	to present (as a gift); to give	L.16a
0994	展出	zhǎnchū	to exhibit; to display	L.12b
0995	展区	zhǎnqū	exhibition section/zone	L.12a
0996	展示	zhǎnshì	to reveal; to show; to display; to exhibit sth.	L.6a
0997	展位	zhǎnwèi	booth (at an exhibition)	L.12a
0998	展销	zhǎnxiāo	to exhibit and sell	L.12b
0999	张红	Zhāng Hóng	*a name*	L.3b
1000	账户	zhànghù	account	L.13b
1001	招待	zhāodài	to receive/entertain (guests); reception	L.5a
1002	招聘	zhāopìn	to invite applications for a job; recruitment	L.13a
1003	招商	zhāoshāng	inviting investments; investments	L.12b
1004	招商银行	Zhāoshāng Yínháng	China Merchants Bank	L.9b
1005	招手	zhāoshǒu	to wave (the hands); to beckon	L.1a

1006	折扣	zhékòu	discount	L.8a
1007	真诚	zhēnchéng	sincerity; sincere	L.5b
1008	镇	zhèn	small town	L.14a
1009	争议	zhēngyì	dispute; controversy; to dispute	L.15b
1010	正本	zhèngběn	original (of document)	L.15a
1011	正常	zhèngcháng	normal(ly); regular(ly)	L.14a
1012	正经事	zhèngjingshì	serious matters; reputable affairs	L.16b
1013	正式	zhèngshì	formal(ly); official(ly)	L.3a
1014	政策	zhèngcè	policy	L.6b
1015	政府	zhèngfǔ	government	L.7b
1016	之行	zhī xíng	the trip of ...	L.14a
1017	之内	zhīnèi	within	L.10a
1018	之一	zhīyī	one of ...	L.5a
1019	支持	zhīchí	support; to support	L.7b
1020	支付	zhīfù	to pay (money); defray	L.9b
1021	只顾	zhǐgù	be absorbed in; to be concerned only with	L.16b
1022	只有	zhǐyǒu	only	L.6b
1023	知己知彼	zhījǐ-zhībǐ	to know one's self and know the enemy	L.6b
1024	知名度	zhīmíngdù	name recognition; reputation	L.8a
1025	知识密集型	zhīshi mìjí xíng	knowledge-intensive model	L.14b
1026	执行	zhíxíng	to carry out; to execute; to implement	L.15a
1027	值得	zhídé	to deserve; to be worth	L.11b
1028	职能	zhínéng	function	L.14b
1029	职能部门	zhínéng bùmén	functional department	L.14b
1030	职位	zhíwèi	position; post	L.13a
1031	职业	zhíyè	occupation; profession	L.13a
1032	职责	zhízé	duty; obligation; responsibility	L.13a
1033	指出	zhǐchū	to point out	L.15a
1034	指导	zhǐdǎo	to guide; to direct; guidance	L.13b
1035	指定	zhǐdìng	to appoint; to assign	L.10b
1036	指教	zhǐjiào	to give advice/comments	L.3a
1037	至少	zhìshǎo	at (the) least	L.10a
1038	制定	zhìdìng	to draw up; to formulate; to establish	L.11a
1039	制度	zhìdù	system	L.8b
1040	制冷	zhìlěng	to refrigerate; to cool; cooling	L.12a

1041	制暖	zhìnuǎn	to make warm; to heat; heating	L.12a
1042	制造	zhìzào	to make; to manufacture	L.7a
1043	质量	zhìliàng	quality	L.6a
1044	智联招聘网	Zhìlián Zhāopìn Wǎng	www.zhaopin.com, an employment website	L.13b
1045	中国（北京）国际服务贸易交易会	Zhōngguó (Běijīng) Guójì Fúwù Màoyì Jiāoyìhuì	China Beijing International Fair for Trade in Services	L.12b
1046	中国（上海）自由贸易试验区	Zhōngguó (Shànghǎi) Zìyóu Màoyì Shìyànqū	China (Shanghai) Pilot Free Trade Zone	L.14b
1047	中国工商银行	Zhōngguó Gōngshāng Yínháng	Industrial and Commercial Bank of China	L.9b
1048	中国国际高新科技成果交易会	Zhōngguó Guójì Gāoxīn Jìshù Chéngguǒ Jiāoyìhuì	China Hi-Tech Fair	L.12b
1049	中国国际投资贸易洽谈会	Zhōngguó Guójì Tóuzī Màoyì Qiàtánhuì	China International Fair for Investment and Trade	L.12b
1050	中国建设银行	Zhōngguó Jiànshè Yínháng	China Construction Bank	L.9b
1051	中国交通银行	Zhōngguó Jiāotōng Yínháng	Bank of Communications	L.9b
1052	中国进出口商品交易会	Zhōngguó Jìn-chūkǒu Shāngpǐn Jiāoyìhuì	China Import and Export Fair	L.12b
1053	中国农业银行	Zhōngguó Nóngyè Yínháng	Agricultural Bank of China	L.9b
1054	中国人民银行	Zhōngguó Rénmín Yínháng	People's Bank of China	L.9b
1055	中国银行	Zhōngguó Yínháng	Bank of China	L.9b
1056	中华人民共和国外资企业法	Zhōnghuá Rénmín Gònghéguó Wàizī Qǐyè Fǎ	The Law of the People's Republic of China on Foreign Capital Enterprises	L.15b
1057	中华英才网	Zhōnghuá Yīngcái Wǎng	www.chinahr.com, an employment website	L.13b
1058	中老年	zhōnglǎonián	middle and old age	L.11b
1059	中年	zhōngnián	middle age	L.11b
1060	中心	zhōngxīn	center	L.2a
1061	中央	zhōngyāng	central (government, etc.)	L.7b

1062	衷心	zhōngxīn	heartfelt; whole-hearted;	L.16a
1063	仲裁	zhòngcái	arbitration; to arbitrate	L.15b
1064	众多	zhòngduō	numerous	L.10b
1065	重合同，守信用	zhòng hétóng, shǒu xìnyòng	take one's contract seriously and keep one's word	L.15a
1066	重量级	zhòngliàngjí	heavyweight; important; influential	L.12b
1067	重视	zhòngshì	to value; to take sth. seriously; to consider important	L.16b
1068	周到	zhōudao	attentive; considerate; thorough	L.3a
1069	珠海	Zhūhǎi	*a city in Guangdong Province*	L.14b
1070	逐渐	zhújiàn	gradually	L.7b
1071	主管	zhǔguǎn	person in charge; to be in charge of	L.3a
1072	主人	zhǔrén	host; master	L.4b
1073	主任	zhǔrèn	director;	L.3a
1074	主题	zhǔtí	subject; theme	L.12b
1075	助理	zhùlǐ	assistant	L.3a
1076	注重	zhùzhòng	to attach great importance to; to pay attention to	L.11b
1077	著名	zhùmíng	famous; celebrated	L.4a
1078	专程	zhuānchéng	special-purpose trip	L.16a
1079	专利	zhuānlì	patent; monopoly	L.14a
1080	专卖权	zhuānmàiquán	exclusive right to sell sth.; a monopoly right	L.10b
1081	专门	zhuānmén	specially; special; specialized	L.4a
1082	专业	zhuānyè	specialty; specialized trade/subject; academic major	L.9b
1083	赚钱	zhuàn qián	to make money; to make a profit	L.10b
1084	装运	zhuāngyùn	to load and transport; to ship	L.9a
1085	资金	zījīn	financial resources; funds	L.7b
1086	资金周转	zījīn zhōuzhuǎn	capital turnover; flow of funds; circulation of funds	L.9a
1087	资料	zīliào	date; means; material	L.6a
1088	资信	zīxìn	crcdit; (capital) credibility	L.10a
1089	仔细	zǐxì	careful(ly); attentive(ly)	L.6a
1090	自从	zìcóng	since	L.6b
1091	自贸区	zìmàoqū	Free Trade Zone	L.13a
1092	自然	zìrán	of course; naturally	L.5b
1093	自我	zìwǒ	self; oneself	L.7a

243

1094	自由	zìyóu	free; freedom	L.14b
1095	自助	zìzhù	self-help; self-serving	L.2a
1096	综合	zōnghé	multiple; comprehensive	L.14b
1097	总裁	zǒngcái	chief executive officer; CEO	L.3a
1098	总代理	zǒngdàilǐ	general agent/agency	L.10b
1099	总经理	zǒngjīnglǐ	president; general manager	L.1a
1100	总算	zǒngsuàn	finally; at last	L.1a
1101	总之	zǒngzhī	in a word; in short	L.16b
1102	走后门	zǒu hòumén	to get in by the back door; to secure advantages through influence	L.16b
1103	租车	zū chē	to rent a car; car rental	L.2b
1104	租赁	zūlìn	to rent; to lease; lease	L.7b
1105	组装	zǔzhuāng	to assemble; assembly	L.7a
1106	组装线	zǔzhuāngxiàn	assembly line	L.7a
1107	最好	zuìhǎo	best; had better; it would be best	L.2b
1108	醉	zuì	drunk	L.5b
1109	尊重	zūnzhòng	to respect; to value; to esteem	L.16b
1110	左右	zuǒyòu	about; around	L.4a
1111	作为	zuòwéi	as; to act/serve as	L.10a
1112	作用	zuòyòng	effect; function	L.15b
1113	座位	zuòwèi	seat	L.5b

句型总表（全二册）
The List of Sentence Patterns (Volume I & II)

A

001	A 对 B 有影响	A has an impact on B; A influences B	L.7b
002	A 分为（/成）……	A can be categorized into...	L.7b
003	A 比 B + Adj. + rough estimation (or specific quantity)	A is + rough estimation (or specific quantity) + Adj. than B	L.2a
004	A 比 B + V. + specific quantity (or rough estimation)	A V. + specific quantity (or rough estimation) than B	L.7a
005	A 比 B 早 / 晚 V. + amount of time	A V. + amount of time earlier/later than B	L.9a
006	A 不比 B + Adj.	A is not more adj. than B (namely, A and B are about same)	L.8a
007	A 代表 B + V.……	A + V. ... on behalf of B	L.3a
008	A 给 B……的印象 /A 给 B 的印象 + Adj.	A makes ... impression on B	L.7a
009	A 离不开 B	A cannot do anything well without B	L.11b
010	A 为 B + V. + sth.	A V. sth. for B	L.2a
011	A 也好，B 也好	no matter whether A or B	L.7b
012	A 有利于 B	A is beneficial/helpful to B	L.10b
013	A 有助于 B	A is conducive/helpful to B	L.4b
014	按照……	according to; on the basis of	L.6a

B

015	（……），不妨 + V. ……	(in case that...,) it might as well V. ...; (for the purpose of...) it's no harm to V. ...	L.13b
016	（你）不是……吧？	(A rhetorical question. For example, you are joking, aren't you?)	L.9a
017	……，便于……	(do sth. which would make) easy to; convenient for...	L.3b
018	把 Obj. 一口气 V. + Complement	do sth. at one go/at a stretch	L.5b
019	把 Obj. 分成……	to divide obj. into ...	L.9a
020	把 sth. V. 成……	V. sth. to/into/as...	L.4a

021	把……视为……	regard...as...; consider...as...	L.13b
022	并不	not at all; by no means (*for emphasizing negation)	L.10b
023	不但……而且……	not only...but also...	L.2a
024	不但不……，反而……	not only not... but instead ...	L.16b
025	不得不	have no choice but to; have to	L.8a
026	不管是……，还是……	no matter A or B	L.13b
027	不仅……而且……	not only ... but also ...	L.4b

C

028	除此之外，（……）还 / 也……	in addition to this, (...) also ...	L.12b
029	除非……，否则……	unless..., otherwise...	L.11a
030	除了……以外，还……	besides/in addition to ..., also ...	L.4a
031	从 A 变成（了）B	to change from A into B	L.14a
032	从……到……	from ... to ...	L.10b
033	从……开始	start from ...	L.15b

D

034	（你）对……有什么要求？	What demands/requirements do (you) have concerning ... ?	L.9a
035	当……的时候	when...	L.1b
036	倒是……不过 / 就是……	actually/really...but/the only thing is...	L.16a
037	到……为止	up to; until...	L.13a
038	对……感兴趣	be interested in ...	L.6a
039	对……满意	be satisfied with ...	L.7a
040	对……熟悉	to be familiar with...	L.11a
041	对……有帮助 / 有利	A is helpful to B; A is profitable to B; A benefits B	L.13a
042	对于……来说	as far as sb./sth. be concerned; as for sb./sth.	L.13a

F

043	凡是……都……	every; any; all (*an all-inclusive sentence structure)	L.15a
044	反正	anyway; anyhow; in any case	L.4a
045	非……不可	(absolutely) must...	L.8b

046	分别是……	be ... respectively (*indicate a list of items)	L.14b

G

047	……供 + sb. + 选择（/参考 etc.）	to be provided to sb. for choosing (/consulting, etc.)	L.12a
048	赶在……前 V.	rush/hurry to V. before ...	L.7a
049	根据……	on the basis of; according to	L.15a
050	跟……打交道	come into contact with...; have dealings with...	L.9b
051	跟……有关系	have something to do with...; related to ...	L.6a
052	关于……	about; with regard to; concerning	L.15a
053	固然……不过……	it is true that ... but ...	L.8b

H

| 054 | 好像……似的 | seem; as if | L.16a |

J

055	（……）即……	namely; to be (with emphasis)	L.10b
056	给予 A 以 B	give B to A	L.15b
057	即使……还是……	even (if) ... still ...	L.8a
058	即使……也……	even (if) ... (still/also) ...	L.3b
059	既……又……	both A and B; A as well as B	L.3b
060	既然……就……	given the fact that/since ... then ...	L.5a
061	借这个（/此）机会 do sth.	take this opportunity to do sth.	L.16b
062	仅限于	be limited to ...	L.9b
063	就	(an adverb, serves as an emphatic marker; it is usually stressed in speaking)	L.1a
064	就……达成（了）协议	reach an agreement on ...	L.10a
065	就……进行（/举行）谈判（/会谈/洽谈）	have negotiations (talk) on ...	L.8a
066	就……进行讨论/交换意见	have discussions on/to exchange opinions on	L.11a
067	就是……也……	even (if)...	L.5b
068	就数……	be reckoned as (the best/worst/etc.)	L.12a
069	据说……	it is said ...; according to (sb./media) said	L.5b

070	据我所知	as far as I know...	L.14a

K

071	看来 / 看起来	it looks like...; to appear; to seem	L.12a
072	可 + Adj. + 了	(可 is an emphatic adverb)	L.2a
073	可是 + V. (or Adj.)	(to emphasizes the tone of the speaker)	L.10a

L

074	离开 A 去 / 回 B	to leave A for/to return to B	L.11a
075	利用 A（来）V.	use A to V.	L.15b
076	连……都 / 也……	even/including...	L.4a

M

077	（sb. V. ……的）目的是……	the purpose (that sb. V. ...) is ...	L.3a
078	面临……	to face/be faced with ...; be up against	L.10b

N

079	难怪	no wonder	L.16a
080	难免	hard to avoid	L.12b
081	能 + V. + 多少 + 就 + V. + 多少	to V. as much/many as one can	L.1b

Q

082	起到……作用	have the effect of ...; play a part in...	L.15b
083	请 A 帮 B + V. ……	ask A to help B to do ...	L.2b
084	取决于……	be decided by ...; depend on ...	L.8b

R

085	让 sb.（来）V. ……	let sb. V./allow sb. to V. (usually provide some sort of service)	L.3a
086	如果……（的话），就……	If..., then...	L.2a

S

087	sb. 有权 do sth.	sb. has the right to do sth.	L.15a
088	善于……	be good at ...	L.8b

089	使 / 让	to make; to cause	L.1b
090	是来 / 去……的	(express purpose in coming or going)	L.1a
091	谁不 V. ……呢?	Who doesn't + V. ...? (*to form a rhetorical question. It means "everyone does," "no exception")	L.11b
092	说到……	speak about; when it comes to ...; when ... is mentioned	L.9a
093	算是……	considered to be ...	L.12a
094	虽然……但是 / 可是……	although ... but/however ...	L.5a
095	随着	along with; in pace with; as ...	L.9b
096	所 + V. + 的	that which ...	L.16a

T

| 097 | 提起…… | to mention ......; to speak of ...... | L.1a |
| 098 | 通过…… | by means of; through | L.9a |

W

| 099 | 位于…… | be located at/in ... | L.14b |
| 100 | 无论……还是……，（……）都…… | no matter ... or ... | L.4b |

X

101	X 不晚于 Y	(the time of ...) is not later than...; X is not later than Y	L.15a
102	习惯 + V.	be used to/accustomed to V.	L.3b
103	先……，再……，最后……	first ... , then ..., lastly ...	L.5b
104	像……等等	such as ...etc.	L.2b
105	谢谢 + clause	thank + clause	L.1a

Y

106	（依）靠……（来）V.	to rely/depend on ... to V.	L.14a
107	……，以便……	in order to; so that; with the aim of...	L.14b
108	……，尤其是 + N. (or nominal phrase)	..., especially + N. (or nominal phrase)	L.2b
109	……，有谁还能 / 还能不……呢?	..., what person still can/still can not...?	L.4b
110	一……就……	as soon as; once...then...	L.11b

111	一方面……，一方面……	on the one hand..., on the other hand...; for one thing..., for another...	L.6b
112	一是……，二是……	one (of the reasons, etc.) is..., the other is...; on the one hand..., on the other hand...	L.7a
113	以……的办法	use the method of ...	L.12b
114	以……的名义	in the name of ...	L.16a
115	以……的形式（/方式）来 + V. + sth.	do sth. in the form of; do sth. by way of	L.11b
116	以……为目的	with the aim of; be aimed at; for the purpose of	L.14b
117	以……为荣／主题	consider/regard ... as an honor/a subject	L.12b
118	由 sb.+V.+ sth.	(由 introduces the person in charge of a given task)	L.6a
119	有关……的情况	with regard to the situation of ...	L.10a
120	又……又……	both ... and ...	L.6b
121	与其 A 不如 B	B is a better choice than A; rather than A, it would be better to B	L.16b
122	越来越……	more and more	L.1b

Z

123	……真不错！	... is not bad; ... is very good	L.1a
124	……之一	one of ...	L.5a
125	在 sb.（的）陪同下	accompanied by sb. (*formal expression)	L.12a
126	在……（的）基础上	based on...; on the basis of...	L.14a
127	在……方面	in terms of...; in the respect of...	L.13a
128	在……过程中	in the process of...	L.7b
129	在……看来	in the view of ...	L.11b
130	在……期间	during (a certain period of time)	L.3a
131	在……上	in terms of ...; as far as ...	L.6b
132	在……推动下	with the impetus of...; pushed forward by...; driven by...	L.13b
133	在……之内	within ...	L.10a
134	在……中	in ...; within ...	L.9b

135	这么多……（我 / sb.）都 V. 不过来了	there are so many ... that one cannot V. all of them	L.5a
136	只要……，就……	as long as... then...	L.1b
137	只有……才……	only if...(then) ...	L.6b
138	值得注意的是 ……	What is worth noting is...	L.11b
139	自从……以后	(ever) since ...	L.6b
140	总之	in a word; in short	L.16b
141	最好 + V.	had better do...; it would be best to do...	L.2b
142	作为……	as ...; act/serve as ...	L.10a